standard catalog of®

HARLEY-DAVIDSON

MOTORCYCLES

1903-2003

Doug Mitchel

Published by

700 East State Street • Iola, WI 54990-0001
715-445-2214 • 888-457-2873
www.krause.com

Our toll-free number to place an order or obtain
a free catalog is (800) 258-0929.

Library of Congress Catalog Number: 2004100731

ISBN: 0-87349-736-8

Edited by Brian Earnest

Designed by Jamie Griffin

Printed in United States of America

Dedication

To Kyle and Jenna, for always making me smile.

Contents

1903..........10
1904..........11
1905..........12
1906..........14
1907..........14
1908..........15
1909..........16

1910..........18
1911..........20
1912..........21
1913..........23
1914..........24
1915..........26
1916..........28
1917..........30
1918..........32
1919..........33

1920..........35
1921..........37
1922..........38
1923..........39
1924..........40
1925..........42
1926..........45
1927..........47
1928..........49
1929..........50

1930..51
1931..53
1932..56
1933..58
1934..59
1935..61
1936..63
1937..66
1938..69
1939..72

1940..75
1941..77
1942..80
1943..83
1944..84
1945..85
1946..86
1947..87
1948..90
1949..93

1950..95
1951..96
1952..97
1953..99
1954..100
1955..103
1956..106
1957..108
1958..111
1959..115

1960..118
1961..120
1962..121
1963..122
1964..125
1965..128
1966..132
1967..134
1968..138
1969..140

1970..141
1971..143
1972..146
1973..148
1974..150
1975..151
1976..152
1977..153
1978..155
1979..158

1980..159
1981..162
1982..165
1983..167
1984..170
1985..173
1986..174
1987..177
1988..178
1989..180

1990..183
1991..185
1992..188
1993..190
1994..192
1995..195
1996..198
1997..199
1998..202
1999..206

2000..208
2001..210
2002..212
2003..216
Harley Davidson Racing............219
Bibliography 224

Acknowledgments

A book of this magnitude requires resources, historical material, and assistance from a variety of places and people. I consider myself lucky to have a long list of people willing to lend me their time and reference information to complete a project as expansive as this. My very special thanks go out to the following people, museums, and dealerships that guided me along the way.

Dr. Marty Rosenblum, Ray Schlee, Tom Bolfert and the entire gang in the Harley-Davidson Archives; Dave Kiesow and the whole crew at Illinois Harley-Davidson; Lee Mattes and his energetic staff at Heritage Harley-Davidson; Mr. Jim Kersting, his family, and his troop of dedicated employees at Kersting's Cycle Center; Dale Walksler and his incomparable Wheels Through Time Museum; Ed and Ginny Rich at American Classic Motorcycle Company; John Parham and The National Motorcycle Museum; Becky, Jerry, and Desmo at Motorcycle Classics, LLC.; Walters brothers Harley-Davidson; John Archacki and his collection of vintage Harleys; Dan Chasteen for his rare assortment of Milwaukee machines; Buzz and Pixie Walneck for the years of telling me where to find what I needed; the many private owners of the fine Motor Company models pictured throughout this book. Without them, the pages would be filled with nothing but words.

Introduction

It is difficult to imagine that two young men with no experience building motorcycles were able to assemble what would become one of America's great success stories. It may have taken 100 years to accomplish, but some things just take more time than others.

As boyhood friends, William Harley and Arthur Davidson were fascinated by the motorized world that was growing around them. Like so many children in their formative years, the pair had a particular fascination with anything mechanical. The motorcycle had yet to make a huge splash in the U.S., but across the pond, two-wheeled transportation had already logged a bit of motorcycle history.

Despite their keen awareness of the pending motorcycle revolution, the 14-year-old boys missed a momentous occasion in their hometown of Milwaukee, Wisconsin in 1895. A gentleman by the name of E.J. Pennington made a stop in the growing Wisconsin city to show off his motorized cycle. Boasting an output of 2 hp, the crudely built machine made two runs on Wisconsin Avenue, amazing the crowd with its speed. Had William and Arthur witnessed this valiant display, The Motor Company may have been born even earlier than 1903.

There were certainly other men toiling with the creation of a new motorcycle, but most were focusing their efforts on a workable power plant. Daimler-Maybach had built a four-stroke, 212cc motor, but it weighed in at 189 lbs., and the 1/2-hp output failed to deliver enough energy to drive a two-wheeled machine with a rider. Two Frenchmen, Compte Albert deDion and Georges Bouton, decided that they could improve on the German's design, and proceeded to prove their own theories.

By 1896, back in the U.S., Harley and Davidson had moved to different cities to pursue non-

motorcycle activities. William Harley found work in a bicycle factory, while Arthur Davidson spent time on his grandmother's farm. Although not his intention, Davidson met another soon-to-be frontrunner in the field of self-propelled vehicles. Ole Oleson Evinrude would prove to play a huge part in the making of what would soon become The Motor Company.

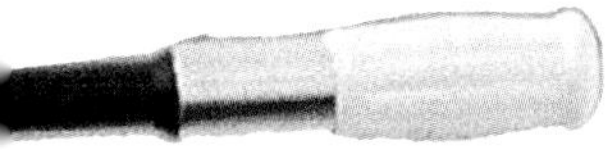

By 1900, several builders of early motorcycles could be found populating the U.S. There had already been scores of builders who had tried and failed, but numerous companies remained afloat, improving their wares with every passing year. Also by 1900, Harley had worked his way up to the position of an apprentice draftsman at a manufacturing facility in Milwaukee. Although he and Davidson lived apart, they stayed in contact by writing letters to each other. Seeing the burgeoning need for skilled labor in the city, Harley urged Davidson to head back and take advantage of the many opportunities.

Once Davidson was settled, the two joined forces to build their own powered cycle. They began by purchasing a kit engine. The mail-order engine was far from the powerhouse they'd hoped for, and the completed motorized bicycle was unable to climb the hills of Milwaukee's streets. Obviously, further labors were required to produce the machine they had dreamed of for so long. This initial failure did little to slow them down, as history would soon prove.

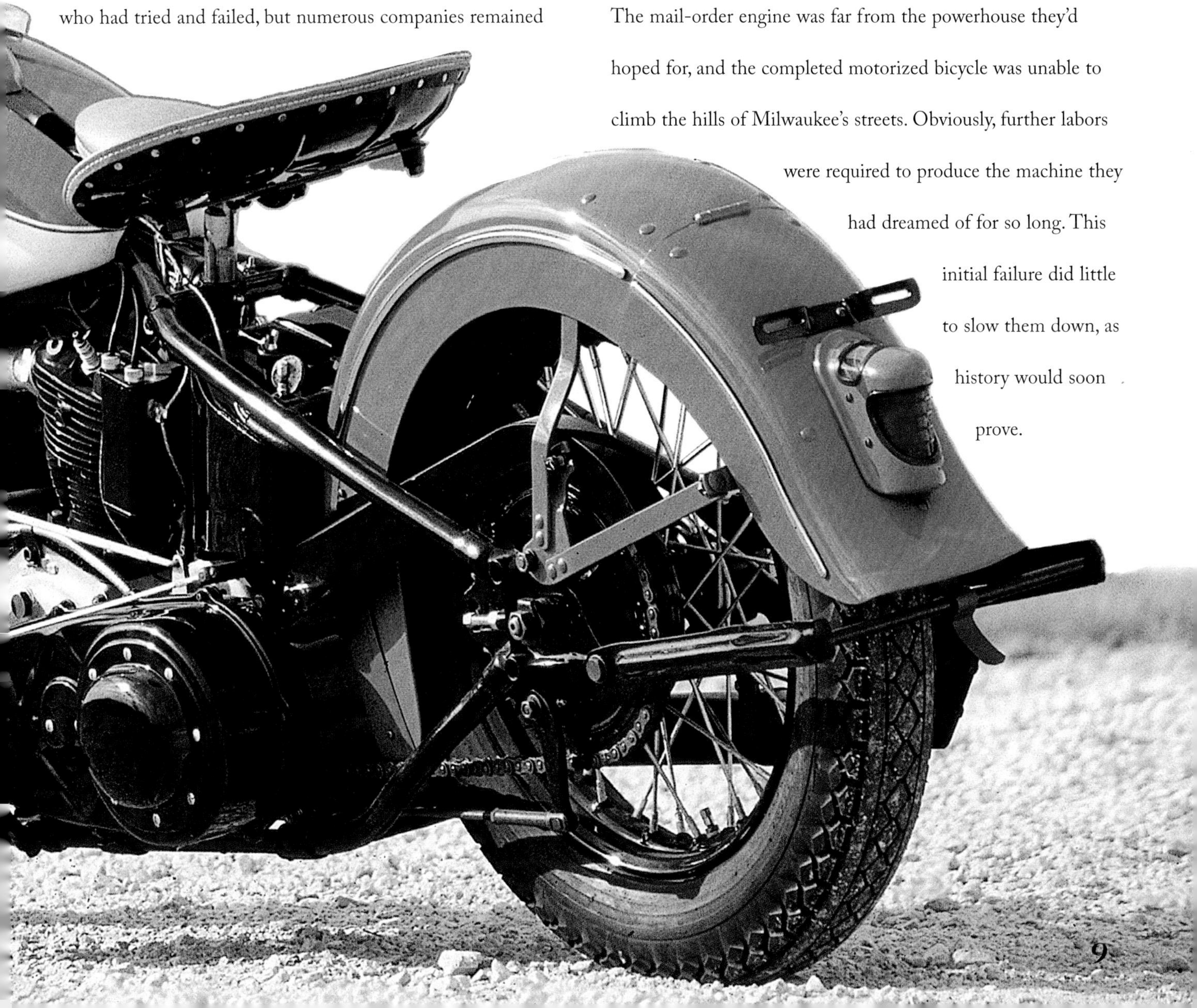

The First Year of "Production"

The machine that started it all, "Serial #1," has been lovingly assembled by the Harley-Davidson restoration staff to preserve its heritage.

1903

While their first attempt to marry an engine to a bicycle frame didn't turn out as they had hoped, Harley and Davidson were not easily deterred. Several other makers of motorcycles were now in existence, and Bill and Arthur learned what they could from the machines coughing around the streets of Milwaukee. Seeing that others had proven it could be done, they became even more determined to build their own variation.

The acquaintance they had made years earlier with Ole Evinrude would prove to be an invaluable tool as they moved ahead with plans to build a machine bearing their names. Despite being only three years older than the young partners, Evinrude's experience was much greater. He was in the business of tooling and engine building when he spoke with the pair again, and he suggested using an air-cooled motor instead of the heavier water-cooled version already on the drawing board. Taking their friend's advice to heart, Harley and Davidson made drawings for just such a motor.

Assembled somewhere between 1902 and 1903, the first new engine looked like a success. With a claimed displacement of 24.74 cubic inches, and a horsepower rating of approximately 3, the engine's power had increased tremendously.

With the newfound power and displacement came increased size, and a new dilemma. The first motor fit easily into a standard bicycle frame, but the second design proved to be too large to be shoe-horned into place using a simple, readily available bike frame. Noted Wisconsin cycle builders Merkel and Mitchell were busy designing their own frames to cradle their newer, larger motors in 1902 and 1903. Harley and Davidson were always on the lookout for new answers to their setbacks, and the Merkel frame seemed to be the perfect fit. The end result was a frame design that closely mimicked the Merkel, which solved the fit problem.

It would be many months before all the required hardware had been fashioned and prepared for final assembly. The first "factory" would be a small wooden shed located behind the Davidsons' home. It was in this humble structure that motorcycle history would be made.

1903 Model Year Lineup

Model	Engine Type	Displacement	Transmission	Special Feature(s)
N/A	F-Head Single	24.74 cid	None	First "production" model

Prices and Production

Model	Production	Price
N/A	1	Not offered for sale

1904

After Harley and Davidson had achieved their initial goal of building their own motorcycle in 1903, 1904 would appear to be a bit anti-climactic. There was an offer to purchase the 1903 model, which surprised the fledging partners. What had begun as an obsessive hobby now looked like an opportunity to create a real business.

Forming a formal partnership was the next step, and with that arrangement completed, William Harley returned to school to enhance his mechanical knowledge. This seemed logical as the pair began a new enterprise that would require a high degree of technical ability.

A lack of record keeping makes it impossible to determine how many '04 units were actually assembled. Figures range from 1 to 8, with the likely number somewhere in between. At this stage of the game, there was no print advertising, no sales department, and no efforts to create either. With Bill still away at school, things slowed to a crawl.

Once again, due to a lack of any formal records, there is no way to determine what, if any changes were made on the 1904 model. It would seem highly unlikely that too much was altered due to the shortage of finances and manpower for the period.

1904 Model Year Lineup

Model	Engine Type	Displacement	Transmission	Special Feature(s)
N/A	F-Head Single	24.74 cid*	None	Unknown

* Assuming no real changes were made on the 1904 edition

Prices and Production

Model	Production	Price
N/A	Between 1 and 8*	N/A

* Without verifiable records, there is no way to claim an actual figure.

The 1905 Model 1 was considered to be the first production machine for the newly formed company. Changes from the previous versions were minor, and virtually impossible to identify.

1905

The new model year would prove to be pivotal in the continuation of the new Harley-Davidson Motor Company history. Beginning in January of that year, a small print ad for "Harley-Davidson Motor Cycle Motors" begin to appear in the *Cycle and Automobile Trade Journal*. In addition to the first printed ad, a sales brochure was also created to boost sales.

For a mere $70, a buyer could now purchase a power plant, including carburetor, for a variety of applications. It is once again impossible to determine how many motors were sold that year, but some were rumored to be installed in watercraft as well as those built for use on terra firma.

Changes in the 1905 motorcycles were becoming obvious as the company improved on the previous models. Both the interior and exterior of the F-Head motor were changed for the '05s. A 1/8-in.-larger bore now put the displacement at 26.84 cubic inches, which boosted horsepower to 3 1/4.

The changes made to the '05 allowed Perry E. Mack to ride his machine to a new speed record at the local racing venue. This single notch in the "win" column persuaded The Motor Co. to cease the sales of its motors and focus its attention on boosting production and sales of motorcycles.

The next boost to Harley-Davidson's reputation and sales came when Carl Lang visited Milwaukee on business. He had seen the print ads for the new company's offerings, and suggested he become H-D's agent in Chicago, his base of operations. Thus, the dealer network had begun. Of the maybe five units built in 1905, Carl took three of them for his new venture.

With these events serving as a springboard, the '05 models were considered the first production units and the company began to track assembled cycles beginning then. The company's newfound confidence in production also led to an expansion of the original "factory." Although still a wooden shed, the space increased to 10 x 30 ft.—nearly doubling work space.

1905 Model Year Lineup

Model	Engine Type	Displacement	Transmission	Special Feature(s)
Model 1	F-Head single	26.84 cid	None	Three-coil Saddle

Prices and Production

Model	Production	Price
Model 1	5*	$200

* As stated before, early record keeping was virtually nonexistent, forcing "educated guesswork."

Displacing just under 27 cubic inches, the '05 single would be the springboard for many future iterations of the same design concept.

With no actual transmissions, the early models were provided with belt-tensioning devices to allow for smooth launches from a standing start.

1906

The new model year brought many changes, but very few were actually made to the motorcycles themselves. Increases in production, building space, and staff were the three most important growth areas of the now bustling concern.

Harley and Davidson didn't need a crystal ball to see their future would revolve around manufacturing motorcycles, so building an even larger facility was now a priority. While the previous shed had already been increased in size, it had outlived its usefulness. An entirely new structure would be needed to keep the company on track. Another location was also needed, and Chestnut Street would be the new home. This street's name would change later to become the now fabled Juneau Ave.

1906 Model Year Lineup

Model	Engine Type	Displacement	Transmission	Special Feature(s)
Model 2	F-Head single	26.84 cid	None	Optional "Renault" gray paint with red pinstripes

The new factory must have seemed immense to the founders and their new hires. The staff was upped to six in 1906 in an effort to meet with the growing demand for the machines. Total production for 1906 would expand tenfold from the previous year, and a few changes were seen on the roster.

A choice was now offered on the new Model 2. The '06s could now be purchased in the standard "Piano" black with gold pinstripes, or the optional "Renault" gray with red pinstripes. The newly available color scheme would bring to life the nickname "Silent Gray Fellow," which remains in use today.

With the progress came added costs, and this was reflected in a small boost in the purchase price. The 1906 Model 2 retailed for $210 per copy—$10 more than the 1905 Model 1.

Prices and Production

Model	Production	Price
Model 2	50	$210

1907

The new model year would also see several alterations to the still young company. With the decision to incorporate in 1907, it was time to raise funds for expansion. Of course, the initial stock offering added some fuel to their coffers, but additional funding would be required to build an even bigger facility and improve the operation. Loans from banks and a Scottish relative would prove to be the push Harley and Davidson needed. Their designs were also aided by Bill Harley's recently earned degree in mechanical engineering. The combination of capital and newfound education set the stage for the next segment of the company's history.

The new factory expanded to include a second story. With the new and improved facility came alterations to the machine

H-D was making famous. The 1907 Model 3s were not radically different from the 2s, but the changes made were considered important enough to help increase sales.

Still powered by a single-cylinder motor displacing 26.84 cubic inches, the Model 3 did show some physical revisions. The cylindrical crankcase of the motor was now assembled with eight bolts instead of the previous 6. The locations of the motor mounts were modified, as was the casting of the Harley-Davidson name on the cases. A new sprung fork was first seen on the '07s as well.

The boys also experimented with a twin-cylinder iteration of the 1907 motor, but it failed to meet their expectations. Very little is known about this early V-twin design, and any evidence of their design efforts is long gone from the Harley archives.

Production of the 1907 Model 3 jumped to 150 for the year, and employment tripled as well. Things were moving very quickly indeed.

1907 Model Year Lineup

Model	Engine Type	Displacement	Transmission	Special Feature(s)
Model 3	F-Head Single	26.84 cid	None	Sprung front fork

Prices and Production

Model	Production	Price
Model 3	150	$210

1908

There were no technical changes to the 1908 Model 4. The employees were kept busy cranking out the two-wheeled machines almost as quickly as the laborers were making additions onto the actual company building. The majority of the previous building was made of lumber, but the architectural limits were being pushed to the edge. In 1908, a brick addition was made to the existing edifice. This two-story appendage was built on the west end of the wooden factory, and added some much-needed space. Management had hoped that the new brick building would suffice, but the need for more square footage would not end for many years to come.

The unchanged '08s remained strong sellers due to their dependable design and sturdy construction. While $210 was a lot of money for what some considered a toy, it proved its mettle on the streets of Milwaukee, and was pressed into service by a wide array of customers.

Even the best of designs need upgrades, but those would not be implemented until the following model years. More work was done to create a twin-cylinder engine, but none of the efforts bore fruit.

1908 Model Year Lineup

Model	Engine Type	Displacement	Transmission	Special Feature(s)
Model 4	F-Head Single	26.84 cid	None	None

Prices and Production

Model	Production	Price
Model 4	450	$210

After two previous attempts at building a twin-cylinder for production, Harley-Davidson appeared to have finally solved the puzzle in 1909.

1909

After several years of minor changes to the Harley-Davidson lineup, something major would be registered in the history books for 1909. Along with yet another doubling of workable factory space, the venerable single-cylinder bike would be sold alongside a twin-cylinder model.

With the existing motor having proven itself to be highly reliable in single-cylinder form, the team at Harley didn't need to start from scratch with its new motor. By adding another cylinder to the existing motor, they realistically boosted power without compromising quality and dependability. At least it looked good on paper.

The new power plant displaced 53.68 cubic inches, and produced 7 hp. This was a drastic improvement over the single's output. The cylinders were splayed at a 45-degree angle, which has become the hallmark of the Harley motors.

The excitement of the new motor was to be short-lived, however, as trouble became evident almost immediately. With documented history being somewhat lax in the early days, the true nature of the '09 twin's demise is somewhat sketchy. Depending on who you ask, it stemmed from either a complication with the automatic intake valve system, or the lack of a belt tensioner. Regardless of what caused the trouble, the twin model would be dropped from the sales catalog for 1910.

To bolster the output of the single, the cylinder bore was increased to 3 5/16 inches, bumping displacement to 30.16 cubic inches for 1909. The option of a magneto ignition was also found in the 1909 sales brochures, adding a new flavor to menu. The 1909s had the optional magneto mounted near the front of the motor, but subsequent placement would be at the backbone of the frame. The '09s could also be had with either 26- or 28-inch wheels.

Styling changes would see the fuel/oil tank shape altered to better fill in the spaces between the frame and previous sheet metal. This was not exactly revolutionary, but at least it makes it easier to identify the previous models.

Even with the loss of the new motor, production would soar to more than 1,000 units for 1909. Thirty-five employees now punched in and out each day, and there seemed to be no end to the company's annual expansion.

1909 Model Year Lineup

Model	Engine Type	Displacement	Transmission	Special Feature(s)
Model 5	F-Head Single	30.16 cid	None	28-in. Wheels & Battery Ignition
Model 5A	F-Head Single	30.16 cid	None	28-in. Wheels & Magneto Ignition
Model 5B	F-Head Single	30.16 cid	None	26-in. Wheels & Battery Ignition
Model 5C	F-Head Single	30.16 cid	None	26-in. Wheels & Magneto Ignition
Model 5D	F-Head Twin	53.68 cid	None	Magneto Ignition

Prices and Production

Model	Production	Price
Model 5	864	$210
Model 5A	54	$250
Model 5B	168	$210
Model 5C	36	$250
Model 5D	27	$325

With the all-new power plant nestled in the looped frame, it looked like the latest power plant would change the world of motorcycling again.

The two cylinders shared a common carburetor, and this model was built with the magneto ignition—a new option for the '09 models.

The addition of the belt idler control was the most obvious change on the 1910 Model 6's.

1910

After the initial excitement of the twin's introduction in 1909, the 1910 catalog would find only a single-cylinder model offered for sale. Still a highly reliable motor, the single would carry the Harley banner for several years to come.

Still attempting to design newer and better machines, Bill Harley designed a two-speed rear hub for use on their cycles. A patent was applied for as well, but the option never found its way onto the 1910 models.

Previously, riders of Harley-Davidsons didn't have a belt idler mechanism at their disposal. The Model 6 would finally allow that luxury, allowing the rider to slow his machine by removing tension from the drive belt with the motor still running.

Nestled beneath the split fuel/oil tanks, the battery was safely mounted on the backbone of the frame of the 1910s.

Additional cooling fins can be found on the 1910 models, helping to differentiate them from the earlier versions.

With the exception of the belt idler, the 1910 models were carry-overs from the previous year's offerings. But dramatic changes were on their way to the motorcycle buyer, especially those desiring a Harley-Davidson.

Alterations to the factory and expansion of the workforce continued, bringing the labor pool up to 149, and workspace to more than 9,200 square feet.

1910 Model Year Lineup

Model	Engine Type	Displacement	Transmission	Special Feature(s)
Model 6	F-Head Single	30.16 cid	None	28-in. Wheels & Battery Ignition
Model 6A	F-Head Single	30.16 cid	None	28-in. Wheels & Magneto Ignition
Model 6B	F-Head Single	30.16 cid	None	26-in. Wheels & Battery Ignition
Model 6C	F-Head Single	30.16 cid	None	26-in. Wheels & Magneto Ignition

Prices and Production

Model	Production	Price
Model 6	2,302	$210
Model 6A	334	$250
Model 6B	443	$210
Model 6C	88	$275

1911

As in each of the previous years of production, the 1911 models were treated to a variety of incremental changes. The ever-expanding production needs took their toll on fresh design work.

Along with the return of an improved single, the twin-cylinder would once again appear for 1911. The last version of the twin was devoid of a belt-tensioner device, the lack of which was rumored to have brought about its premature demise. The new twin featured both a belt-tensioner and an improved valve train. These changes would prove to be exactly what was needed, and their implementation kept the twin-cylinder concept alive.

The newest version of the V-twin motor now featured horizontal cooling fins on the cylinder walls, and vertical fins on the heads. Displacement on the 1911 twin was 50 cubic inches—four less than in 1909.

The singles were also fitted with horizontal and vertical cooling fins, but the motor remained the same within the new one-piece castings. The previous two-part exhaust valve was supplanted by a single-piece steel unit. Both battery and magneto ignition models were offered.

In addition to the developments in the power plants, the frames were now found with a straight front downtube where a curved section had been in earlier years. Several colors of fuel tank striping were also available, allowing the buyer more options to customize his machine.

Factory and workforce expansion continued unabated, with output now exceeding 5,600 units. The Silent Gray Fellow was proving to be a popular choice amongst American buyers, and the constant improvements only added to its appeal.

1911 Model Year Lineup

Model	Engine Type	Displacement	Transmission	Special Feature(s)
Model 7	F-Head Single	30.16 cid	None	28-in. Wheels & Battery Ignition
Model 7A	F-Head Single	30.16 cid	None	28-in. Wheels & Magneto Ignition
Model 7B	F-Head Single	30.16 cid	None	26-in. Wheels & Battery Ignition
Model 7C	F-Head Single	30.16 cid	None	26-in. Wheels & Magneto Ignition
Model 7D	F-Head Twin	50 cid	None	28-in. Wheels & Magneto Ignition

Prices and Production

Model	Production	Price
Model 7	***	$225
Model 7A	***	$250
Model 7B	***	$225
Model 7C	***	$250
Model 7D	***	$300

*** Individual production figures were not available for this, and many other years.

Although cast in one piece with the cylinder, the 1911 cylinder heads featured horizontal cooling fins.

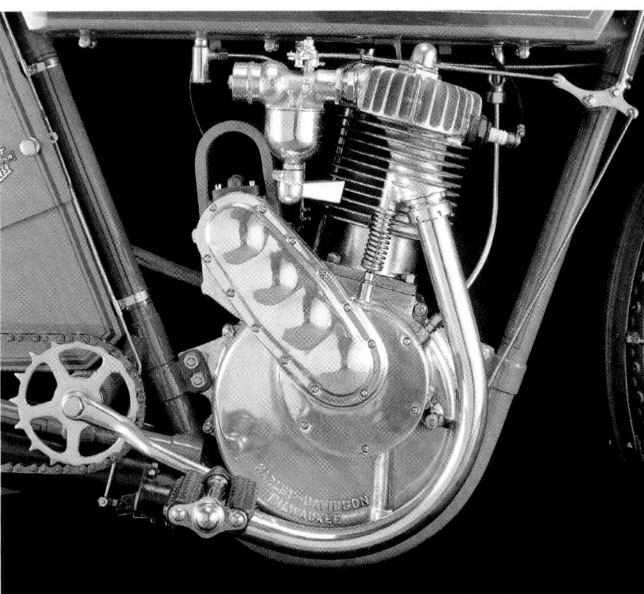

Despite the added power available from the twin-cylinder model, the time-tested single remained a strong seller in 1911.

This X8A carried its rider with a new level of comfort and convenience.

1912

Until now, applying the term "motorcycle" to motorized, two-wheeled machines was stretching the truth somewhat. Since nearly every builder of these machines used a bicycle-style frame to house their chosen motors, "motorized bicycle" seems more accurate. This would prove to be the year, however, that Harley-Davidson took a turn towards building real motorcycles.

By placing a downward bend to the top tube of its latest frames, Harley could now provide the rider with a lower seat height, curing a problem found on the previous models. In addition to the lowered seat height, the vertical frame tube now housed a long spring which, when attached to the seat, provided a modicum of suspension to the hard saddle. Lower saddle height and the greater comfort pushed sales even higher.

Rider comfort was not the only agenda H-D would address for 1912. The new models were now offered with an actual clutch for the drive wheel. This rudimentary clutch was located in the rear hub and was controlled by hand using a lever mounted on the left side of the fuel tank. While the pedals were still in place, they were no longer needed for a smooth getaway from stops.

Also new for 1912 were easier-adjusting pedals and their chain. Previous editions required the rider to adjust the location of the rear wheel to modify the chain tension. This also meant the drive belt would be affected even though its tension might have been correct. The 1912s offered a method of adjusting the pedal chain independently from the drive belt, and provided yet another touch of modernization to the expanding line.

The twin-cylinder models were still found on the roster, and could now be had in one of two different displacements. The "D" models displaced 49.48 cubic inches, while the "E" version was bumped to 60.34 cubic inches. The bigger "E" produced up to two additional horsepower over the D's. Yet another first for the "E" models were connecting rods fitted with roller bearings inside the large-diameter crankshaft end. Ball bearings were also used on the main shaft, but only on the sprocket side.

The newfound power of the "E" was providing private racers with numerous checkered flags as racing grew in popularity.

Harley-Davidson now had a dealer network of 200 members, and the factory was again expanded in an effort to keep up with higher sales.

1912 Model Year Lineup

Model	Engine Type	Displacement	Transmission	Special Feature(s)
Model 8	F-Head Single	30.16 cid	None	Battery Ignition
Model X8	F-Head Single	30.16 cid	None	Rear Wheel Clutch
Model 8A	F-Head Single	30.16 cid	None	Magneto Ignition
Model X8A	F-Head Single	30.16 cid	None	Magneto Ignition & Rear Wheel Clutch
Model 8D	F-Head Twin	49.48 cid	None	Magneto Ignition
Model X8D	F-Head Twin	49.48 cid	None	Magneto Ignition & Rear Wheel Clutch
Model X8E	F-Head Twin	60.34 cid	None	Magneto Ignition & Rear Wheel Clutch

Prices and Production

Model	Production	Price
Model 8	***	$200
Model X8	***	$210
Model 8A	***	$225
Model X8A	***	$235
Model 8D	***	$275
Model X8D	***	$285
Model X8E	***	$285
TOTAL	9,571	

*** As in the previous year, production numbers for individual models were not recorded

The single-cylinder motor would remain unchanged while the twin got all the attention.

The belt tensioner and rear-wheel clutch lever gave the rider more control than ever.

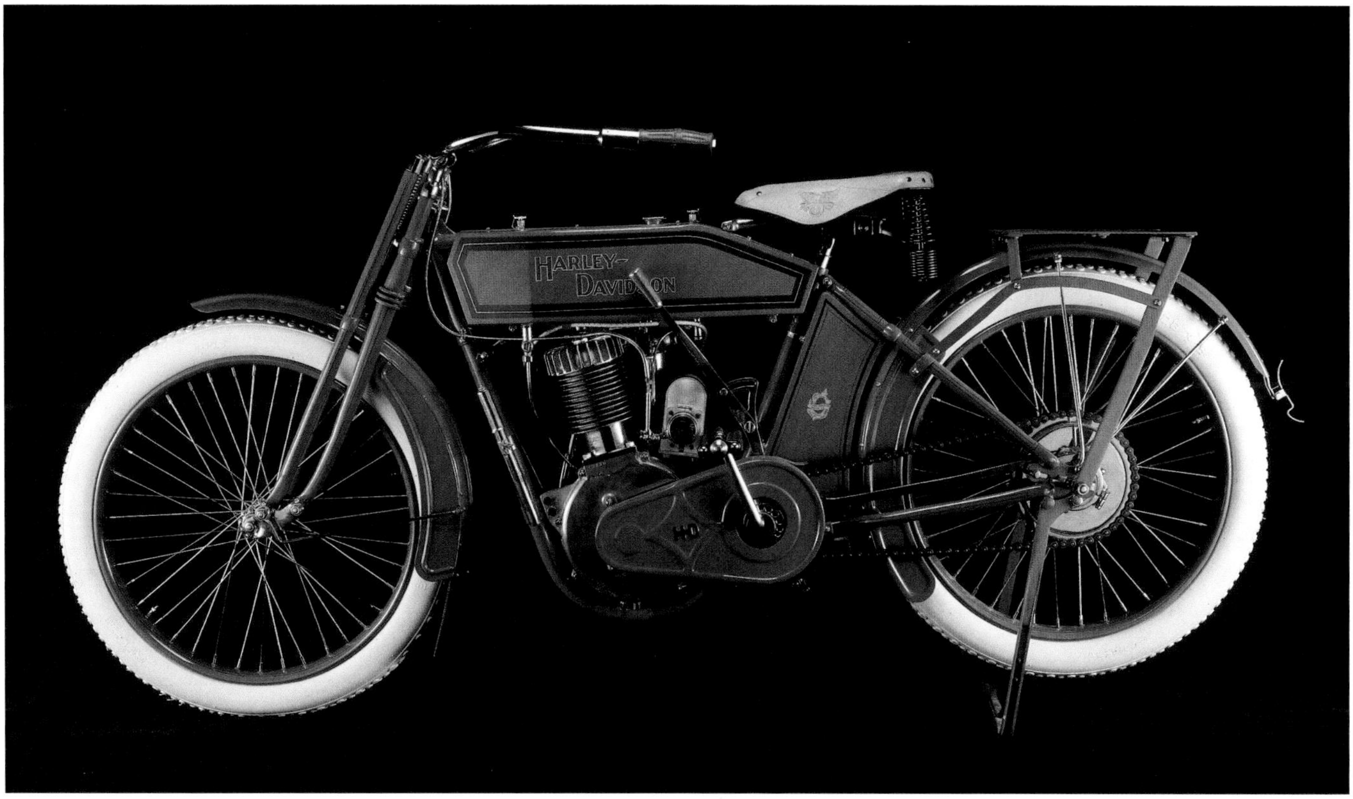

This 1913 Model 9B sports the chain drive that was new for the model year.

1913

While significant changes were looming large on the horizon, 1913 would prove to be a year of evolution and improvement for Harley-Davidson. For the first time, the leather drive belt of the previous years could now be supplanted by a chain drive. The wide, leather belts had delivered quiet power to the rear wheel, but often slipped when wet. The new chain drive amended that shortcoming.

The singles were altered in several ways to improve power. The stroke was enhanced by 1/2 inch to a total of 4 inches, which bumped the displacement to 35 cubic inches. The larger jugs also delivered more horsepower with a new rating of 5. The new single cylinder designation was the "5-35" denoting the latest level of size and power.

The inlet valves on the singles were now of the mechanical variety, much like the twin cylinder models since 1911. Internal components were better balanced to deliver the new level of power with added smoothness.

Harley-Davidson sales continued to climb sharply, though the industry as a whole was beginning to experience some downturns. The Ford automobile was getting more affordable and popular. Due to the strength of its products, H-D handled this challenge better than many other motorcycle makers. Nearly 100 motorcycle companies would disappear from the history books by 1913, leaving Harley among the top 3 producers.

1913 Model Year Lineup

Model	Engine Type	Displacement	Transmission	Special Feature(s)
Model 9A	F-Head Single	35 cid	None	—
Model 9B	F-Head Single	35 cid	None	Chain Drive
Model 9E	F-Head Twin	60.34 cid	None	Chain Drive
Model 9F	F-Head Twin	60.34 cid	None	Chain Drive
Model 9G	F-Head Twin	60.34 cid	None	Chain Drive & Front Delivery Box

Prices and Production

Model	Production	Price
Model 9A	1,510	$290
Model 9B	4,601	$290
Model 9E	6,732	$350
Model 9F	49	N/A
Model 9G	63	N/A

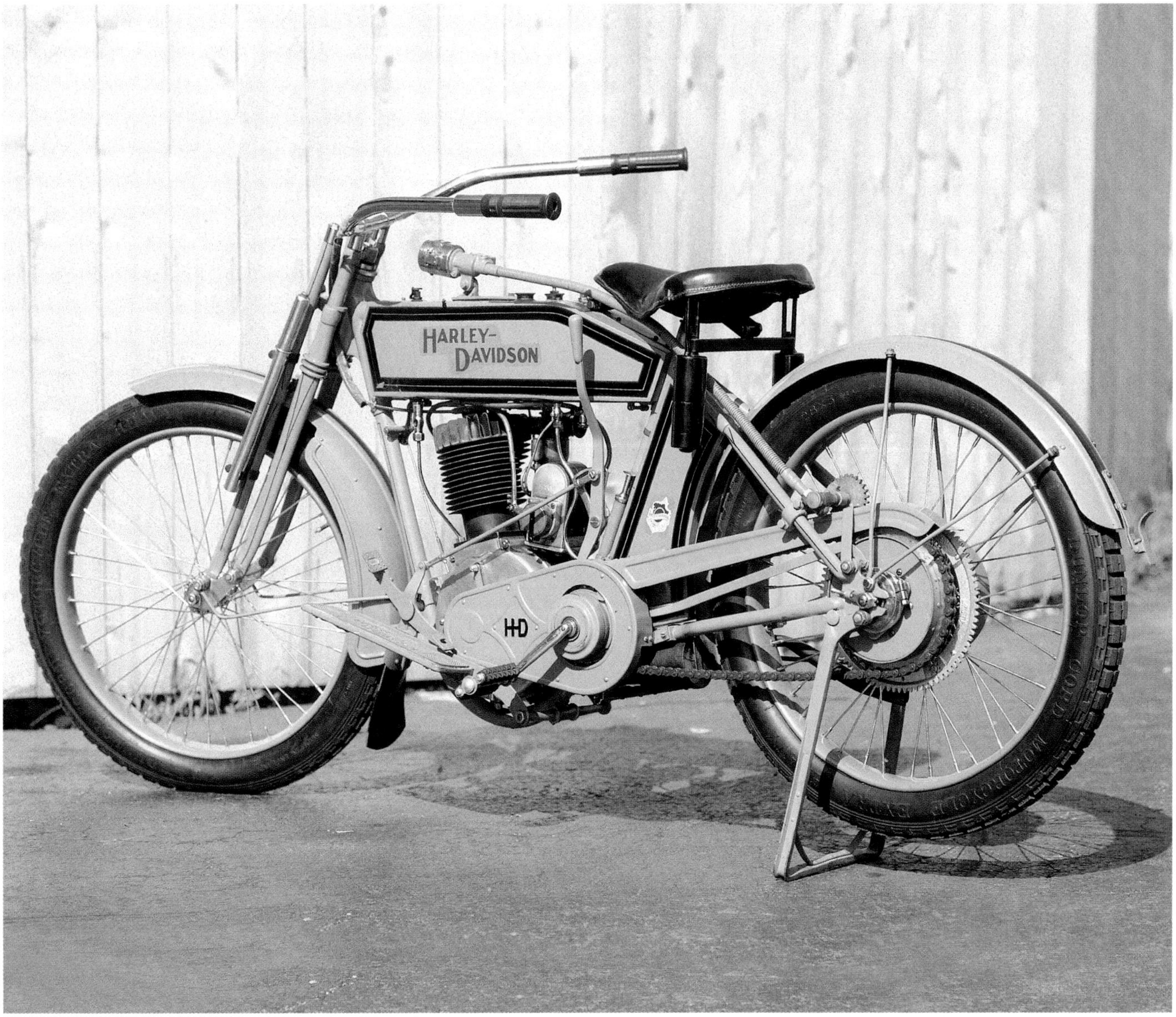

The Model 10C was the top-of-the-line single for 1914, and came equipped with chain drive and the new two-speed rear hub.

1914

The 1914 models would be fitted with a variety of new hardware and improvements, and would set a new standard for the two-wheeled marketplace.

Starting earlier models required the rider to peddle the motor to life while astride the machine. H-D added a new step-starter to simplify the procedure. The rider could now stand beside his Harley and apply pressure to a single pedal, even if it wasn't on the center stand. It would be many decades before electric starting became a reality, but this new method was a vast improvement.

The business end of the gear-driven speedometer allowed the rider to monitor his velocity.

1914 would mark the first appearance of a two-speed transmission mounted in the rear hub. The additional gearing could now deliver a higher level of flexibility for diverse riding conditions. A foot-operated clutch lever permitted the rider to easily change gears while moving. The installation of footboards provided plenty of space for riding boots, and a brake pedal was added to help provide a new level of comfort and convenience. Exhaust valve springs were exposed to the elements until the 1914 models came along. The new motorcycle was fitted with enclosures to protect the coils from dust and dirt. Since paved roads were still scarce, these coil covers help keep the bikes in top condition with less maintenance. Internal changes to the motors were minor.

1914 Model Year Lineup

Model	Engine Type	Displacement	Transmission	Special Feature(s)
Model 10A	F-Head Single	35 cid	None	Final Belt-Drive Model
Model 10B	F-Head Single	35 cid	None	Chain Drive
Model 10C	F-Head Single	35 cid	Two-Speed Rear Hub	Chain Drive
Model 10E	F-Head Twin	60.34 cid	None	Chain Drive
Model 10F	F-Head Twin	60.34 cid	Two-Speed Rear Hub	Chain Drive
Model 10G	F-Head Twin	60.34 cid	Two-Speed Rear Hub	Front Delivery Box

The 1914 Model 10A would be the final Harley-Davidson offered with belt drive as the newer chain drives had proven their mettle.

In the racing department, H-D would finally enter the performance realm with a stealth "factory" effort in the early part of the year. Since many riders had piloted their privately owned H-Ds to victories as the competition scene expanded, it seemed to make sense that the actual factory take part in some of the glory. By late 1914, Harley-Davidson unveiled its official factory team, and the gauntlet was dropped. The performance race was on.

Prices and Production

Model	Production	Price
Model 10A	316	$200
Model 10B	2,034	$210
Model 10C	877	$245
Model 10E	5,055	$25
Model 10F	7,956	$285
Model 10G	171	N/A

The two-speed gearing was housed within the steel drum on the rear wheel. The gear-driven speedometer is also fitted to this 1914 example.

The 1914 "5-35" single was trimmed with covered exhaust springs.

A pristine example of an 11F Model, complete with the new three-speed transmission.

1915

The 1915 models were loaded with new features that enhanced power and usability. The major focus of the upgrades was in the motor, but there were changes in many other areas as well.

First on the list of alterations on the twin was more power. The "guaranteed" horsepower rating of 11 was achieved through the adaptation of several components. The latest cylinder castings featured larger inlet ports, which were in turn fed through larger-diameter inlet valves. The increased ports and valves breathed through an improved Y-shaped manifold. Harley claimed a 31-percent boost at 2500 rpm with this new configuration.

Connecting rods now rode on a pair of roller bearings at the bottom end, and were manufactured by Harley-Davidson on the initial models. This brought a claimed friction reduction of 46 percent.

Lubrication of the motor's internals was done somewhat imperfectly by the rider on earlier models. With no real way of sensing the oil level, a rider could easily over or under lubricate his engine. Neither situation was ideal. The 1915s were delivered with

The three-speed transmission was another first for 1915.

The F model came equipped with gas-operated lighting, and this tank was for storage of the acetylene.

automatic oilers. The gear-driven pump fed into the crankcase through a glass sight-tube to confirm the presence of the proper lubrication.

This new level of power was delivered to the rear wheels using a true three-speed transmission. No longer a rear-hub mounted affair, the three-speed box sat directly behind the crankcase in its own cast housing. The three-speed was on option, but proved to be very popular with buyers. Nearly 10,000 Model F's were sold in 1915, eclipsing sales of all other models combined.

1915 Model Year Lineup

Model	Engine Type	Displacement	Transmission	Special Feature(s)
Model 11B	F-Head Single	35 cid	None	—
Model 11C	F-Head Single	35 cid	Two-Speed Rear Hub	—
Model 11E	F-Head Twin	60.34 cid	Single-Speed	—
Model 11F	F-Head Twin	60.34 cid	Three-Speed	—
Model 11G	F-Head Twin	60.34 cid	Three-Speed	Delivery Van
Model 11H	F-Head Twin	60.34 cid	Single-Speed	Electric Lighting
Model 11J	F-Head Twin	60.34 cid	Three-Speed	Electric Lighting
Model 11K	F-Head Twin	60.34 cid	Three-Speed	Stripped Stock
Model 11-K4	F-Head Single	N/A	N/A	Track Racer with Magneto
Model 11-K5	F-Head Single	N/A	N/A	Roadster Racer w/Magneto
Model 11-K12	F-Head Twin	N/A	N/A	"Fast Motor" with Magneto
Model 11-K12H	F-Head Twin	N/A	N/A	"Fast Motor" with Electrical
Model 11-KT	F-Head Twin	N/A	N/A	Track Racer with Magneto
Model 11-KR	F-Head Twin	N/A	N/A	Roadster Racer w/Magneto
Model 11-KRH	F-Head Twin	N/A	N/A	Roadster Racer w/Electrical
Model 11-KTH	F-Head Twin	N/A	N/A	Track Racer w/Electrical

In addition to all the latest mechanical improvements, an electric lighting system was now available. Before the advent of electric lighting, both head and taillights were powered by acetylene gas stored in a tank mounted on the frame. The electric system would offer the rider increased light, and there were no tanks to refill. The taillight could also be removed from its mount and used as a handheld service light.

Motorcycle owners were finding more ways to incorporate their machines into their daily travels, and some longed for more fuel capacity. For 1915, the twin-cylinder H-Ds could be ordered with extra-large oil and fuel tanks to meet the growing needs of the consumer.

Motorcycle racing continued to play a part in Harley-Davidson's development, and to meet rider's requests, several special models were built for racing use only. The factory team continued its winning ways, and many privateers could also be found in the winner's circle bearing the Harley-Davidson logo on their attire.

Production and Prices

Model	Production	Price
Model 11B	70	$200
Model 11C	545	$230
Model 11E	127	$240
Model 11F	9,855	$275
Model 11G	98	N/A
Model 11H	140	$275
Model 11J	3,719	$310
Model 11-KR	121	$250
Model 11-KT	37	$250
Model 11-K4	3	$250
Model 11-K5	3	N/A

The Model 16J was the best all-around street-going version offered by Harley-Davidson in 1916. Twin-cylinder power linked to a three-speed transmission, as well as a complete electrical system, made the "J" a jack-of-all-trades.

1916

As was the case with many of Harley-Davidson's early years, the 1916 models would only improve in small increments, but design and construction continued to advance.

The most prominent change was the new shape of the fuel/oil tank. Previous models wore sheet metal formed with crisp edges at every bend, but the 1916 versions were formed with plenty of gentle curves. The latest shape also provided for two additional pints of capacity, which was another welcome change. Even the filler caps were increased in size to allow for easier access at fill-ups.

For the first time, the single and twin models would share the same frame. Only minor modifications were needed to install either

This J Model is equipped with an oversized horn mounted above the headlight.

motor. Henry Ford was teaching the world about streamlining manufacturing techniques, and Harley-Davidson was not blind to the obvious benefits. The front fork tubes were now spaced further apart to allow wider fenders. These new "mudguards" provided additional spacing between the sheet metal and the tires. A newly designed tire rim claimed a 50-percent boost in strength. Roads of the time were crude and not kind to tires and suspension, and any durability and handling improvements were greeted with open arms.

In their efforts to improve the longevity of their machines, a new heat-treating process was used on nearly all moving parts. Not only did this add to their durability, but shortened break-in periods.

1916 Model Year Lineup

Model	Engine Type	Displacement	Transmission	Special Feature(s)
Model 16B	F-Head Single	35 cid	None	—
Model 16C	F-Head Single	35 cid	Three-Speed	"Solo" model
Model 16E	F-Head Twin	60.34 cid	Single-Speed	—
Model 16F	F-Head Twin	60.34 cid	Three-Speed	Stock Competition
Model 16J	F-Head Twin	60.34 cid	Three-Speed	Electrical System
Model 16S	F-Head Single	35 cid	None	Stripped Stock Racer
Model 16R	F-Head Twin	60.34 cid	None	Roadster Racer
Model 16T	F-Head Twin	60.34 cid	None	Track Racer

For the first time since it started applying model designations to its products, H-D prefaced models with a "16" in the moniker. This meant you no longer had to subtract four years from the current offerings' identifying numbers to determine year of make.

The Harley-Davidson racing team continued its winning ways and the company continued to gain a reputation for having race-proven cycles.

The Enthusiast Magazine was delivered to all registered Harley owners and dealers for the first time in 1916. The official publication of the company sold for a nickel and provided a variety of information for all of those interested in the marque. This publishing tradition continues today.

World War I was in full swing in 1916, and several military sidecars and special-purpose side-mounted accoutrements were used in the conflict overseas.

Prices and Production

Model	Production	Price
Model 16B	292	$200
Model 16C	862	$230
Model 16E	252	$240
Model 16F	9,496	$265
Model 16J	5,898	$295

The 1916 Model 16J was powered with a 61-cubic inch F-head motor, as well as an electrical system.

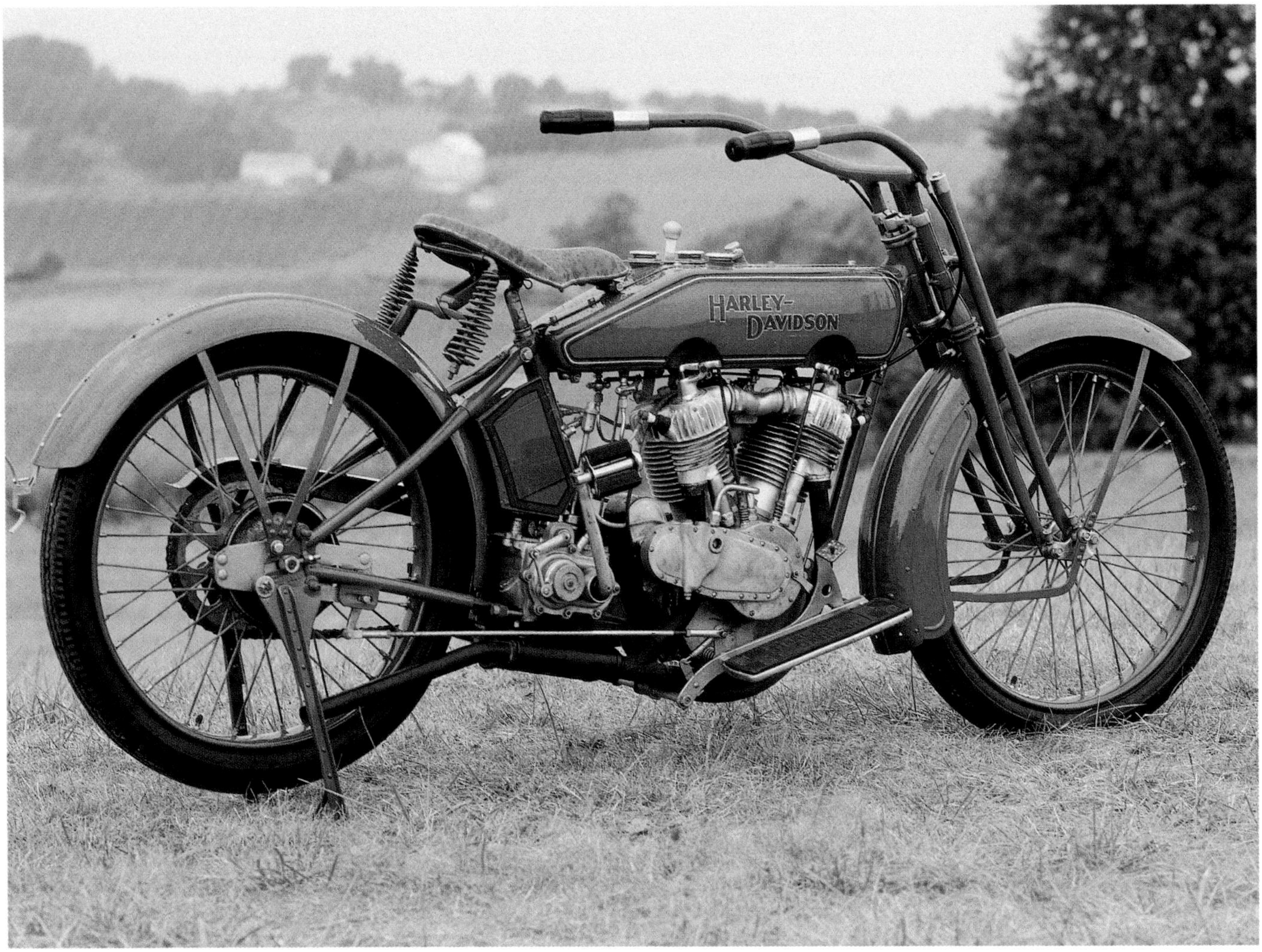

The Model 17F was the second-best seller for 1917, and was only exceeded by the "J," which featured an electrical system.

1917

With the pending entry of U.S into WW I, only minor changes were made to the 1917 models.

A majority of the changes were made to the internals of the twin-cylinder motors, and many dealt with attempts at maintaining durability for machines that were being used in a variety of unforeseen ways. Previously, only the eight-valve twins had a four-lobe cam arrangement. This system was implemented on the F-heads in 1917. Clearance between the lift pins and exhaust valves was doubled to .008 for both cylinders. This new clearance allowed for greater tolerance during high-demand usage. Valve timing was also altered to match that of the

Featuring enclosed valve springs for inlet and exhaust valves, the '17 motors were the most dependable mills available.

"special" motors. The externally mounted inlet valve springs were enclosed starting with the 1917 models.

In its efforts to continue its domination at the racetracks, Harley offered new "Fast" motors in 1917. With motor numbers beginning with "500", these new power plants were specially built for performance use. Greater precision and care were used when assembling the engines, and less stringent tolerances allowed for the abuses of racing. A full compliment of new components were used in the assembly of the fast motors, and each was tested rigorously before being installed.

1917 Model Year Lineup

Model	Engine Type	Displacement	Transmission	Special Feature(s)
Model 17B	F-Head Single	35 cid	None	—
Model 17C	F-Head Single	35 cid	Three-Speed	—
Model 17E	F-Head Twin	60.34 cid	Single-Speed	—
Model 17F	F-Head Twin	60.34 cid	Three-Speed	—
Model 17J	F-Head Twin	60.34 cid	Three-Speed	Electrical System
Model 17S	F-Head Single	35 cid	None	—
Model 17R	F-Head Twin	60.34 cid	None	—
Model 17T	F-Head Twin	60.34 cid	None	—

The most obvious change to the '17 models was the new green color. According to the factory literature, the new olive paint was "the snappiest and most attractive color ever used on a motorcycle." Some have attributed the change to H-D showing its support for the troops about to enter the war, but the olive green paint would remain standard for almost every one of the next 16 years.

Foreseeing widespread use of its machines in the war overseas, Harley-Davidson created its Service School to train military personnel in the art of H-D maintenance. This factory training continues today to keep the world's fleet of Milwaukee machines rolling.

Prices and Production

Model	Production	Price
Model 17B	124	$215
Model 17C	605	$240
Model 17E	68	$255
Model 17F	8,527	$275
Model 17J	9,180	$310
Model 17S	5	$225
Model 17R	12	$280
Model 17T	1	$280

This Model 17C is paired with an unusual wicker sidecar rig. Motorcycles were being pressed into a variety of duties, and there seemed to be no end to the options available.

1918

World War I was now accounting for much of the country's production capabilities, and Harley-Davidson was not excluded. Production of Harleys continued, but nearly 20,000 units went straight into the war effort. Dealers still had bikes to sell, but not in the quantities of years previous. As perhaps the first nail in Indian's coffin, very few of their nationwide dealers received any units to sell during the war. These customers made their way to the competing brands, of which Harley was most common.

The Dixie brand magnetos, which had supplanted the Bosch units in 1917, were now replaced with Remy models. The majority of the twins were fitted with the Model 250 from Remy. A mechanically operated circuit breaker was also added to the '18s.

A raft of new components were found on the 1918 models, all of which improved the breed, albeit subtly. Previous Harley bikes required dealer service to lubricate the clutch bearings. The 1918 models provided the owner with simple access to the bearings through the actuator plate. Although it was required every 1,000 miles, the rider could now lubricate his machine in the comfort of his own garage.

The color variations on the contrasting pin striping also changed in 1918. The green finish was introduced in 1917, but was accented with "Pullman Green" stripes with gold detail. The '18 models wore the same green base color, but were now decorated with light green stripes and black details.

Perhaps the biggest news for 1918 was the War Department's decision to request a "standard" military motorcycle for use in battle. Each of the major manufacturers contributed their own bits of hardware for review in this new conglomerated machine. Harley-Davidson's role was crucial, since it supplied the "Liberty" motor for review. The choice of an H-S power plant only heightened the demand for the green machines at U.S. dealerships. The USA motorcycle project never bore fruit, but Harley had still scored big points in the sales race.

1918 Model Year Lineup

Model	Engine Type	Displacement	Transmission	Special feature(s)
Model 18B	F-Head Single	35 cid	None	High-Tension Magneto
Model 18C	F-Head Single	35 cid	Three-Speed	Solo Model with Magneto
Model 18E	F-Head Twin	60.34 cid	Single-Speed	High-Tension Magneto
Model 18F	F-Head Twin	60.34 cid	Three-Speed	Solo Model with Magneto
Model 18J	F-Head Twin	60.34 cid	Three-Speed	Electrical System
Model 18R	F-Head Twin	60.34 cid	Three-Speed	—
Model 18FUS	F-Head Twin	60.34 cid	Three-Speed	Government Use Model

Production and Prices

Model	Production	Price
Model 18B	19	$235
Model 18C	251	$260
Model 18E	5	$275
Model 18F	11,764	$290
Model 18J	6,571	$320
Model 18R	3	NA
Model 18FUS	8,095	NA

The 1919 Sport Model represented a big leap of faith for Harley, but sold poorly in its short life.

1919

While World War I had ended in 1918, it had a lingering effect on the production of 1919 models. With the military's needs still a consideration, production models were simplified in the early part of the model year. Only twin-cylinder models with three-speed transmissions were assembled for public sale.

Even with the limited range of models available in 1919, Harley-Davidson found itself in an even stronger position than before the war began. The devastation and aftermath of the war ended production completely for motorcycle builders in Europe. This vacuum allowed the Milwaukee machines to step right in and fill the void.

Only minor alterations were made to '19s built later in the model year. The previous worm-actuated clutch was replaced by a cam-actuated mechanism. The handlebars were now wider by 2 1/2 inches and came to the owner wearing enamel matching the bike's sheet metal.

The trailing-link front fork was another attempt to produce an entirely new platform for Harley buyers in 1919. Not every idea Harley tried was a success.

In an attempt to bring diversity and excitement to the line, Harley added an entirely new model in the latter part of the season. The new 1919 Sport Model was assembled around a twin-cylinder engine, but the usual V format was not used. The new motor featured cylinders that were horizontally opposed, inline with the new frame. The motor was actually a stressed member of the structure, delivering strength and lighter weight. Displacing 35.64 cubic inches, the twin's combined capacity barely exceeded the 1918 single cylinder's capacity of 35. The new motor was of the side-valve variety, and looked like nothing seen before in a Harley dealership. The 6-hp motor was mated to a three-speed transmission, and easy maintenance was a key selling point.

The Sport Model was also delivered with a different front fork design. The trailing-link setup was similar to other machines available, but was tidier in its appearance. Electric lighting was not an option on the first Sport Models, but acetylene-powered units could be ordered.

Despite the bike's radical appearance, or maybe because of it, the machine received a lukewarm reception. The cost of entry was also deemed a bit high at $325 per copy. It seemed that Americans had come to love their V-twin Harleys above all others in the previous 20 years. The Sport Model trundled on for several years, but would disappear from the 1924 catalog.

The factory racing team was provided with an all-new eight-valve motor with promises of new levels of power. The eight-valve motors were also driven by the first two-cam mechanisms. The idea behind the double cam was to reduce the excessive motion a single came caused when driving both cylinders. For additional weight savings, the eight-valve motors sported drilled connecting rods.

1919 Model Year Lineup

Model	Engine Type	Displacement	Transmission	Special Feature(s)
Model 19F	F-Head Twin	60.34 cid	Three-Speed	Solo Model w/Magneto
Model 19FUS	F-Head Twin	60.34 cid	Three-Speed	Government Use Only
Model 19J	F-Head Twin	60.34 cid	Three-Speed	Solo Model
Model 19WF	Horiz.-Opp. Twin	35.64 cid	Three-Speed	Sport Model

Production and Prices

Model	Production	Price
Model 19F	5,064	$350
Model 19FUS	7,521	NA
Model 19J	9,941	$370
Model 19WF	753	$325

The horizontally opposed cylinders were a radical departure when compared to the tried-and-true V-twin design. Benefits of the early design proved to be minimal.

This 1920 Model 20J was the year's best seller.

1920

After WWI, Harley-Davidson found itself in first place in the race of the "Big 3" American cycle manufacturers. Indian was second, and Excelsior an aggressive third. This was no time for complacency, and Harley was ready.

Changes to the venerable V-twin motor were numerous, yet not radical. Harley was afraid to mess with the success it had achieved, so minor improvements seemed more proper.

The 1920 models were fitted with new cylinder castings. In an effort to provide the smoothest-running motor possible, H-D gave some of the front or rear cylinders compression plates. Other motors bore no plates at all. With high-quality metal casting still a thing of the future, the motors often needed the plates to provide equal compression to each cylinder. There was no other way to monitor and control the volume of the combustion chambers at the time.

The "Fast" motors were now named with an "E" instead of the previous "500" designation. Aluminum pistons and drilled connecting rods were but a few of the performance modifications made to the "E" motors. Looser tolerances were still in force, and teardowns and inspection were suggested every 100 miles. Factory specs also recommended different compression ratios for the different types of tracks being raced on.

The toolbox resided atop the tank, along with filler caps and the ammeter.

A special frame was offered to "dealers" and was delivered with a removable plate near the bottom. This plate was removed to allow the installation of either the new "E" motors, or the earlier "500" series. Once the chosen motor was in place, the plate was bolted back in to complete the assembly.

Late in the model year, H-D began to add electric components of its own design and manufacture. Generators and coils would be "home made" and come from within the expanding bowels of the factory. The Sport model was also fitted with electrics, a new battery box, and toolbox cover with locks.

Another addition to the factory was completed in 1920, and brought the total square footage to more than 542,000. This made the Harley-Davidson headquarters the largest motorcycle assembly plant in the U.S. Annual capacity was now 35,000 units. Indian was stuck at 520,000 square feet, and production capabilities of only 30,000 units. The gap began to widen with every passing year.

1920 Model Year Lineup

Model	Engine Type	Displacement	Transmission	Special Feature(s)
Model 20F	F-Head Twin	60.34 cid	Three-Speed	Magneto Ignition
Model 20FS	F-Head Twin	60.34 cid	Three-Speed	Sidecar Gearing w/Magneto
Model 20J	F-Head Twin	60.34 cid	Three-Speed	Electrical System
Model 20JS	F-Head Twin	60.34 cid	Three-Speed	Sidecar Gearing w/Electrics
Model 20WF	Horiz.-Opp. Twin	35.64 cid	Three-Speed	—
Model 20WJ	Horiz.-Opp. Twin	35.64 cid	Three-Speed	Electrical System

Production and Prices

Model	Production	Price
Model 20F	7,579	$370
Model 20J	14,192	$395
Model 20WF	4,459	$335
Model 20WJ	810	NA

The 20J cylinder castings featured more rounded fins around the sparkplugs.

The 1921 Model J outsold the new Seventy-Four model, despite its smaller displacement.

1921

The big news for the 1921 models was the introduction of the 74-cubic inch motor. The Seventy-Four was now offered alongside the Sixty-One motor from previous years.

Changes in the new motor were not extensive, save for the increase in capacity. The Seventy-Four drew its breath through a 1/4-inch larger-diameter Schebler carburetor.

The Sixty-One motors were still fitted with chrome-nickel exhaust valves, but the Seventy-Four would get something better. Metalurgy was becoming more precise every year, and the creation of new alloys made all sorts of things possible. The latest metal-hardening techniques created silchrome, a harder yet smoother material. This new alloy was chosen for use on the Seventy-Four exhaust valves.

The Seventy-Fours were assembled using solid flywheels, replacing the previous spoked and webbed varieties. Later in the model year, the Sixty-One motor was also fitted with the solid flywheels. A bevy of updated parts could be found within the new motor, along with several changes to the sheet metal and fenders. Right and left crankcases, as well as front and rear exhaust pipes, were required for the new motor, but made for a better-running product.

The Sport model received a few cosmetic alterations, but remained mechanically unchanged.

Another new motor variation was the Model CD, which touted 37 cubic inches of displacement from a single cylinder. The bike was used mostly for commercial applications.

Temporary plant closings and reductions in production numbers helped to curb excess inventory, but it was obvious that the market was changing. Even racing victories no longer seemed to drive people into the showrooms as they once did.

1921 Model Year Lineup

Model	Engine Type	Displacement	Transmission	Special Feature(s)
Model 21F	F-Head Twin	60.34 cid	Three-Speed	Magneto Ignition
Model 21FS	F-Head Twin	60.34 cid	Three-Speed	Sidecar Gearing w/Magneto
Model 21J	F-Head Twin	60.34 cid	Three-Speed	Electrical System
Model 21JS	F-Head Twin	60.34 cid	Three-Speed	Sidecar Gearing w/Electrics
Model 21FD	F-Head Twin	74 cid	Three-Speed	Magneto Ignition
Model 21FDS	F-Head Twin	74 cid	Three-Speed	Sidecar Gearing w/Magneto
Model 21JD	F-Head Twin	74 cid	Three-Speed	Electrical System
Model 21JDS	F-Head Twin	74 cid	Three-Speed	Sidecar gearing w/Electrics
Model 21CD	F-Head Single	37 cid	Three-Speed	Magneto Ignition
Model 21WF	Horiz.-Opp. Twin	35.64 cid	Three-Speed	Magneto Ignition
Model 21WJ	Horiz.-Opp. Twin	35.64 cid	Three-Speed	Electrical System

Production and Prices

Model	Production	Price
Model 21F	2,413	$450
Model 21FS	NA	$450
Model 21J	4,526	$485
Model 21JS	NA	$485
Model 21FD	277	$485
Model 21FDS	NA	$485
Model 21JD	2,321	$520
Model 21JDS	NA	$520
Model 21CD	NA	$430
Model 21WF	1,100	$415
Model 21WJ	823	$445

1922

Mechanical changes for the 1922s were few and far between. Constant improvement without drastic alterations seemed to be the name of the game at this stage in Harley-Davidson history.

The most obvious change in the line's appearance was the switch from olive green to a darker Brewster green. The previous green accent stripes were now seen as fine, gold pinstripes. Since very few other changes were obvious, this makes for a great way to identify the '22 models.

Both the Sixty-One and Seventy-Four motors were still available. The Seventy-Fours now featured cylinders that were 1/16 inch taller to eliminate the need for the earlier compression plates. The Sixty-One motors did, however, utilize the plates to lower compression in 1922. The V-twins of 1922 featured new crankcases on the left and right, as well as an updated gearbox and cover. New front forks were implemented in both the sprung and rigid variations.

The Sixty-Ones were fitted with solid flywheels late in the 1921 production, and would remain for 1922. Late in the 1922 run, a double-plunger oil pump was found on all V-twins. Proper lubrication remained a dominant factor in a machine's life span, so every effort was made to improve and simplify the process.

The higher-performance "E" motors were still offered on the Sixty-Ones, and about mid-year a similar "DCA" option was added to the Seventy-Fours. Both variations featured aluminum pistons, drilled connecting rods, and a bevy of other performance tweaks.

With the exception of minor design changes, the Sport model continued to be offered. Sales still lagged, and Harley didn't seem interested in spending wildly on such a poor performer. Speaking of which, the Model 37 CD single-cylinder variation would appear for the last time in 1922. It was only able to exist for two model years before being eliminated from the lineup.

When they first appeared, motorcycles offered a low-cost alternative to the "horseless carriages" being offered by the Ford Motor Company. By the end of 1920, a Sixty-One from Harley and a Model T Runabout both cost $395. By the end of 1922, the same Model T sold for $71 LESS than a Seventy-Four model. It was obvious that changes would have to be made for motorcycles to remain competitive in the expanding world of four-wheeled transportation.

1922 Model Year Lineup

Model	Engine Type	Displacement	Transmission	Special Feature(s)
Model 22F	F-Head Twin	60.34 cid	Three-Speed	Magneto Ignition
Model 22FS	F-Head Twin	60.34 cid	Three-Speed	Sidecar Gearing w/Magneto
Model 22J	F-Head Twin	60.34 cid	Three-Speed	Electrical System
Model 22JS	F-Head Twin	60.34 cid	Three-Speed	Sidecar Gearing w/Electrics
Model 22FD	F-Head Twin	74 cid	Three-Speed	Magneto Ignition
Model 22FDS	F-Head Twin	74 cid	Three-Speed	Sidecar Gearing w/Magneto
Model 22JD	F-Head Twin	74 cid	Three-Speed	Electrical System
Model 22JDS	F-Head Twin	74 cid	Three-Speed	Sidecar Gearing w/Electrics
Model 22CD	F-Head Single	37 cid	Three-Speed	Commercial Use
Model 22WF	Horiz.-Opp. Twin	35.64 cid	Three-Speed	Magneto Ignition
Model 22WJ	Horiz.-Opp. Twin	35.64 cid	Three-Speed	Electrical System

Production and Prices

Model	Production	Price
Model 22F	1,824	$335
Model 22FS	NA	$335
Model 22J	3,183	$365
Model 22JS	NA	$365
Model 22FD	909	$360
Model 22FDS	NA	$360
Model 22JD	3,988	$390
Model 22JDS	NA	$390
Model 22CD	39	$315
Model 22WF	388	$310
Model 22WJ	455	$340

1923

While changes in the last few years had been minimal, they were positively miserly for the 1923 lineup. Period advertising claimed a total of 11 improvements for the latest offerings.

The Sixty-Ones were now treated to the same silchrome exhaust valves used in the Seventy-Fours in a previous year. The exterior shape of the Seventy-Four's cylinders was altered, giving the cylinder head cooling fins a more angular appearance. The number of exhaust manifold fins increased from five to seven.

1923 Model Year Lineup

Model	Engine Type	Displacement	Transmission	Special Feature(s)
Model 23F	F-Head Twin	60.34 cid	Three-Speed	Magneto Ignition
Model 23FS	F-Head Twin	60.34 cid	Three-Speed	Sidecar Gearing w/Magneto
Model 23J	F-Head Twin	60.34 cid	Three-Speed	Electrical System
Model 23JS	F-Head Twin	60.34 cid	Three-Speed	Sidecar gearing w/Electrics
Model 23FD	F-Head Twin	74 cid	Three-Speed	Magneto Ignition
Model 23FDS	F-Head Twin	74 cid	Three-Speed	Sidecar Gearing w/Magneto
Model 23JD	F-Head Twin	74 cid	Three-Speed	Electrical System
Model 23JDS	F-Head Twin	74 cid	Three-Speed	Sidecar Gearing w/Electrics
Model 23 WF	Horiz.-Opp. Twin	35.64 cid	Three-Speed	Magneto Ignition
Model 23WJ	Horiz.-Opp. Twin	35.64 cid	Three-Speed	Electrical System

The improved double-plunger oiler became a fixture on all 1923 models after its introduction on mid-year '22s. An enhanced generator now provided more output for the Staylit taillight, and provided a charge anytime the cycle exceeded 12 mph. The rear fender was now hinged to facilitate easier tire changes, and the rear hub featured roller bearings.

Seeing the writing on the wall, H-D made no changes to the Sport models, and 1923 would be their last year. As before, it appeared that the V-twin variation was what people wanted most. Even the twin-cylinder Indian Scout was outselling the Sport, driving in the last nail in its coffin.

Production and Prices

Model	Production	Price
Model 23F	2,822	$285
Model 23FS	NA	$285
Model 23J	4,802	$305
Model 23JS	NA	$305
Model 23FD	869	$310
Model 23FDS	NA	$310
Model 23JD	7,458	$330
Model 23JDS	NA	$330
Model 23WF	614	$275
Model 23WJ	481	$295

The 1924 24JE seen here is a perfect example of the most popular model for that year.

1924

The new model year would offer more options to the Harley-Davidson buyer than ever before. The lineup hadn't changed much, but now you could build one of the remaining models to meet you specific needs.

The Sixty-One was only built using the aluminum pistons, but the Seventy-Four allowed for several choices. The choices, including the aluminum slugs, were a pair of cast-iron, or the new iron alloy pistons. The latest alloy pistons promised more durability. Both the front and rear cylinders were also new for 1924.

Once your piston selection had been made, the carburetion was next on the list. Assuming the standard Schebler Model H was not your cup of tea, The Schebler Deluxe could be added. The third choice was a unit by Zenith.

There were numerous improvements made to the V-twins. As always, reliable chassis lubrication was critical in the longevity of a motorcycle, and the addition of 12 grease fittings made the chore far less arduous. The owner was no longer forced to disassemble anything to get the Alemite lube to its critical locations.

The previous three-plate battery was upgraded to four plates, providing a huge increase in capacity. The three brushes within the generator were also increased in size to feed the newly improved electrics.

The 1924s were also delivered wearing a new, one-year-only, box-shaped muffler. This exhaust component could even be retrofitted to models dating back to 1915 with a set of factory brackets.

Both exhaust pipes on the Seventy-Four were new, as was the front pipe on the Sixty-One. 1924 would also mark the final year for the horizontal top frame rail.

Front fenders sported a more aggressive center rib, and the side panels continued further forward than the earlier versions. Paint for the line was once again returned to olive green, but the earlier striping colors were not re-issued. The latest accent stripes were maroon in color with black borders. A gold pinstripe divided the narrower maroon striping.

While the American buyer loved the power and sound of a V-Twin, the European market clamored for a smaller, lighter, single-cylinder Harley. A team of four Harley-Davidson executives

Sweeping changes would make it easy to differentiate between the 1924 and 1925 models.

1924 Model Year Lineup

Model	Engine Type	Displacement	Transmission	Special Feature(s)
Model 24FE	F-Head Twin	60.34 cid	Three-Speed	Magento Ig./ Alum. Pistons
Model 24FES	F-Head Twin	60.34 cid	Three-Speed	Sidecar Gear./ Mag./Alum. Pist.
Model 24JE	Head Twin	60.34 cid	Three-Speed	Electric Sys./ Alum. Pistons
Model 24JES	F-Head Twin	60.34 cid	Three-Speed	Sidecar Gear./ Elec./Alum. Pist.
Model 24FD	F-Head Twin	74 cid	Three-Speed	Mag. Ig./Cast-Iron Pistons
Model 24FDS	F-Head Twin	74 cid	Three-Speed	Sidecar Gear./ Mag. Ig./Cast-Iron Pistons
Model 24FDCA	F-Head Twin	74 cid	Three-Speed	Mag. Ig./Alum. Pistons
Model 24FDSCA	F-Head Twin	74 cid	Three-Speed	Sidecar Gear./ Mag. Ig./Alum. Pistons
Model 24FDCB	F-Head Twin	74 cid	Three-Speed	Mag. Ig./Iron Alloy Pistons
Model 24JD	F-Head Twin	74 cid	Three-Speed	Elec. Sys./Cast-Iron Pistons
Model 24JDS	F-Head Twin	74 cid	Three-Speed	Sidecar Gear./ Elec/Cast-Iron Pistons
Model 24JDCA	F-Head Twin	74 cid	Three-Speed	Elec. Sys./ Alum. Pistons
Model 24JDSCA	F-Head Twin	74 cid	Three-Speed	Sidecar Gear./ Elec. Sys./Alum. Pistons
Model 24JDCB	F-Head Twin	74 cid	Three-Speed	Elec. Sys./Iron-Alloy Pistons

traveled overseas to gauge the marketplace for such a machine. What they learned was surprising, and convinced them that a smaller model needed to be added to the Harley catalog.

The Sport model was no more, and had been a bit disappointing. It offered several unique characteristics, many of which would never be seen again on a Harley. With the factory running at about 50 percent of capacity, the loss of any production was painful. Commercial, police, and overseas orders were keeping the company busy.

Production and Prices

Model	Production	Prices
Model 24FE	2,708	$300
Model 24FES	NA	$300
Model 24JE	4,994	$320
Model 24JES	NA	$320
Model 24FD	502	$315
Model 24FDS	NA	$315
Model 24FDCA	51	$325
Model 24FDSCA	NA	$325
Model 24FDCB	90	NA
Model 24JD	2,995	$335
Model 24JDS	NA	$335
Model 24JDCA	3,014	$345
Model 24JDSCA	NA	$345
Model 24JDCB	3,034	NA

The 1925 models sported new frames and tank designs, along with enhanced comfort.

1925

For this year, Harley provided customers with an all-new frame for the V-twin line. It offered several advantages in comfort and convenience. Factory advertising referred to the new design as the "Stream-Line," and touted "27 big improvements" and "new low prices!"

The new frame design provided the rider a seating position that was 3 inches closer to the ground. This opened up the market to many who had been hampered by the taller saddle height. The lower frame layout also permitted designers to incorporate sleeker, more rounded fuel tanks. The front downtube was now "double butted" for additional strength, and terminated just below the engine cases. This bolted to a rigid steel channel, which now served as the base for the motor's mounting platform.

The latest frame iteration allowed for several related improvements. The tires and wheels could be wider, which improved both handling and comfort. Mounted at the front of the frame, the forks now featured recoil and cushion springs with softer response. The newly shaped handlebars and repositioned gearshift

The sleek fuel tank and upright battery position make the '25s easy to spot.

lever made the '25s more rider-friendly than ever. Yet another added comfort feature was the saddle-shaped seat, complete with six mounting positions. The rider could now choose the position of the seat, and the seat post cushion spring was increased in length from 9 to 14 inches.

Inside the motor, both aluminum and cast-iron pistons were eliminated from the options sheet. The iron-alloy versions were now installed on all Sixty-One and Seventy-Four models. The optional Schebler DeLuxe carburetor provided a low-speed position that allowed for easier cold-weather starting. The Zenith

The 1925 handlebars reached towards the rider, offering more comfort.

The overall balance of form and function was improving every year for Harley.

The Single Passenger Sidecar, Model LT, sold for $100 in 1925 and provided a modicum of comfort for a passenger.

was also offered if the standard Schebler Model H was not desired.

Four more Alemite grease fittings were added, bringing the total to 16. Required maintenance was getting easier with every passing year.

There were two headlight lenses in use for the 1925s. One was a simple clear lens, and the other a diffusing unit with vertical ribs on the inside surface. The front surface remained flat, but provided a wider splay of light for riding after dark. Adjustable headlight brackets and a vastly improved headlight switch were also added. The taillight was also brighter than the previous year, with a clip to hold the wire in place.

1925 Model Year Lineup

Model	Engine Type	Displacement	Transmission	Special Feature(s)
Model 25FE	F-Head Twin	60.34 cid	Three-Speed	Magneto Ignition
Model 25FES	F-Head Twin	60.34 cid	Three-Speed	Sidecar Gearing/ Magneto
Model 25JE	F-Head Twin	60.34 cid	Three-Speed	Electrical System
Model 25JES	F-Head Twin	60.34 cid	Three-Speed	Sidecar Gearing/ Electrics
Model 25FDCB	F-Head Twin	74 cid	Three-Speed	Magneto Ignition
Model 25FDCBS	F-Head Twin	74 cid	Three-Speed	Sidecar Gearing/ Magneto
Model 25JDCB	F-Head Twin	74 cid	Three-Speed	Electrical System
Model 25JDCBS	F-Head Twin	74 cid	Three-Speed	Sidecar Gearing/ Electrics

Production and Prices

Model	Production	Price
Model 25FE	1,318	$295
Model 25FES	NA	$295
Model 25JE	4,114	$315
Model 25JES	NA	$315
Model 25FDCB	433	$315
Model 25FDCBS	NA	$315
Model 25JDCB	9,506	$335
Model 25JDCBS	NA	$335

Model 26B was by far the most popular of the new single-cylinder offerings.

1926

After their trip to Europe in 1924, H-D executives decided they needed to build a single-cylinder model for both U.S. and overseas markets. Despite its ongoing patent infringement lawsuit with Eclipse, H-D decided it was time to enter the fray. 1926 would see four different versions offered, and they were priced about $100 lower than the twin-cylinder models.

Each of the four models displaced 21.35 cubic inches, and were of the side-valve variety. Trim levels were the only options available, and H-D hoped to entice a new audience of buyers with these simple machines. With a mileage rating of 80 mph and a top speed reaching nearly 60 mph, the singles were not suggested to be toys.

The front fenders on the new singles were fully sprung, and you could order standard or the shorter Speedster handlebars. A new box located at the front of the fuel tank housed control levers and a key lock. This was only used on the battery-equipped B and BA variants.

The 21-cubic inch 26B motor was mated to a three-speed transmission.

The singles equipped with the optional electrical system came equipped with this neat dash panel. The same panel was also seen on the twins for 1926.

The twin-cylinder models were equipped with electrics, and the batteries provided double the capacity of earlier versions. The generators were also improved with larger brushes and a new armature. V-twin models received wider fenders with the latest "balloon" tires riding underneath. This style tire was also used on the new single models. Enhanced rust proofing was applied to the spokes and nipples of the wheels, adding life to the tried-and-true format.

Buyers could now order a big twin in either white or cream motifs. Very little in the way of official listings is available, but examples of the newly colored machines began appearing in *The Enthusiast* on a regular basis.

1926 Model Year Lineup

Model	Engine Type	Displacement	Transmission	Special Feature(s)
Model 26A	Side-Valve Single	21.35 cid	Three-Speed	Magneto Ignition
Model 26B	Side-Valve Single	21.35 cid	Three-Speed	Electrical System
Model 26AA	Overhead-Valve Single	21.35 cid	Three-Speed	Magneto Ignition
Model 26BA	Overhead-Valve Single	21.35 cid	Three-Speed	Electrical System
Model 26S	Overhead-Valve Single	21.35 cid	NA	Race Model/ Magneto
Model 26J	F-Head Twin	60.34 cid	Three-Speed	Electrical System
Model 26JS	F-Head Twin	60.34 cid	Three-Speed	Sidecar Gearing/ Electrics
Model 26JD	F-Head Twin	74 cid	Three-Speed	Electrical System
Model 26JDS	F-Head Twin	74 cid	Three-Speed	Sidecar Gearing/ Electrics

Production and Prices

Model	Production	Price
Model 26A	1,128	$210
Model 26B	5,979	$235
Model 26AA	61	$250
Model 26BA	515	$275
Model 26S	NA	$300
Model 26J	3,749	$315
Model 26JS NA	NA	$315
Model 26JD	9,544	$335
Model 26JDS	NA	$335

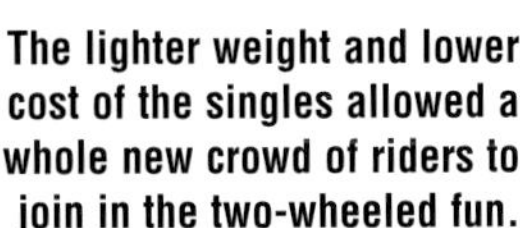

The lighter weight and lower cost of the singles allowed a whole new crowd of riders to join in the two-wheeled fun.

Despite the popularity of the new singles, the JD outsold them by nearly 3 to 1.

1927

After the excitement of the new single models being introduced in 1926, the following model year was a bit anticlimactic. A minimum of changes would be made to the existing lineup, and no new models would be offered to the public.

In an effort to eliminate poor engine performance under wet conditions, H-D introduced a distributor-less ignition on the twin-cylinder models for 1927. Both Harley and Indian had been plagued by problems with their magnetos in wet weather, and Harley decided this system would improve results.

But the new ignition system exposed a new problem when tested on prototypes. When running the engine with the spark fully retarded, there was an excessive amount of backfiring. By adjusting the level of spark retard available to the rider, the problem was solved.

1927 was the final year for the olive green crankcases.

Of the singles offered in 1927, the B model was the hot seller.

The single-cylinder models were also given a small selection of upgrades. Both the frame and fuel tank received additional structural support, and the lugs on the crankcase were enlarged. A new muffler was installed, reducing back pressure, and the saddle was given a more comfortable contour. Included in the puchase price was an Alemite lubrication gun used to service the 10 grease fittings found on the singles.

1927 Model Year Lineup

Model	Engine Type	Displacement	Transmission	Special Feature(s)
Model 27A	Side-Valve Single	21.35 cid	Three-Speed	Magneto Ignition
Model 27B	Side-Valve Single	21.35 cid	Three-Speed	Electric System
Model 27AA	Overhead-Valve Single	21.35 cid	Three-Speed	Magneto Ignition
Model 27BA	Overhead-Valve Single	21.35 cid	Three-Speed	Electric System
Model 27S	Overhead-Valve Single	21.35 cid	NA	Magneto Ignition
Model 27J	F-Head Twin	60.34 cid	Three-Speed	Electric System
Model 27JS	F-Head Twin	60.34 cid	Three-Speed	Electric System
Model 27JD	F-Head Twin	74 cid	Three-Speed	Electric System
Model 27JDS	F-Head Twin	74 cid	Three-Speed	Electric System

Production and Prices

Model	Production	Price
Model 27A	444	$210
Model 27B	3,711	$235
Model 27AA	32	$250
Model 27BA	481	$275
Model 27S	6	$300
Model 27J	3,561	$310
Model 27JS	NA	$310
Model 27JD	9,691	$320
Model 27JDS	NA	$320

The compact size and weight of the singles appealed to some, but not as many as H-D had hoped.

1928

Big performance news could be heard echoing up and down the halls of the Harley-Davidson headquarters as the 1928 models were announced. Only so much power could be squeezed from a single-cam motor, so a second variation, complete with twin cams, was now available to the public. Twin-cam motors had dominated the field at racing venues since 1919, but were never offered to John Q. Public before.

The twin-cam Sixty-One was the JH version, while the twin-cam Seventy-Four was the JDH variant. To mimicking the twin-cam racing engines, a direct-action valve gear system was implemented. This layout had been around since 1924 on the race bikes. Both of the twin-cam models were now fitted with domed, magnesium alloy (Dow Metal) pistons. The domed slugs added to the performance blend by increasing compression.

The two-cam machines also featured slimmer fuel tanks to help project the appearance of a svelte racing machine. Fuel capacity was reduced to 4.75 gallons from 5.3 as a result of the new look. Wheel diameter was also smaller at 18 inches, which dropped the performance bikes lower to the ground. Beginning early in the model year, H-D began installing larger spokes on the rear wheels of its machines, and this would apply to all units after January 1, 1928.

1928 Model Year Lineup

Model	Engine Type	Displacement	Transmission	Special Feature(s)
Model 28B	Side-Valve Single	21.35 cid	Three-Speed	Electric System
Model 28BA	Overhead-Valve Single	21.35 cid	Three-Speed	Electric System
Model 28J	F-Head Twin	60.34 cid	Three-Speed	Electric System
Model 28JS	F-Head Twin	60.34 cid	Three-Speed	Sidecar Gearing/ Electrics
Model 28JL	F-Head Twin	60.34 cid	Three-Speed	Spec. Sport Solo/ Dow Met. Pist.
Model 28JH	Twin-Cam/F-Head Twin	60.34 cid	Three-Speed	Dow Metal Pistons/Electrics
Model 28JD	F-Head Twin	74 cid	Three-Speed	Electric System
Model 28JDS	F-Head Twin	74 cid	Three-Speed	Sidecar Gearing/ Electrics
Model 28JDL	F-Head Twin	74 cid	Three-Speed	Spec. Sport Solo/ Dow Metal Pist.
Model 28JDH	Twin-Cam/F-Head Twin	74 cid	Three-Speed	Dow Metal Pistons/Electrics

Along with the more potent engine options, Harley-Davidson introduced several additional firsts for the '28 models. All bikes had an air cleaner as standard equipment. Pulling clean air into the motor saved on maintenance, and the new device proved worthy of the task.

Rear-wheel brakes had been a fixture on all motorcycles for many years while the front wheel remained unfettered. Many riders thought a front-wheel brake would be dangerous, but H-D decided to buck that trend by adding a binder to the front wheel of all the 1928 models. These were primitive compared to today's systems, but still offered the rider additional stopping power.

A throttle-controlled oil pump was also new on the '28s, and reduced the need to keep an eye on daily oil consumption. Since oil requirements were now partially controlled by throttle use, the rider had a far better chance of keeping the motor from going dry.

In the styling department, a wide variety of colors were available. You could now get your new twin in Azure Blue, Coach Green, Police Blue, or Maroon for only $3 extra. Cream and White were also available, but at a price of $27. The real breakthrough in the palette was the option of getting your Harley in any color. This $24 choice was covered by the "all other colors" category. Similar color selections were also available on the singles for a lower cost than the twins.

Production and Prices

Model	Production	Price
Model 28B	3,483	$235
Model 28BA	943	$255
Model 28J	4,184	$310
Model 28JS	NA	$310
Model 28JL	NA	$325
Model 28JH	NA	$360
Model 28JD	11,007	$320
Model 28JDS	NA	$320
Model 28JDL	NA	$335
Model 28JDH	NA	$390

1929

The minor changes H-D made to its motorcycle lineup seemed especially insignificant in 1929. By the end of the calendar year, the financial stability of the country would be rocked by the stock market collapse, which causing a domino that certainly affected the motorcycle market.

Both the Sixty-One and Seventy-Four motors received larger bushings on the inlet rocker arms, and the other twins were fitted with stronger inlet housing caps. The OHV single-cylinder models now functioned with Dow Metal pistons within their cylinder walls, just like the side-valve models had beginning in 1928. Pending changes to the V-twin power plant would mark 1929 as the final year for the F-head twins, and the 21-cubic inch single would soon disappear as well.

Two new motor options were offered for the 1929 models: A 30.50-cubic inch single, and a 45-cubic inch twin. Both engines featured side-valve technology.

1929 Model Year Lineup

Model	Engine Type	Displacement	Transmission	Special Feature(s)
Model 29B	Side-Valve Single	21.35 cid	Three-Speed	—
Model 29BA	Overhead-Valve Single	21.35 cid	Three-Speed	—
Model 29C	Side-Valve Single	30.50 cid	Three-Speed	—
Model 29D	Side-Valve Twin	45 cid	Three-Speed	Low Comp./Dow Met. Pist.
Model 29DL	Side-Valve Twin	45 cid	Three-Speed	High Comp./Dow Met. Pist.
Model 29J	F-Head Twin	60.34 cid	Three-Speed	—
Model 29JS	F-Head Twin	60.34 cid	Three-Speed	Sidecar Gear/ Dow Met. Pist.
Model 29JH	Twin-Cam/F-Head Twin	60.34 cid	Three-Speed	Dow Metal Pistons
Model 29JD	F-Head Twin	74 cid	Three-Speed	Iron Alloy Pistons
Model 29JDS	F-Head twin	74 cid	Three-Speed	Sidecar Gear./ Iron All. Pist.
Model 29JDH	Twin Cam/F-Head Twin	74 cid	Three-Speed	Dow Metal Pistons

Clutch springs in the singles were changed twice. The first configuration consisted of 12 springs, while the updated version sported 14 longer units. Commercial machines were found with larger spokes on the front wheels to boost durability.

A new, four-tube "Pipes O'Pan" muffler was installed to reduce noise without compromising performance. This unique format was only used on the 1929 models due to its lack of popularity with riders. The available retrofit kits were even less popular, and were also dropped from the parts catalog for 1930.

Up front, a pair of bullet-shaped headlights blazed the way for the '29s. This styling feature would be dropped from some of the lineup for 1930. The rest were scrapped the year after that. Olive green paint would remain as the standard selection, but additional optional hues were offered as in years past.

Factory options continued to flourish, and for 1929, a new handlebar windshield was shown in the January issue of *The Enthusiast*. Selling for $16, the windshield offered weather protection to the rider while still allowing ample air to cool the motor. They were used on the 61- and 74-inch twins. A few examples of these "fairings" can be seen today.

Production and Prices

Model	Production	Price
Model 29B	1,592	$235
Model 29BA	191	$255
Model 29C	1,570	$255
Model 29D	4,513	$290
Model 29DL	2,343	$290
Model 29J	2,866	$310
Model 29JS	NA	$310
Model 29JH	NA	NA
Model 29JD	10,182	$320
Model 29JDS	NA	$320
Model 29JDH	NA	$370

The 74-cubic inch VS made a perfect match for a sidecar, even this unusual left-side model.

1930

The H-D model lineup for 1930 was comprised of nearly all new versions of the previous offerings, but the timing was not great—the bikes hit the showroom floors only two months before the stock market crashed. Of course, the changes had been penned many months before becoming reality, and proved Harley's insistence on bringing improved machines to the market.

The newly offered 74 was well received by customers in 1930.

Sales brochures for the year claimed, "The Greatest Sport of Them All—MOTORCYCLING!" The new "74s" were the centerpiece for the year, and Harley-Davidson was obviously proud of its latest motor.

1929 would mark the final year for the F-head motors that had appeared in Harleys for so many years. The side-valve and overhead-valve versions had already proved their mettle, and would be implemented in every model for 1930. Of course, there were many who bemoaned the loss of their beloved F-heads, but time and change marches on.

With respect to hardware, there were very few carry-overs from the previous model year. The Forty-Five power plant made the transition, but the new Seventy-Four motors, frames, suspension, and convenience features were all new for the 1930 models. A few internal components from earlier examples were also still in use, but only those that had proved their worth. Every motor in the 1930 catalog featured Ricardo heads. This enabled the owner to easily remove the heads to allow for at-home service of the valves and pistons. The Ricardo heads also pledged proper turbulence and complete combustion.

The all-new frames on the big twin Seventy-Fours allowed the rider to sit 2 inches closer to the ground, but still provided additional ground clearance. The Forty-Five twin models provided a seat height nearly 3 inches lower to the pavement. The upper

Sidecars were available in one- or two-person capacities, and provided a fairly comfortable perch for passengers.

frame tubes were spaced to allow for the lower seat height, as well as easier access to the battery located beneath the hinged saddles. The frames were strengthened for the 1930 models, and were becoming more rugged with each passing year. Dealer brochures claimed the new frames were "...now at least 100 percent stronger." The front forks were also constructed using "double-strength drop-forged sides," and promised to deliver performance no matter how rugged the terrain.

The Forty-Five models were now available in a new DLD version. The DLD motor featured higher 6:1 compression, a larger inlet port, and a 28-tooth sprocket on the rear wheel, all of which was claimed to add an additional 10 to 15 mph. The Thirty-Fifty single-cylinders were once again on the roster, but now featured the frame used on the bigger Forty-Fives.

1930 Model Year Lineup

Model	Engine type	Displacement	Transmission	Special Feature(s)
Model 30B	Side-Valve Single	21.35 cid	Three-Speed	Export Model Only
Model 30C	Side-Valve Single	30.50 cid	Three-Speed	Dow Metal Pistons
Model 30D	Side-Valve Twin	45 cid	Three-Speed	Dow Metal Pistons
Model 30DS	Side-Valve Twin	45 cid	Three-Speed	Sidecar gearing
Model 30DL	Side-Valve Twin	45 cid	Three-Speed	High Compression
Model 30DLD	Side-Valve Twin	45 cid	Three-Speed	High Comp./28 Tooth Gear
Model 30V	Side-Valve Twin	74 cid	Three-Speed	Dow Metal Pistons
Model 30VL	Side-Valve Twin	74 cid	Three-Speed	High Compression
Model 30VS	Side-Valve Twin	74 cid	Three-Speed	Sidecar Gearing
Model 30VC	Side-Valve Twin	74 cid	Three-Speed	Nickel-Iron Pistons

All 1930 models were fitted with a greatly enhanced electrical system, which provided nearly twice the power to illuminate the twin headlights while not compromising operation of the machine. The previous troubles with over- or under-charged batteries were now a thing of the past.

A "most startling, revolutionary" feature was now found on the complete line. Interchangeable, quickly detachable wheels provided the rider with a way to repair a flat tire on the road. By simply carrying a replacement wheel and tire on the machine, one could simply swap out the old for the new. Considering the numerous ways motorcycles were being used, this feature brought a whole new level of convenience to the owner.

Sadly, as new buyers of Harleys joined the ranks, thieves found the two-wheeled machines terrific items for their plunder. In an effort to curb the thefts, a steering head lock was also added to the 1930 models. A twist of a key would lock the steering head in a turned position, making it impossible to ride away on the cycle.

Production and Prices

Model	Production	Price
Model 30B	577	$235
Model 30C	1,483	$260
Model 30D	2,000	$310
Model 30DS	213	$310
Model 30DL	3,191	$310
Model 30DLD	206	$310
Model 30V	1,960	$340
Model 30VL	3,246	$340
Model 30VS	3,612	$340
Model 30VC	1,174	$340

This 1931 Model D features the wild graphics and two-toned paint that was offered, but not detailed in any of the factory materials.

1931

After the introduction of the nearly all-new models for 1930, things were quieter at H-D the following year.

The most obvious across-the-board change was the return to single headlights on all models. The new light measured 7 inches in diameter, and was fitted with a flat diffuser lens. The "John Brown Motolamp" featured a uniquely shaped rim holding the flat lens in position. The previous cylindrical toolbox was also changed to a rounded teardrop configuration. Still located beneath the headlight assembly, the new box was easy to access.

The mostly unpopular four-tube muffler on the Seventy-Fours and Forty-Fives was replaced with a single-tube Burgess variant. The Thirty-Fifties still exhaled through the four-tube

The new muffler was of single-tube design and finished in cadmium.

style. The previous Klaxon horns had been faced with a black plate, but all the '31s received a bright chrome piece in its place. Same horn, different look. The Fifty-Five and Thirty-Fifty models also received larger rear brakes and newly shaped handlebars.

The Seventy-Four and Forty-Fives also received new die-cast Schebler carburetors. This new process provided smoother interior surfaces, allowing for a better flow of air and fuel. The Seventy-Fours could also be ordered with a three-speed transmission complete with a reverse gear—needed mainly for bikes with sidecars.

To meet the changing demands of the niche markets, H-D rolled out four new variations for the 1931 model year. The VC was the latest commercial model, the VCR was designed for use as a road marking machine, the VMG was run utilizing a magneto-generator, and the VS was primarily geared for use with a sidecar or delivery box.

The 1931 models featured vertically mounted generators.

The new graphics really added a splash of color and flair for those who ordered them.

The brake pedal and kickstarters were also treated to a cadmium finish in 1931.

Additional minor changes were the finish of the clutch and brake pedals from parkerized black to cadmium silver. Chrome plating was also used on a limited number of small parts in an effort to add a touch of flash to the lineup. "Other colors" were again offered on all models, with no definition of what "other" pertained to. A very small number of machines were finished with graphic, multi-color paint schemes on their fuel tanks. Once again, these options were not shown on any dealer order sheet, but could still be had through factory channels.

The post-market crash pinch was being felt by everyone, and Harley-Davidson was no exception. Reductions in pay were made to staunch the flow of red ink, but sales and profits continued to plummet. Few workers were actually eliminated, but all felt the pain being experienced by their employer. The poor condition of the financial world made the Henderson brand extinct and left only Harley and Indian to duke it out for the few scraps of sales available.

A single 7-inch headlight and chrome-faced horn were new on the '31 models.

1931 Model Year Lineup

Model	Engine Type	Displacement	Transmission	Special Feature(s)
Model 31C	Side-Valve Single	30.50 cid	Three-Speed	—
Model 31D	Side-Valve Twin	45 cid	Three-Speed	Low Compression
Model 31DS	Side-Valve Twin	45 cid	Three-Speed	Sidecar gearing
Model 31DL	Side-Valve Twin	45 cid	Three-Speed	High Compression
Model 31DLD	Side-Valve Twin	45 cid	Three-Speed	Performance Clutch
Model 31V	Side-Valve Twin	74 cid	Three-Speed	Medium Compression
Model 31VS	Side-Valve Twin	74 cid	Three-Speed	Medium Comp./ Sidecar Gear
Model 31VL	Side-Valve Twin	74 cid	Three-Speed	High Compression
Model 31VC	Side-Valve Twin	74 cid	Three-Speed	Low Compression

Production and Prices

Model	Production	Price
Model 31C	874	$260
Model 31D	715	$310
Model 31DS	276	$310
Model 31DL	1,306	$310
Model 31DLD	241	$325
Model 31V	825	$340
Model 31VS	1,994	$340
Model 31VL	3,477	$340
Model 31VC	NA	$340

1932

With the Great Depression gripping the nation, Harley-Davidson needed to find methods to continue production and sell some machines. Sales of the bigger, more-expensive twins continued to wane, and an earlier model was reborn and added to the dealer books for the '32 model year.

The "Twenty-One" featured the diminutive 21-cubic-inch single-cylinder motor used in the previously offered B models. This variant had been removed from the export books a year earlier, and from the domestic scene two years previous.

H-D assembled the '32 Twenty-Ones from an abundance of parts and leftover inventory. Listed at only $195, the "new" Twenty-Ones were the least expensive units ever offered by Harley-Davidson. Despite the fact that each model was probably sold at a loss, they kept the remaining employees busy, and kept a few dollars flowing to the dealers.

Of the Forty-Five and Seventy-Four models, the smaller twin received the most extensive upgrades for 1932. Model designations for the 45 were changed from "D" to "R" across the model line. A new set of crankcases held larger flywheels, and the cylinders housed updated pistons. The latest slugs were aluminum, and the piston pins now featured lock rings. The oil pump was improved for easier removal.

The previous Forty-Fives featured vertical-mount generators, but that would change to a horizontal mount for 1932. The front down tube of the frame was now curved to provide additional space for the new mounting position. The generator itself was also used on the Seventy-Four models, and included larger brushes and a bolstered bearing housing.

The exhaust assembly on the Forty-Fives now included a Burgess muffler that was comparable to that of the one found on the bigger Seventy-Fours.

Changes to the Seventy-Fours were minimal, but continued to improve the breed. To avoid further catastrophe when a chain broke while riding, mounting tabs for the chain guard were altered to allow more space between the two components. Earlier versions caused the chain to get jammed between them.

A fuel strainer was another addition found on both the Forty-Fives and Seventy-Fours. The length of the air intake pipe was increased, and treated to a layer of chrome plating on both versions as well.

The smaller Thirty-Fifty twin variant was still offered, but with only minimal alterations. Frame tubing had been strengthened on the Forty-Fives, and the Thirty-Fifty shared the new design, albeit with a straight front down tube.

The model year would see the introduction of the new three-wheeled variant called the Servi-Car. It was not officially listed until 1933, and was sold largely to police departments and service stations. Housed between the two rear wheels was a storage compartment that was available in two different capacities. The tow bar-equipped models helped dealers and garages return bikes to customers' homes more conveniently. The service station would pull the Servi-Car behind the auto, then disconnect it and ride it back to the shop after the delivery was made.

It was obvious that production would need to lowered for the '32 model year, but initial forecasts were off target. The company hoped to build and sell 9,000 units for 1932, but that became increasingly unlikely as the calendar year dragged on. The total number reached was shy of 7,000, and things looked even worse for the following year. Discussions were had about discontinuing the production of the industrial motors that had been offered since 1931. As fate would have it, 1932 would be the final year for assembly of these stand-alone power plants.

Salary reductions were implemented for any employee who earned more than $100 a month, and the four founding members took a 50-percent cut themselves. Even these measures failed to rescue company earnings, and Harley-Davidson posted an annual loss of more than $321,000.

1932 Model Year Lineup

Model	Engine Type	Displacement	Transmission	Special Feature(s)
Model 32B	Side-Valve Single	21.35 cid	Three-Speed	Low Cost at $195
Model 32C	Side-Valve Single	30.50 cid	Three-Speed	—
Model 32R	Side-Valve Twin	45 cid	Three-Speed	Low Compression
Model 32RS	Side-Valve Twin	45 cid	Three-Speed	Sidecar Gear./ Low Comp.
Model 32RL	Side-Valve Twin	45 cid	Three-Speed	Dow Metal Pist./ Med. Comp.
Model 32RLD	Side-Valve Twin	45 cid	Three-Speed	High Compression
Model 32V	Side-Valve Twin	74 cid	Three-Speed	Med. Compression
Model 32VS	Side-Valve Twin	74 cid	Three-Speed	Sidecar Gear./ Med. Comp.
Model 32VL	Side-Valve Twin	74 cid	Three-Speed	High Compression
Model 32VC	Side-Valve Twin	74 cid	Three-Speed	Commercial Use/ Low Comp.
Model 32G	Side-Valve Twin	45 cid	Three-Speed	Servi-Car with Tow Bar
Model 32GA	Side-Valve Twin	45 cid	Three-Speed	Servi-Car without Tow Bar
Model 32GD	Side-Valve Twin	45 cid	Three-Speed	Servi-Car w/ Large Cap. Box & Tow Bar
Model 32GE	Side-Valve Twin	45 cid	Three-Speed	Servi-Car w/ Large Cap. Box & Air Tank

Production and Prices

Model	Production	Price
Model 32B	535	$195
Model 32C	213	$235
Model 32R	410	$295
Model 32RS	111	$295
Model 32RL	628	$295
Model 32RLD	98	$310
Model 32V	478	$320
Model 32VS	1,233	$320
Model 32VL	2,684	$320
Model 32VC	239	$320
Model 32G	NA	$450
Model 32GA	NA	$450
Model 32GD	36	$450
Model 32GE	5	$450

1933

With The Depression still choking the country, Harley-Davidson's finances did not allow for many changes to the 1933 lineup. The factory was only running at about 20 percent of its capacity, and total production for the model year was set at 3,700 units. Numbers approaching 20,000 were seen only a few scant years before.

There were three new variations in the lineup, each based on previous models. The new VLE came complete with magnesium alloy (Dow Metal) pistons, as did the latest VLD. The VLD also boasted a higher performance rating of 36 hp. The other new model, the CB, combined the 30.50 motor with the frame of the Twenty-One.

The three-wheeled Servi-Car became an official offering, and was mated to a revised gearbox that included a reverse gear. This model would remain in the catalog until 1973.

Linkert carburetors would be the latest brand to grace the late '33 models, replacing the Scheblers used on previous examples. Although from a different manufacturer, the units were still die cast in brass.

A notable new option was offered on the '33 models. "Ride Control" consisted of a pair of slotted steel plates mounted on the front fork assembly. By changing the position of the slotted plates, the suspension could, in theory, be customized to meet the rider's specific tastes. The actual value of the arrangement was questionable, but it became a popular choice for buyers. In the comfort department, the two-place "Buddy Seat" was also added to the options list. The elongated saddle allowed enough space for a rear-mounted partner, but without any partition the rider and passenger had better be the best of friends.

Another popular option was the new graphics and color schemes. The '33s were available with two-tone paint and the latest "bird's-head" graphics as the company tried to liven things up in the face of a dreary economy. A package of chrome-plated components was also an opportunity to add some flash, and personalized machines were becoming more valuable to consumers.

The lingering effects of The Depression took its toll on the Harley dealer network. Many shops were forced to close their doors forever as sales fell. The Indian brand was doing no better, and actually faced a more dire situation than the Milwaukee company.

1933 Model Year Lineup

Model	Engine Type	Displacement	Transmission	Special Feature(s)
Model 33B	Side-Valve Single	21.35 cid	Three-Speed	
Model 33C	Side-Valve Single	30.50 cid	Three-Speed	
Model 33CB	Side-Valve Single	30.50 cid	Three-Speed	Motor Mtd. in "21" Frame
Model 33R	Side-Valve Twin	45 cid	Three-Speed	Low Compression
Model 33RS	Side-Valve Twin	45 cid	Three-Speed	Sidecar Gear/Low Comp.
Model 33RL	Side-Valve Twin	45 cid	Three-Speed	High Compression
Model 33RLD	Side-Valve Twin	45 cid	Three-Speed	Magnesium Alloy Pistons
Model 33V	Side-Valve Twin	74 cid	Three-Speed	Medium Compression
Model 33VS	Side-Valve Twin	74 cid	Three-Speed	Sidecar Gear./ Med. Comp.
Model 33VL	Side-Valve Twin	74 cid	Three-Speed	High Compression
Model 33VLD	Side-Valve Twin	74 cid	Three-Speed	Mag. Alloy Pist./ High Comp.
Model 33VC	Side-Valve Twin	74 cid	Three-Speed	—
Model 33G	Side-Valve Twin	45 cid	Three-Speed	w/Reverse Tow Bar
Model 33GA	Side-Valve Twin	45 cid	Three-Speed	w/Reverse No Tow Bar
Model 33GD	Side-Valve Twin	45 cid	Three-Speed	w/Reverse Large Box/No Tow Bar
Model 33GDT	Side-Valve Twin	45 cid	Three-Speed	w/Reverse Large Box/Tow Bar
Model 33GE	Side-Valve Twin	45 cid	Three-Speed	w/Reverse Large Box/Air Tank

Production and Prices

Model	Production	Price
Model 33B	123	$187.50
Model 33C	112	$225
Model 33CB	51	NA
Model 33R	162	$280
Model 33RS	37	$280
Model 33RL	264	$280
Model 33RLD	68	$290
Model 33V	233	$310
Model 33VS	164	$310
Model 33VL	886	$310
Model 33VLD	780	$320
Model 33VC	106	$310
Model 33G	80	NA
Model 33GA	12	NA
Model 33GD	60	NA
Model 33GDT	18	NA
Model 33GE	12	NA

This VL found its way into service with law enforcement.

1934

This year would feature drastic changes for the Harley-Davidson lineup. The Sixty-One side-valve was still in the process of being finalized, so the general catalog didn't appear too different for the new year.

Proper lubrication remained critical in the life of an internal combustion engine, and 1934 models would receive improvements to their total loss systems. While messy, the total loss oil process did deliver fresh oil to all internal components. The fact that many external items, like the rider himself, also received a healthy dose of oil remained a part of the two-wheeled experience. A new oil pump was installed on every Forty-Five and Seventy-Four model, promising improved delivery of the lubrication. The new version of the pump was located beneath a revised gear case cover.

The steel frames and forks were all strengthened with a new heat-treating process and exuberant claims of improvement were all a part of the game. Aluminum alloy pistons were now used in place of the previous magnesium alloy versions. The new slugs were slightly heavier, but offered additional reliability.

The most apparent change to the '34 twin-cylinder models were the curvaceous new fenders both front and rear. The fender on the Forty-Five had a leading edge that did not reach the top edge of the chain guard. This was the only year for this peculiar design. Finishing off the rear fender sheet metal was the latest Airflow taillight unit. The twins also received the upswept High-Flo exhaust, and a freshly shaped bucket saddle. Two-tone paint schemes were coming on strong, as well as angular graphics on the tank panels. Harley was doing its best to drum up sales amidst the still unstable economy.

As was typically the case, the 1934 models were available in the fall of 1933. To help sell the existing inventory, they were sold through the end of the 1934 calendar year. Extending the sales year to 16 months helped boost total sales to nearly 10,000 units. This figure was still below expectations, but beat the previous year's numbers by nearly three fold.

This would also mark the final year of production for the single-cylinder models. Sales had never reached desired levels, and it made more sense to focus on more serious changes to the twin-cylinder variants. As any fan of Harley-Davidson history is aware, 1936 would see the introduction of an entirely new power plant for the Milwaukee manufacturer.

1934 Model Year Lineup

Model	Engine Type	Displacement	Transmission	Special Feature(s)
Model 34B	Side-Valve Single	21.35 cid	Three-Speed	—
Model 34C	Side-Valve Single	30.50 cid	Three-Speed	—
Model 34CB	Side-Valve Single	30.50 cid	Three-Speed	Motor Mtd. In "21" Frame
Model 34RL	Side-Valve Twin	45 cid	Three-Speed	—
Model 34R	Side-Valve Twin	45 cid	Three-Speed	Low Compression
Model 34RLD	Side-Valve Twin	45 cid	Three-Speed	Extra-High Compression
Model 34VLD	Side-Valve Twin	74 cid	Three-Speed	High Compression
Model 34VD	Side-Valve Twin	74 cid	Three-Speed	Low Compression
Model 34VDS	Side-Valve Twin	74 cid	Three-Speed	Sidecar Gear/Low Compression
Model 34VFDS	Side-Valve Twin	74 cid	Three-Speed	Sidecar Gear/ Nickel-Iron Pist.
Model 34G	Side-Valve Twin	45 cid	Three-Speed w/Reverse	Tow Bar
Model 34GA	Side-Valve Twin	45 cid	Three-Speed w/Reverse	No Tow Bar
Model 34GD	Side-Valve Twin	45 cid	Three-Speed w/Reverse	Large Box/No Tow Bar
Model 34GDT	Side-Valve Twin	45 cid	Three-Speed w/Reverse	Large Box/Tow Bar
Model 34GE	Side-Valve Twin	45 cid	Three-Speed w/Reverse	Large Box/Air Tank

Production and Prices

Model	Production	Price
Model 34B	424	$187.50
Model 34C	220	$225
Model 34CB	310	$197.50
Model 34RL	743	$280
Model 34R	450	$280
Model 34RLD	240	$290
Model 34VLD	4,527	$310
Model 34VD	664	$310
Model 34VDS	1,029	$310
Model 34VFDS	1,330	$310
Model 34G	317	$430
Model 34GA	40	$415
Model 34GD	104	$430
Model 34GDT	58	$445
Model 34GE	27	$485

The latest in tank graphics added a touch of style to even the standard olive paint.

The 1934 VLD model featured a high-compression motor that mated well with sidecars.

1935

With the introduction of a new motor looming, changes to the 1935 H-D line would be minimal, both inside and out. Sales continued to improve as the world's economy rebounded, and things were looking brighter for the crew at Harley-Davidson.

With only twin-cylinder models in the catalog for 1935, it was easier to adapt model-wide alterations. The Forty-Five and Seventy-Four engines were now fitted with straight-bore cylinders, and elliptical, T-slot pistons. This change supplanted the previous tapered bores and round piston layout. The new Lynite pistons promised a perfect fit within the cylinder walls, and reduced noise and friction. The latest "mirror finish cylinders" claimed to offer easier kick starting and "snappier acceleration."

Late in the model year, 80-cubic inch motors were offered to the public. As motorcycles continued to find expanded duty on the roads, a bump in displacement and power was welcomed.

1935 Model Year Lineup

Model	Engine Type	Displacement	Transmission	Special Feature(s)
Model 35RL	Side-Valve Twin	45 cid	Three-Speed	—
Model 35R	Side-Valve Twin	45 cid	Three-Speed	Low Compression
Model 35RS	Side-Valve Twin	45 cid	Three-Speed	Sidecar Gear/Low Comp.
Model 35RLD	Side-Valve Twin	45 cid	Three-Speed	—
Model 35RLDR	Side-Valve Twin	45 cid	Three-Speed	Competition Model
Model 35VLD	Side-Valve Twin	74 cid	Three-Speed	High Compression
Model 35VD	Side-Valve Twin	74 cid	Three-Speed	Low Compression
Model 35VDS	Side-Valve Twin	74 cid	Three-Speed	Sidecar Gear/Low Comp.
Model 35VLDJ	Side-Valve Twin	74 cid	Three-Speed	Competition Special
Model 35VLDD	Side-Valve Twin	80 cid	Three-Speed	—
Model 35VDDS	Side-Valve Twin	80 cid	Three-Speed	Sidecar Bars
Model 35G	Side-Valve Twin	45 cid	Three-Speed w/Reverse	Tow Bar
Model 35GA	Side-Valve Twin	45 cid	Three-Speed w/Reverse	No Tow Bar
Model 35GD	Side-Valve Twin	45 cid	Three-Speed w/Reverse	Large Box/No Tow Bar
Model 35GDT	Side-Valve Twin	45 cid	Three-Speed w/Reverse	Large Box/Tow Bar
Model 35GE	Side-Valve Twin	45 cid	Three-Speed w/Reverse	Large Box/Air Tank

The Forty-Fives were now shifted through a constant-mesh three-speed transmission. This gearbox had first been pressed into duty on the '33 Servi-Cars. A new and improved air intake helped the machine breathe, and a gas deflecting muffler tip kept the rider's oxygen healthier.

The rear wheels on the Forty-Fives slowed the bike with the help of the newly installed internal expanding brake. The quick-release rear wheel made tire changes a much simpler process than in previous years.

The Airflow taillight assembly introduced in 1934 was now finished off with a new beehive lens that promised better visibility from side angles. Up front, the headlight was installed with refocused bulbs. By fixing the mounting location of replacement bulbs within the housing, H-D was able to align the bulb with the lens. This accuracy improved output and focus of the beam. The grips were shortened and were more sporty than the last versions. Larger "man-size" oil and fuel caps resided on the top of the tank.

New colors and splashier graphics continued to be offered on the 1935 models. It was hoped that the more intense visuals would help to boost sales and, when combined with the improving economy, it seemed to be working.

Production and Prices

Model	Production	Prices
Model 35RL	819	$295
Model 35R	543	$295
Model 35RS	392	$295
Model 35RLD	177	$305
Model 35RLDR	29	$322
Model 35VLD	3,963	$320
Model 35VD	585	$320
Model 35VDS	1,189	$320
Model 35VLDJ	102	$333.50
Model 35VLDD	179	$347
Model 35VDDS	NA	$347
Model 35G	323	$440
Model 35GA	64	$425
Model 35GD	91	$440
Model 35GDT	72	$445
Model 35GE	17	$495

The "Knucklehead" Arrives

While the side-valve motors had served Harley well for more than decades, newer technology was needed to continue growing the product line. The obvious choice was a V-twin with overhead valves, and the Sixty-One had been in development for several years before making its debut. Instead of simply taking an existing power plant and making the required changes, Harley created a new overhead-valve motor from scratch. European builders were already implementing the overhead-valve mills on their motors, so the new motor was not totally new technology, but was a first for Harley.

The latest motor design used several techniques to simplify the operation of the engine. A single-camshaft arrangement was selected in an effort to reduce noise and components. With all four of the cam lobes located on a single cam, valve timing was more precise. The valve stems and springs were largely exposed to the elements on the early examples, much to the disdain of the rider. Without adequate protection, oil flew everywhere. Exposed valve trains were all the rage on European machines, so this unpleasant drawback was not limited to Harleys.

The newly designed rocker housings gave the "Knucklehead" engine its moniker. Seated atop the twin cylinders, the cast form resembled a closed fist with its "knuckles" exposed. It may not have been the most flattering of terms, but has come to be a common phrase for Harley fans.

The cylinders on the new Sixty-Ones claimed a bore of 3 5/16 inches and a stroke of 3 1/2 inches, providing a ratio of 0.946:1, which was similar to other high-end machines being sold. Horsepower on the new OHV motor was rated at 40 at 4800 rpm when using the 7:1 compression ratio. This was considered typical for a motor of this design and displacement.

A dry sump lubrication system provided a constant flow of oil between the engine and oil tank. The gear driven oil pump delivered the lube at an adjustable rate, not exceeding 15 psi. Pressures above that rating would cause a seated ball fitting to open, releasing the excess oil to the gear case below. Problems with excessive oil usage on the early '36s were solved by the addition of a large nut on each of the rocker arm shafts. These replaced the previous caps that were secured with center-mounted retaining screws.

The cover for the timing case was altered three times during the model year, with each variation appearing smoother than the previous iteration. Minor changes to the front chain guard and kickstart covers were also implemented during the production year. By the end of the model year the new Sixty-Ones had become a complete and competent machine.

Ultimately, the knucklehead motor from Harley-Davidson pushed the company to new heights as many eager new riders joined the ranks of two-wheeled fanatics already tooling around the streets of the U.S.

The new "Knucklehead" motor would be the first in a long line of OHV power plants for Harley-Davidson.

Mechanically and cosmetically, the new EL model was the best Harley yet.

1936

Changes to the latest Sixty-Ones were not limited to the new V-twin motor, and additions were also found throughout the 1936 model lineup.

Power delivery on the Sixty-Ones was handled by a new clutch and transmission. The latest clutch featured six splines used to mount the outer disc and springs, and a larger center hub. The four-speed transmission featured constant-mesh shifting, which provided vastly improved gear changes. The new speedometer gear had a spiral design that eliminated the need for re-alignment after changing the rear rubber.

The styling on the latest model from H-D made it an instant classic, and it remains so today. From the shape of the new fuel tanks to the modern front forks, the new model offered a fresh look to the revered marque.

A new instrument panel was mounted on top of the now welded fuel tank. The large cylindrical speedometer face would stand the test of time, although undergoing numerous changes in the decades that followed its introduction. The latest frame design had a double-loop theme, and added an air of strength to the freshly minted machines. The front fork was also beefed up and provided improved steering. The rear-facing intake stamping made the latest Milwaukee machines instantly recognizable to the world of motorcycling.

Changes to the balance of the '36 models were minimal, but continued to improve performance, appearance and reliability.

The Forty-Five motors now inhaled through a Y-shaped inlet manifold that boosted performance as well as adding a touch of style. Cooling fins were enlarged, and seemed to embrace the new manifold as they curved around the casting. The inlet manifolds of the RL and RLD models were enlarged to 1 1/4 inches from the previous 1 inch. The venturi of the carburetor was also enlarged from 7/8 inch to 1 1/4 inches. The cylinder heads were retained with an eight-bolt pattern, an increase of one, and the size of the cooling fins was increased. Improved combustion was delivered with reshaped cylinder heads.

Of the three side-valve twin models, only the Forty-Fives had their drive chains on the right. The Eighty models were now an official model in the catalog, but had been available since the middle of the 1935 offerings. Both the Seventy-Four and Eighty motors had nine-bolt cylinder heads with improved internal contours for higher combustion. The cylinders and their respective heads were found with larger cooling fins.

The side-valve models were still sold with the earlier three-speed transmissions, but the newer four-speed, constant-mesh variation could be added as a special-order item.

Cosmetics differed with a new set of tank transfers, chrome-plated air inlet, and tubular rear wheel stands.

The Servi-Cars with tow bars now came with an additional safety cable to meet with stricter motor vehicle laws. The two locks found on the previous covers had been supplanted with a large spring latching device.

The tank-mounted instrument pod was another all-new feature for 1936, and remains a fixture on today's models from Harley-Davidson.

The latest overhead-valve motor made the Sixty-One a terrific seller, even in its first year.

1936 Model Year Lineup

Model	Engine Type	Displacement	Transmission	Special Feature(s)
Model 36R	Side-Valve Twin	45 cid	Three-Speed	Low Compression
Model 36RL	Side-Valve Twin	45 cid	Three-Speed	High Compression
Model 36RLD	Side-Valve Twin	45 cid	Three-Speed	Extra-High Compress.
Model 36RLDR	Side-Valve Twin	45 cid	Three-Speed	Competition Model
Model 36RS	Side-Valve Twin	45 cid	Three-Speed	Sidecar Gearing
Model 36E	Overhead-Valve Twin	61 cid	Four-Speed	Medium Compression
Model 36ES	Overhead-Valve Twin	61 cid	Four-Speed	Sidecar Gearing
Model 36EL	Overhead-Valve Twin	61 cid	Four-Speed	High Compression
Model 36VLD	Side-Valve Twin	74 cid	Three-Speed	High Compression
Model 36VD	Side-Valve Twin	74 cid	Three-Speed	Low Compression
Model 36VDS	Side-Valve Twin	74 cid	Three-Speed	Sidecar Gearing
Model 36VLH	Side-Valve Twin	80 cid	Three-Speed	Solo Bars
Model 36VHS	Side-Valve Twin	80 cid	Three-Speed	Sidecar Gearing
Model 36G	Side-Valve Twin	45 cid	Three-Speed w/Reverse	Tow Bar
Model 36GA	Side-Valve Twin	45 cid	Three-Speed w/Reverse	No Tow Bar
Model 36GD	Side-Valve Twin	45 cid	Three-Speed w/Reverse	Large Box/No Tow Bar
Model 36GDT	Side-Valve Twin	45 cid	Three-Speed w/Reverse	Large Box w/Tow Bar
Model 36GE	Side-Valve Twin	45 cid	Three-Speed w/Reverse	Large Box w/Air Tank

Production and Prices

Model	Production	Price
Model 36R	539	$295
Model 36RL	355	$295
Model 36RLD	540	$295
Model 36RLDR	79	$320
Model 36RS	437	$295
Model 36E	152	$380
Model 36ES	26	$380
Model 36EL	1,526	$380
Model 36VLD	1,577	$320
Model 36VD	176	$320
Model 36VDS	623	$320
Model 36VLH	2,046	$340
Model 36VHS	305	$340
Model 36G	382	$440
Model 36GA	55	$425
Model 36GD	96	$440
Model 36GDT	85	$455
Model 36GE	30	$495

The EL model was changed only slightly for its second year of production.

1937

Having rolled out the all-new OHV Sixty-One in 1936, The 1937 model year would prove to be a year of numerous minor changes for Harley-Davidson, which had rolled out is new overhead-valve Sixty-One just one year earlier. The new OHV model was barely touched while the rest of the line was spruced up to make it more appealing when compared to the new machine.

New colors were offered on all available models, and the Sixty-One was seen with a new air intake horn that mimicked that of the Seventy-Four and Eighty models. The '37 ELs also had a cumbersome oil tank supply line that was combined with the drain plug. A valve was needed to keep the lubricant in the motor until the owner was ready to drain it. This awkward design was only seen on the '37 models. The size of the rear brake on the Sixty-Ones was increased, and the gearshift gate now claimed more distinctive stops for each gear position. The shift lever now featured a flat-section profile for use with the new gate.

The newly shaped air intake horn helped to distinguish the 1937 model from the previous edition.

The balance of the lineup received a raft of alterations as H-D tried to keep the playing field even amongst its own machines. The most obvious of these changes was the re-styling of the Forty-Five, Seventy-Four, and Eighty models. The popular fuel and oil tank design from the EL was carried over to the side-valve machines, as well as the black instrument panel. In addition to the refreshed styling, the Seventy-Four and Eighty models now rode on double-loop frames with tubular front forks. All models now came with Harley's "Ride Control," although the hardware differed slightly from the Sixty-One's setup. The adjustment knob on the Forty-Fives was mounted on the left side of the forks, allowing the rider to make adjustments without taking his hand off of the throttle. The Ride Control option was included on both the standard and deluxe accessory packages. These two option groups were purchased with 90 percent of all new Harleys sold.

Engine lubrication was improved on the side-valve motors with the installation of a dry sump system much like the one found on the OHV engines. A new method of delineating the models was the use of the "W" prefix on the Forty-Fives, and "U" on the Seventy-Fours and Eighties. Forty-Five motors also now wore a ribbed timing case cover.

The Servi-Car continued to be a popular choice for police departments and service stations, and the three-wheeler now featured a separate brake on each of the two rear wheels. Large-diameter hubcaps and an extended box apron were also new additions to the model.

The big side-valve models received the biggest makeover for the new year. The newest styling was created to match that of the OHV model, and the motor was also upgraded with new features and improvements. Internally, there were few parts that weren't changed. Crankpin diameter grew by 1/8 inch to a new diameter of 1 1/8 inch, and the connecting rods were forged from stronger steel to mate with the bigger pins. The flywheel diameter was also enhanced by 9/32 inch and improved balancing resulted in a smoother running engine.

The ULH model was the second-best seller for the 1937 model year.

Cylinder bores were altered to simplify inventory and manufacturing. The Seventy-Four's pistons now traveled in a cylinder that had a longer stroke of 4 9/32 inches, which matched the dimension in the Eighty's. The diameter of the Seventy-Four bore was reduced to 3 5/16 inches to mirror that of the Sixty-One OHV. This change allowed the big twins to share pistons and rings. The latest cylinders on the Seventy-Four and Eighty models had thicker walls, and more effective cooling fins that were deeper and ran all the way to their base.

Frames on the big side-valve models were fortified through reinforcements in several key locations. The backbones of the frames were treated to an 11-inch support that ran from the seat bar mount and the seat post. The transmission mounting bracket was enhanced and the stabilizer bushing in the seat post was of sterner stock. All of these improvements added up to a stiffer frame and improved handling.

For the record books, Joe Petrali rode a specially built Sixty-One OHV model to a new American record of 136.183 mph. The strong new OHV motor was making itself heard all across the U.S.

Production and Prices

Model	Production	Price
Model 37W	509	$355
Model 37WS	232	$355
Model 37WL	560	$355
Model 37WLD	581	$355
Model 37WLDR	145	$380
Model 37E	126	$435
Model 37ES	70	$435
Model 37EL	1,829	$435
Model 37U	612	$395
Model 37US	1,080	$395
Model 37UL	2,861	$395
Model 37UH	185	$415
Model 37UHS	400	$415
Model 37ULH	1,513	$415
Model 37G	491	$515
Model 37GA	55	$500
Model 37GD	112	$515
Model 37GDT	136	$530
Model 37GE	22	$570

1937 Model Year Lineup

Model	Engine Type	Displacement	Transmission	Special Feature(s)
Model 37W	Side-Valve Twin	45 cid	Three-Speed	Low Compression
Model 37WS	Side-Valve Twin	45 cid	Three-Speed	Sidecar Gear/Low Comp.
Model 37WL	Side-Valve Twin	45 cid	Three-Speed	High Compression
Model 37WLD	Side-Valve Twin	45 cid	Three-Speed	Extra-High Compression
Model 37WLDR	Side-Valve Twin	45 cid	Three-Speed	Competition Special
Model 37E	Overhead-Valve Twin	61 cid	Four-Speed	Medium Compression
Model 37ES	Overhead-Valve Twin	61 cid	Four-Speed	Sidecar Gear/ Med. Comp.
Model 37EL	Overhead-Valve Twin	61 cid	Four-Speed	High Compression
Model 37U	Side-Valve Twin	74 cid	Four-Speed	Medium Compression
Model 37US	Side-Valve Twin	74 cid	Four-Speed	Sidecar Gear/ Med. Comp.
Model 37UL	Side-Valve Twin	74 cid	Four-Speed	High Compression
Model 37UH	Side-Valve Twin	80 cid	Four-Speed	Medium Compression
Model 37UHS	Side-Valve Twin	80 cid	Four-Speed	Sidecar Gear/ Med. Comp.
Model 37ULH	Side-Valve Twin	80 cid	Four-Speed	High Compression
Model 37G	Side-Valve Twin	45 cid	Three-Speed w/Reverse	Tow Bar
Model 37GA	Side-Valve Twin	45 cid	Three-Speed w/Reverse	No Tow Bar
Model 37GD	Side-Valve Twin	45 cid	Three-Speed w/Reverse	Large Box/No Tow Bar
Model 37GDT	Side-Valve Twin	45 cid	Three-Speed w/Reverse	Large Box / Tow bar
Model 37GE	Side-Valve Twin	45 cid	Three-Speed w/Reverse	Large Box w/Air Tank

Like its OHV sibling, the Side-Valve ULH was now fitted with the instrument panel atop the fuel tank.

The UL was the third-best seller for H-D in 1938.

1938

As was often the case, there were changes across the board for the Harley-Davidson models for 1938. Interchangeable components between models were becoming more common as the company sought ways to improve efficiency. Thoughts of wartime production would not enter into the picture until late in the model year, and would be a huge factor in H-D's future.

As a result of so many components being interchangeable between the OHV, Seventy-Four, and Eighty models, the three were now referred to as the "big twins." Only the Forty-Five would remain in its own class.

The biggest news for the Sixty-One OHV was the implementation of fully enclosed valves. This was attained through an assembly of sheet metal stampings and gaskets. This new compilation of hardware allowed for a cleaner operation and more efficient lubrication. The new components could also be installed on earlier knucklehead motors with only minor alterations.

Additional measures were taken to reinforce the frames on the big twin models. Heavier-gauge steel was used on some existing parts, and larger-diameter tubing was also implemented. Higher handlebars provided a more natural riding position, and the bars were fitted into a self-aligning steering head cone. Clutches on the big twins were beefed up as well as the transmissions they were mated to. The previous eight-ball clutch thrust bearing was replaced with a ten-ball version and a more resilient clutch releasing finger was installed. The transmissions on the newer versions sported new starter covers, and carried improved gearing for smoother shifts.

The Forty-Five clutches received two additional balls on their clutch thrust bearings, bringing the total to eight, and the clutch was now activated with a rocking foot pedal like the one found on the big twins. Transmissions on the Forty-Fives were also fitted with better shifting gears that resided within a new housing.

The Servi-Car was not without changes, and the '38s received a quieter muffler, enclosed rear chain, and a tow bar with a clamping mechanism.

Several changes were made to all the models in the catalog. To provide universal lubrication regardless of location, Zerk-Alemite grease fittings were added. These fittings were compatible with the lubrication gear found at commercial service stations, allowing for lubing on the road. Horn and lighting wiring on the earlier models had been prone to rubbing and chaffing, so the 1938s carried an improved harness designed to prevent shorts. The tank-mounted instrument panel was changed, replacing the small indicator gauges with warning lights. All speedometers, except those on the Servi-Car, now indicated miles per hour in increments of two. The Servi-Car's unit retained the older five-increment markings.

To further streamline the building process, all 1938 models came standard with one of two option packages. The "standard" or "deluxe" groups of options still provided the buyer with a nice selection of upgrades. The Package Truck, Sidecar and Servi-Cars were also sold with the option packages.

In only its third year of production, the EL was Harley's sales leader.

Outfitted with a Package Delivery unit, the 1938 U model was highly versatile.

1938 Model Year Lineup

Model	Engine Type	Displacement	Transmission	Special Feature(s)
Model 38WL	Side-Valve Twin	45 cid	Three-Speed	High Compression
Model 38WLD	Side-Valve Twin	45 cid	Three-Speed	Extra-High Compression
Model 38WLDR	Side-Valve Twin	45 cid	Three-Speed	Competition Model
Model 38EL	Overhead-Valve Twin	61 cid	Four-Speed	High Compression
Model 38ES	Overhead-Valve Twin	61 cid	Four-Speed	Sidecar Model
Model 38U	Side-Valve Twin	74 cid	Four-Speed	Medium Compression
Model 38UL	Side-Valve Twin	74 cid	Four-Speed	High Compression
Model 38US	Side-Valve Twin	74 cid	Four-Speed	Sidecar Gearing
Model 38UH	Side-Valve Twin	80 cid	Four-Speed	Medium Compression
Model 38ULH	Side-Valve Twin	80 cid	Four-Speed	High Compression
Model 38UHS	Side-Valve Twin	80 cid	Four-Speed	Sidecar Gearing
Model 38G	Side-Valve Twin	45 cid	Three-Speed w/Reverse	Tow Bar
Model 38GA	Side-Valve Twin	45 cid	Three-Speed w/Reverse	No Tow Bar
Model 38GD	Side-Valve Twin	45 cid	Three-Speed w/Reverse	Large Box/No Tow Bar
Model 38GDT	Side-Valve Twin	45 cid	Three-Speed w/Reverse	Large Box/Tow Bar

Production and Prices

Model	Production	Prices
Model 38WL	309	$355
Model 38WLD	402	$355
Model 38WLDR	139	$380
Model 38EL	2,289	$435
Model 38ES	189	$435
Model 38U	504	$395
Model 38UL	1,099	$395
Model 38US	1,193	$395
Model 38UH	108	$415
Model 38ULH	579	$415
Model 38UHS	132	$415
Model 38G	259	$515
Model 38GA	83	$500
Model 38GD	81	$515
Model 38GDT	102	$530

The EL of 1939 was Harley's top-selling model, despite only minor improvements over the 1938.

1939

Changes were made to all models for the 1939 catalog, but none were radical. Improving the breed seemed more important than reinventing the wheel each model year, and with another big war looming on the horizon, that strategy seemed to make the most sense. Ongoing efforts to reduce weight and increase dependability resulted in most of the changes.

The Forty-Five models touted a few basic changes, both internally and externally. Valve springs were now of a design that promised longer life. The manifold breathed through unpolished, cadmium-plated tubes that were secured with hardware to match. The knob for the Ride Control was also lowered for easier access for the rider. A newly designed steering damper lever was also crafted to aid the rider's needs. The old cast version of the foot brake lever was stamped from steel to save a few precious ounces.

The big twin lineup had a few notable changes of its own. Both the clutches and transmissions were improved on all the big twin variants. Increased strength of individual parts, as well as improved surfaces, resulted in better-shifting machines. Alterations to the internal crankcase baffles helped to eliminate the air pressure caused by the running engine. A small boost in horsepower was the net gain of this effort. The layout of the connecting rods had to be reversed as a result of the baffle-less design, but the change wasn't monumental.

On the Seventy-Four and Eighty models, the intake manifold's length was increased by 3/4 inch, and an asbestos washer was installed to help reduce vapor lockup under hot conditions. The earlier three-piece valve covers were supplanted by simpler two-section units. Harley-Davidson was quickly learning that fewer parts meant less things to break and fewer items during assembly.

The Sixty-One OHV motor powered the EL to the top of the sales charts.

Front forks on the side-valve models now carried improved springs to enhance comfort.

The Sixty-One OHVs began running with a single-piece pinion gearshift that helped alignment of the components. The front pistons were wrapped with three compression rings while the rear slug had two compression rings and one oil control ring. Internal lubrication was vital to the stronger-running power plants, and H-D was continually finding new ways to keep the moving parts slippery. The EL and ES models were also mated with improved springs on the front suspension to increase rider comfort.

The Servi-Cars now came with their tubular tow bars permanently attached. Early bars needed to be stowed, taking up storage space and time. The G and GA models were fitted with larger boxes, and dual taillights were found on all levels of the Servi-Car.

Several changes were universal on Harleys. Perhaps the most obvious was the new "cat's eye" dashboard atop the fuel tank. The indicator lights of the previous year were still in place, but were now almond-shaped, which led to the feline reference. The instrument panel was also now painted the same color as the body of the tank, instead of basic black. More attention was given to colors and artistic values with every passing model year. Even the saddles on the '39s were different this year. The new "Rhino-grain" leather was finished in a ruddy brown color. This variation would appear only on the 1939 models.

A drain plug could now be found under each carburetor, and a smaller gas strainer was used. The ignition cable's dependability was improved by a neoprene cover that kept out moisture. The switch used to operate the stop light was now made by Harley-Davidson, and was smaller. The previous pinstripes adorning each side of the fenders were replaced with a section of curved stainless steel, adding another touch of design flare to the line. To complete the latest styling, a new "boat tail" taillight was applied to all models except the Servi-Car.

In August of 1939, two specially made Forty-Fives were assembled for the military, and shipped to Fort Knox for review by the Mechanized Calvary Board. The two examples sent would turn out to be the first samples of the soon-to-be-famous WLA model

Stainless-steel trim replaced last year's painted fender trim in 1939.

1939 Model Year Lineup

Model	Engine Type	Displacement	Transmission	Special Feature(s)
Model 39WL	Side-Valve Twin	45 cid	Three-Speed	High Compression
Model 39WLD	Side-Valve Twin	45 cid	Three-Speed	Extra-High Compression
Model 39WLDR	Side-Valve Twin	45 cid	Three-Speed	Competition Model
Model 39EL	Overhead-Valve Twin	61 cid	Four-Speed	High Compression
Model 39ES	Overhead-Valve Twin	61 cid	Four-Speed	Medium Comp./ Sidecar Gear
Model 39U	Side-Valve Twin	74 cid	Four-Speed	Medium Compression
Model 39UL	Side-Valve Twin	74 cid	Four-Speed	High Compression
Model 39US	Side-Valve Twin	74 cid	Four-Speed	Medium Comp./ Sidecar Gear
Model 39UH	Side-Valve Twin	80 cid	Four-Speed	Medium Compression
Model 39ULH	Side-Valve Twin	80 cid	Four-Speed	High Compression
Model 39UHS	Side-Valve Twin	80 cid	Four-Speed	Medium Comp./ Sidecar Gear
Model 39G	Side-Valve Twin	45 cid	Three-Speed	w/Reverse Tow Bar
Model 39GA	Side-Valve Twin	45 cid	Three-Speed	w/Reverse No Tow Bar
Model 39GD	Side-Valve Twin	45 cid	Three-Speed	w/Reverse Large Box/No Tow Bar
Model 39GDT	Side-Valve Twin	45 cid	Three-Speed	w/Reverse Large Box w/Tow Bar

that was used extensively in World War II. Finished in glossy olive green paint with a few shiny bits for appearance sake, they would undergo extensive testing before assembly could commence.

Overall sales at Harley-Davidson had slumped since the peak in 1929, but company brass was convinced H-D would ride out the war and continue on.

Production and Prices

Model	Production	Prices
Model 39WL	212	$355
Model 39WLD	326	$355
Model 39WLDR	173	$380
Model 39EL	2,695	$435
Model 39ES	214	$435
Model 39U	421	$395
Model 39UL	902	$395
Model 39US	1,327	$395
Model 39UH	92	$415
Model 39ULH	384	$415
Model 39UHS	109	$415
Model 39G	320	$515
Model 39GA	126	$500
Model 39GD	90	$515
Model 39GDT	114	$530

The ribbed side cover and cast tear-drop tank badge identified the 1940 Big Twins.

1940

Changes to the 1940 lineup were once again evolutionary, not revolutionary. Constant improvement and refinement was still the name of the game. Seeing a potential presence in the pending war, Harley-Davidson was spending a fair amount of time refining its existing machines to meet with the military's more rugged needs.

The Forty-Five side-valve models were becoming more like their bigger siblings with every passing year. 1940 would find them fitted with the latest tubular front forks instead of the I-beam variation used before. Motor baffling and the reversed connecting rod arrangement was now applied to the smaller motor as well. Shifting was made easier by adopting the same upgrades given to the Big Twins the past year.

The performance-level WLDR was now found with combustion chambers that were highly polished, along with new cylinders and valve components. These enhancements made the WLDR as close to a street-legal race machine as it could be.

The bigger Eighty models wore cylinder heads forged from aluminum, and deeper finning assisted in heat dissipation. These silicon-aluminum heads could be ordered on the Seventy-Fours as an option. The alloy heads weighed less, and provided vastly enhanced cooling. Brass sparkplug inserts were cast in to eliminate stripped threads when changing plugs.

The OHV models had a few minor changes of their own. Much like the side-valve variations, the OHV now ran without internal oil baffles. While the side-valve models still retained some baffling on the front cylinder, the OHV had none for either cylinder. The Linkert carburetor diameter on the Sixty-Ones was enlarged by 1/4 inch to a new dimension of 1 1/2 inches. The venturi was enhanced by 1/4 inch as well, while the intake manifold diameter was now 1 9/16 inches, and "T" shaped. Larger openings provided better breathing, which led to a stronger-running motor.

The Servi-Car was dealt a few minor tweaks, too. The rear axle housing was strengthened, and additional clearance for the chain was allowed to reduce noise. Brake adjustments were now simpler due to a turnbuckle mechanism, and the rear drums were

The OHV design was proving to be the favorite among consumers and racers alike by 1940.

1940 Model Year Lineup

Model	Engine Type	Displacement	Transmission	Special Feauture(s)
Model 40WL	Side-Valve Twin	45 cid	Three-Speed	High Compression
Model 40WLD	Side-Valve Twin	45 cid	Three-Speed	Aluminum Heads
Model 40WLDR	Side-Valve Twin	45 cid	Three-Speed	Competition/ Alum. Heads
Model 40EL	Overhead Valve Twin	61 cid	Four-Speed	High Compression
Model 40ES	Overhead Valve Twin	61 cid	Four-Speed	Medium Comp/ Sidecar Gear
Model 40U	Side-Valve Twin	74 cid	Four-Speed	Medium Compression
Model 40UL	Side-Valve Twin	74 cid	Four-Speed	High Compression
Model 40US	Side-Valve Twin	74 cid	Four-Speed	Medium Comp/ Sidecar Gear
Model 40UH	Side-Valve Twin	80 cid	Four-Speed	Medium Compression
Model 40ULH	Side-Valve Twin	80 cid	Four-Speed	High Compression
Model 40UHS	Side-Valve Twin	80 cid	Four-Speed	Medium Comp/ Sidecar Gear
Model 40G	Side-Valve Twin	45 cid	Three-Speed w/Reverse	Tow Bar
Model 40GA	Side-Valve Twin	45 cid	Three-Speed w/Reverse	No Tow Bar
Model 40GD	Side-Valve Twin	45 cid	Three-Speed w/Reverse	Large box/No Tow Bar
Model 40GDT	Side-Valve Twin	45 cid	Three-Speed w/Reverse	Large Box/Tow Bar

now nickel-iron castings, replacing the previous stamped editions. The tow bar was widened to function with the wider front forks, and had an improved jaw clamp.

The entire big twin family was also treated to a few enhancements. Along with the number of rollers within the crankpin being increased to forty-four, the diameter was increased to 1 1/4 inches. Ribs were cast into the timing cases of the Big Twins to provide an extra measure of cooling. The front bike stand was of a new design, and used on all big-twin models. The drum of the front wheel brakes was also now cast versus stamped, and helped to reduce chatter upon use. Semi-circular footboards were applied to the entire lineup, replacing the rectangular variety.

Instant access to the reserve fuel supply was now available with the newly designed valve mounted on the tank. When the primary fuel was depleted, a simple pull on the valve would open it, allowing the reserve fuel to flow to the carburetor.

Fuel tank décor was changed from colorful appliqués to a cast teardrop shape, with the Harley-Davidson name recessed in the face.

After some brisk discussions with the military about H-D's resistance to building smaller, 30-inch motors, the decision was made to utilize the proven Forty-Five variant for wartime machinery. Additional requirements of the military found the WLAs with longer forks, providing an extra 2 inches of ground clearance beneath the motor. The government's first order for the new WLA was for 745 units, all identically equipped.

Along with this order, the military also requested the construction of 16 three-wheeled, shaft-driven machines. These three-wheelers would be powered by a 69-inch version of the Sixty-One OHV motor. Only 16 of these were ever built as the military found the new four-wheeled Jeep to be a far more versatile machine.

Production and Prices

Model	Production	Prices
Model 40WL	569	$350
Model 40WLD	567	$365
Model 40WLDR	87	$395
Model 40EL	3,893	$430
Model 40ES	176	$430
Model 40U	260	$385
Model 40UL	822	$385
Model 40US	1,516	$385
Model 40UH	187	$410
Model 40ULH	672	$410
Model 40UHS	163	$410
Model 40G	468	$515
Model 40GA	156	$500
Model 40GD	158	$515
Model 40GDT	126	$530

Harley-Davidson produced 2,280 EL models for 1941, but the bikes became a scarce commodity the next year as the U.S. entered World War II.

1941

Two new machines were introduced for the 1941 model year—one for the civilian market, and the other for military applications. Along with these two models, the usual round of updates and improvements were made on the remaining models.

For the civilian market, the new Seventy-Four OHV motor was rolled out with much fanfare. The bigger motor was largely due to a cry from law enforcement agencies that claimed they needed more power in their patrol units. The new motors were also sold to the public.

The new V-twin motor was produced by increasing bore and stroke of the Sixty-One OHV, and adding material to certain key components. Early examples of the new Seventy-Four had a problem with breaking crankcases, so additional steel was added to bolster the package. This simple fix kept the motors intact. With a bore of 3 7/16 inches and a stroke of 3 31/32 inches, the pistons had to be trimmed to provide clearance at the lower edge. This minor relief kept the connecting rods from coming in contact with the sides of the pistons. Both the F and FL variations were rated at 48 hp at 5000 rpm.

The bigger twin breathed through the same carburetor found on the 1940 Sixty-One models, and featured a 1 5/16-inch venturi. The 1941 Sixty-Ones were still using the smaller 1 1/8-inch

To add flexibility to the EL models, many owners attached sidecars to their machines. Both rider and passenger are protected from the elements by full-size windshields.

venturi carbs that were mounted during the previous year's production. The flywheels of the Seventy-Four models were both heavier and larger in diameter than the 1940 Sixty-Ones.

The Forty-Fives were also being introduced to some changes for the latest year. Cast-iron variants of the WL line, as well as the Servi-Car motors, now ran with the same compression ratio of 4.75:1. This allowed the same cast-iron heads to be used on both models. In an effort to improve valve spring reliability, the length was increased to 2 19/32 inches on all Forty-Five motors. The new spring length mandated the need for new upper valve spring covers.

Numerous changes to the Forty-Five and Servi-Car clutch and transmissions made shifting a smoother task. A straighter and stronger clutch release lever was now connected to a stranded steel cable that ran through a tubular guide, providing a more controlled movement. Gears in the transmission were larger and more robust. The spacing between gears was also increased to simplify the adjustment process. A wider gearbox was used to house the new gears and their more casual spacing.

The Sixty-One OHV was also found with a variety of revisions for the new year. The heavier flywheel used on the Seventy-Four OHV was now put into service on the Sixty-One models. Another 1/2 inch of length was added to the intake manifold to combat vapor lock, and the carburetor now had a venturi measuring 1 1/8 inches in diameter.

All Big Twin models were fitted with vastly improved clutches that featured increased frictional surfaces. The 65-percent boost in surface was augmented by an improved system of retaining the plates in their locations. To help the rider with the new clutch, a longer foot lever bearing was added to the equation.

The Big Twins were made quieter by a larger muffler that held no packing material. Earlier examples used a steel wool packing to reduce noise, but over time this material would work itself free, and the bikes grew louder.

Fuel reserve was increased to 1 gallon for all models. Improved grounding for the batteries was achieved by changing the grounding point to the frame from the previous oil line location. A new face was found on the speedometer, and it featured large, silver numerals and a white indicator needle. A bright band of steel was added to all fuel tanks for the 1941 models as well.

In response to the government's call for a new military-based machine, Harley-Davidson submitted its bid to build a new motorcycle that was driven by an all-new motor configuration—all-new for Harley, anyway. The XA would be powered by a horizontally opposed, twin-cylinder engine. This variation was based on a design that had proven popular by the German cycle maker BMW. Displacing just over 45 cubic inches, the new XA delivered 23 hp at 4600 rpm. A four-speed transmission would provide the rider with enough gearing for a variety of riding conditions.

This engine design was a different way of building motors for Harley, but made sense in several arenas. The exposed cylinders helped the motor to run much cooler than the V-twin variations, and could go anywhere from 10,000 to 15,000 miles without the need for extensive repair work. The bike weighed 538 lbs., but the cylinder location provided a much lower center of gravity, giving riders a more stable platform.

Harley-Davidson was awarded a contract to build 1,000 copies of the new XA, along with several thousand WLA and WLC models for the military. The 1,000 XAs had to be completed by July of 1942, and were not considered to be official until that model year.

The WLC was intended for use by the Canada military, and differed from the U.S. models significantly. Some initial difficulties over tooling rights for the XA were soon overcome, and production went into full swing. Even though the U.S. had not yet entered the war, material shortages were already making themselves apparent. Aluminum was especially scarce, and H-D was allowed to build only 2,500 civilian WLC models with aluminum heads.

Civilian sales eventually diminished to a mere trickle as Harley-Davidson ramped up production of the olive green military machines.

1941 Model Year Lineup

Model	Engine Type	Displacement	Transmission	Special Feature(s)
Model 41WL	Side-Valve Twin	45 cid	Three-Speed	—
Model 41WLA	Side-Valve Twin	45 cid	Three-Speed	Military Sale Only
Model 41WLD	Side-Valve Twin	45 cid	Three-Speed	Sport Solo
Model 41WLDR	Side-Valve Twin	45 cid	Three-Speed	Special Sport Solo
Model 41U	Side-Valve Twin	74 cid	Four-Speed	Medium Compression
Model 41UL	Side-Valve Twin	74 cid	Four-Speed	High Compression
Model 41US	Side-Valve Twin	74 cid	Four-Speed	Medium Comp./ Sidecar Gear
Model 41UH	Side-Valve Twin	80 cid	Four-Speed	Medium Compression
Model 41ULH	Side-Valve Twin	80 cid	Four-Speed	High Compression
Model 41UHS	Side-Valve Twin	80 cid	Four-Speed	Medium Comp./ Sidecar Gear
Model 41EL	Overhead-Valve Twin	61 cid	Four-Speed	High Compression
Model 41ES	Overhead-Valve Twin	61 cid	Four-Speed	Medium Comp./ Sidecar Gear
Model 41FL	Overhead-Valve Twin	74 cid	Four-Speed	High Compression
Model 41FS	Overhead-Valve Twin	74 cid	Four-Speed	Medium Comp./ Sidecar Gear
Model 41G	Side-Valve Twin	45 cid	Three-Speed w/Reverse	Tow Bar
Model 41GA	Side-Valve Twin	45 cid	Three-Speed w/Reverse	No Tow Bar
Model 41GD	Side-Valve Twin	45 cid	Three-Speed w/Reverse	Large Box/No Tow Bar
Model 41GDT	Side-Valve Twin	45 cid	Three-Speed w/Reverse	Large Box/Tow Bar

Production and Prices

Model	Production	Price
Model 41WL	4,277	$350
Model 41WLA	2,282	Gov't. Contract
Model 41WLD	455	$365
Model 41WLDR	171	$385
Model 41U	884	$385
Model 41UL	715	$385
Model 41US	1,888	$385
Model 41UH	126	$410
Model 41ULH	420	$410
Model 41UHS	112	$410
Model 41EL	2,280	$425
Model 41ES	261	$425
Model 41FL	2,452	$465
Model 41G	607	$515
Model 41GA	221	$500
Model 41GD	195	$515
Model 41GDT	136	$530

The 1942 WLA proved itself to be a worthy machine during World War II.

1942

Due to Harley-Davidson's involvement in wartime production, civilian models were few and far between. Several 1941 models were eliminated from the lineup completely, while remaining examples were available in small numbers.

The Forty-Five WLDR was eliminated from the catalog in the fall of 1941, and the race-going WR disappeared in December of the same year. The Servi-Cars were all fitted with a box of the same capacity, versus the two sizes offered in previous year. The newly sized box had a storage capacity of 7 cubic feet, which was slightly smaller than the 1941 GD and GDT compartment.

A new rectangular air filter was installed on 1942 models.

All civilian machines wore 5.00x16 tires, with a few special-order exceptions. The standard saddle had previously been a deluxe option, complete with whipped latex filling.

Harely-Davidson was awarded a contract to build 31,393 motorcycles in January of 1942. It would need to fulfill this order by December of the following year. While getting large orders

The cargo rack was improved and made more durable on the '42 WLA models.

was always welcomed, the slim 6-percent, pre-tax profit margin didn't do much for the company's bottom line. This number would include both WLA and XA models, with the XA proving its worth in initial testing.

As an indicator of how serious the war effort had become, all civilian production of Harley-Davidsons was ceased on February 9, 1942. Any changes made from then on applied strictly to military bikes.

At the peak of production in June of 1942, 750 completed motorcycles rolled off the assembly line each week. By August, the continuing materials shortage reduced that number to 675 units per week Even this diminished figure would be nearly triple that of 1941, when H-D built mainly civilian models.

A third military-directed reduction took effect in September. The total weekly output dropped to about 475 motorcycles per week. Production in the previous year only reached about half of this figure.

Beginning in the middle of June, 1942, the WLA models got most of the attention. The extended forks and rear frame that provided an additional 2 inches of ground clearance were reverted back to stock components for the balance of production. During crashes, the headlight was prone to damage, so it was relocated to a fender-mounted position. Additional crash-related problems were also addressed as production continued. Frame castings were enhanced, and the rider now gripped thicker handlebar tubes built to resist bending—a problem on earlier units. A sturdier toolbox mounting bracket was employed, along with a heavier-duty cargo rack over the rear wheel. Previous cylindrical oil-bath air cleaners were supplanted by rectangular versions.

The continuing dearth of natural resources made manufacturing difficult. Fuel supplies were very tight and related materials such as rubber were nearly impossible to obtain.

The 1942 WLA headlight was mounted to the front fender to reduce damage during a crash.

1942 Model Year Lineup

Model	Engine Type	Displacement	Transmission	Special Feature(s)
Model 42WL	Side-Valve Twin	45 cid	Three-Speed	High Compression
Model 42WLA	Side-Valve Twin	45 cid	Three-Speed	Military Sale Only
Model 42WLC	Side-Valve Twin	45 cid	Three-Speed	Canadian Military Sale Only
Model 42WLD	Side-Valve Twin	45 cid	Three-Speed	Aluminum Cylinder Heads
Model 42U	Side-Valve Twin	74 cid	Four-Speed	Medium Compression
Model 42UL	Side-Valve Twin	74 cid	Four-Speed	High Compression
Model 42E	Overhead-Valve Twin	61 cid	Four-Speed	Medium Compression
Model 42EL	Overhead-Valve Twin	61 cid	Four-Speed	High Compression
Model 42F	Overhead-Valve Twin	74 cid	Four-Speed	Medium Compression
Model 42FL	Overhead-Valve Twin	74 cid	Four-Speed	High Compression
Model 42G	Side-Valve Twin	45 cid	Three-Speed w/Reverse	Tow Bar
Model 42GA	Side-Valve Twin	45 cid	Three-Speed w/Reverse	No Tow Bar
Model 42XA	Horiz.-Opposed Twin	45 cid	Four-Speed	Military Sale Only

Production and Prices

Model	Production	Price
Model 42WL	142	$350
Model 42WLA	13,051	Gov't Contract
Model 42WLC	9,020	Canadian Gov't Contract
Model 42WLD	133	$365
Model 42U	421	$385
Model 42UL	405	$385
Model 42E	NA	$425
Model 42EL	620	$425
Model 42F	NA	$465
Model 42FL	799	$465
Model 42G	138	$525
Model 42GA	261	$510
Model 42XA	1,011	Gov't Contract

The balloon tires and rugged suspension were invaluable on desert terrain.

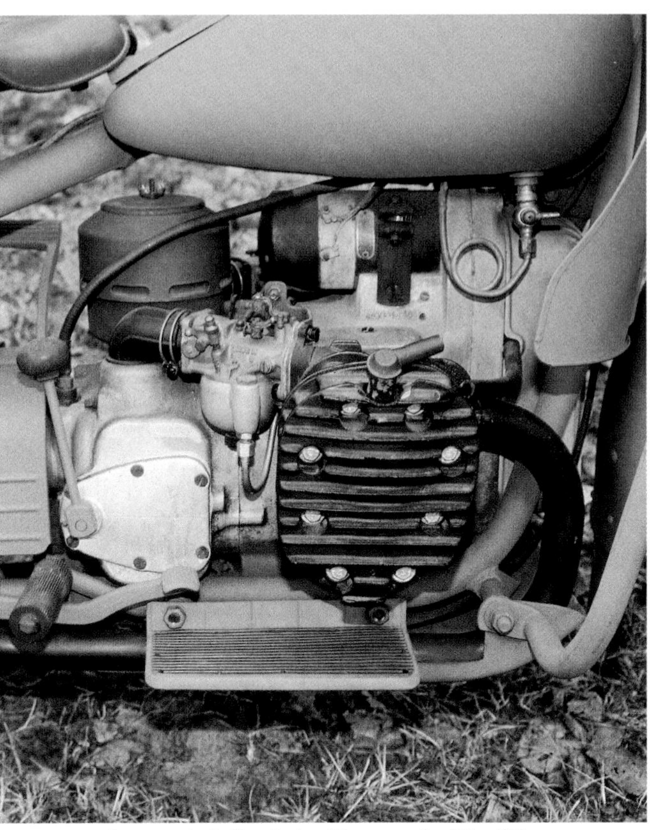

Improved air flow helped keep each of the XA's horizontally opposed cylinders cool.

The XA was designed to meet specific government guidelines for military use.

1943

Civilian bike production was again an afterthought in 1943 military based WLAs and similar variants rolled off the lines. A proposed government purchase of 25,000 shaft-driven motorcycles was dangled in front of both Harley and Indian. The choice came down to the Harley XA or Indian's 841 model. After a prolonged period of deliberation, neither unit was selected. The WLA, however, would go on to be the official cycle purchased for military use.

Although the XA was no longer produced as a complete motorcycle, the horizontally opposed engine would be pressed into a variety of duties outside the theatre of war. The XA mill went on to find work in generators, as well as drive units for other forms of land vehicles.

Non-military motorcycle sales were allowed, but the only buyers were police departments across the U.S. Even this process was cumbersome as the government deemed any non-military assembly to be a waste of valuable resources. Automobile sales were also restricted in the country. Ultimately, 1943 and 1944 would be the only years in U.S. history when fewer automobiles were built than cycles.

1943 Model Year Lineup

Model	Engine Type	Displacement	Transmission	Special Feature(s)
Model 43WLA	Side-Valve Twin	45 cid	Three-Speed	Military Sale Only
Model 43WLC	Side-Valve Twin	45 cid	Three-Speed	Canadian Military Sale Only
Model 43U	Side-Valve Twin	74 cid	Four-Speed	Medium Compression
Model 43UL	Side-Valve Twin	74 cid	Four-Speed	High Compression
Model 43E	Overhead-Valve Twin	61 cid	Four-Speed	Medium Compression
Model 43EL	Overhead-Valve Twin	61 cid	Four-Speed	High Compression
Model 43F	Overhead-Valve Twin	74 cid	Four-Speed	Medium Compression
Model 43FL	Overhead-Valve Twin	74 cid	Four-Speed	High Compression
Model 43G	Side-Valve Twin	45 cid	Three-Speed w/Reverse	Tow Bar
Model 43GA	Side-Valve Twin	45 cid	Three-Speed w/Reverse	No Tow Bar
Model 43XA	Horiz. Opposed Twin	45 cid	Four-Speed	Military Sale Only

With the demise of the XA, the WLA would soldier on with only minimal alterations. Early examples of the WLA and WLC were found to have rubber mats mounted to the steel floorboards. The mats proudly announced the maker as Harley-Davidson. A new regulation forbade any company branding on government machines, forcing H-D to fit WLAs and WLCs with steel versions of the floorboards that were ribbed to provide a modicum of traction.

The shortage of rubber-related products was reflected in several components on the WL models. Some WLCs had grips of green plastic in place of the black rubber units. Kickstarter levers, previously adorned with bicycle-style rubber fittings, were simply a cylindrical steel shaft.

Rubber components were not the only ones being replaced with substitutes. Nickel alloy had proven itself to be the best material for use in cylinder construction, but restrictions on its use forced the implementation of silicon alloy. While this alloy was acceptable for normal riding, police departments were wearing out cylinder rings in less than 1,000 miles. By substituting chrome rings, the problem was solved, and the motor even improved. Police models began getting closer to 20,000 miles on a set of rings before replacement was required.

As the war effort began to wind down, so did production at H-D. Still predicting a rosy future beyond the war, the designers at Harley-Davidson were already busy planning for new post-war models that would bring attract the next generation of riders.

Production and Prices

Model	Production	Price
Model 43WLA	24,717	Gov't Contract
Model 43WLC	2,647	Canadian Gov't Contract
Model 43U	493	$385
Model 43UL	11	$385
Model 43E	105	$425
Model 43EL	53	$425
Model 43F	12	$465
Model 43FL	33	$465
Model 43G	22	$515
Model 43GA	113	$500
Model 43XA	NA	Gov't Contract

1944

This would hardly be remembered as a year of breathtaking changes to the Harley lineup, but history would be made elsewhere as the war drew to an end. Civilian machines remained a rare commodity for most of the period, but as time went by things began to change.

As expected, the WLA accounted for the bulk of Harley-Davidson assembly work. Although no radical changes were made, the 1944 models did vary somewhat from the '42 and '43 WLAs. The front fender was no more than a curved length of steel, with no edge or tip details. Crankcases remained the same shade of olive drab with the cylinders and heads done in black as they were before. The previously cast air intake elbow was now stamped from steel. Keys were no longer needed for the ignition, and noise reduction components were added to assist in radio communications.

Late in the 1943 model year production run the federal government reduced its order for the WLA significantly, putting a definite kink in Harley's post-war plans. In stark contrast to their earlier order reduction, new orders were placed for only about 9,000 more units, as well as the additional parts required for each machine.

To help offset the reduction in government orders, H-D began to subcontract its workforce to assemble machinery for outside companies. Between large orders for power take-off transmissions, winches, and airplane components, Harley was able to secure nearly $1 million worth of business outside of the motorcycle assembly world.

In another sign of a better tomorrow, the allocation of "essential" civilian motorcycles was first increased by 450 units, and again by another 600 in the fall. Once the new orders for WLAs and higher levels of civilian production were allowed, H-D put a rapid stop to outsourcing its employees. With plenty of work doing what they did best, there was no need to water down the manufacturing potential of the factory.

While being able to build more cycles for civilian sales was a terrific sign for H-D, all 1944 machines built for the public were delivered with black frames and forks, mated to silver or gray sheet metal. Still, all in all, a drab motorcycle was better than none at all. October of 1944 saw yet a third increase in the allowed civilian machines, this time with another 6,000 units added to the parade.

1944 Model Year Lineup

Model	Engine Type	Displacement	Transmission	Special Feature(s)
Model 44WLA	Side-Valve Twin	45 cid	Three-Speed	Military Sale Only
Model 44WLC	Side-Valve Twin	45 cid	Three-Speed	Canadian Military Sale Only
Model 44U	Side-Valve Twin	74 cid	Four-Speed	Medium Compression
Model 44UL	Side-Valve Twin	74 cid	Four-Speed	High Compression
Model 44E	Overhead-Valve Twin	61 cid	Four-Speed	Medium Compression
Model 44EL	Overhead-Valve Twin	61 cid	Four-Speed	High Compression
Model 44F	Overhead-Valve Twin	74 cid	Four-Speed	Medium Compression
Model 44FL	Overhead-Valve Twin	74 cid	Four-Speed	High Compression
Model 44G	Side-Valve Twin	45 cid	Three-Speed w/Reverse	Tow Bar
Model 44GA	Side-Valve Twin	45 cid	Three-Speed w/Reverse	No Tow Bar

Production and Prices

Model	Production	Price
Model 44WLA	11,531	Gov't Contract
Model 44WLC	5,356	Canadian Gov't Contract
Model 44U	580	$385
Model 44UL	366	$385
Model 44E	NA	$425
Model 44EL	116	$425
Model 44F	67	$465
Model 44FL	172	$465
Model 44G	6	$515
Model 44GA	51	$500

1945

Being the first model year following the war, 1945 would prove to be a very quiet time for Harley-Davidson. The company was finally allowed to assemble large numbers of civilian machines, but the factory had to get back to full strength before doing so.

Total production of military bikes totaled nearly 88,000 units between the years of 1940 and 1945. Civilian models had basically ceased to exist, except for police and other official applications. Despite these circumstances, Harley came through the war with flying colors. The same could not be said for its rival, Indian. During the war, Harley concentrated on the assembly of motorcycles, which is what the company was best suited for. Indian had done a lot in the subcontracting field, and seemed to have lost sight of its prime market.

When the war ended, Harley was poised to re-enter the market at full strength. Consumers could buy surplus military motorcycles for a song, and many did. These buyers then needed a dealership for service, and many of the existing Harley shops were waiting with open arms. Assembly of real road-ready machines would start soon after, keeping the post-war momentum rolling.

During the war, Harley-Davidson had invested more than $1 million in plant improvements and new tooling. This would also help the company bring fresh offerings to a cycle-starved market. Two potential models based on the XA were discussed while the war raged on. A three-wheeled, XA-powered Servi-Car, and a sport model were considered, but neither saw the sales floor of the dealers. Additional applications for the versatile XA motor had been penned throughout the conflict, and many would remain in service for years to come.

1945 Model Year Lineup

Model	Engine Type	Displacement	Transmission	Special Feature(s)
Model 45WL	Side-Valve Twin	45 cid	Three-Speed	—
Model 45WLA	Side-Valve Twin	45 cid	Three-Speed	Military Sale Only**
Model 45U	Side-Valve Twin	74 cid	Four-Speed	Medium Compression
Model45UL	Side-Valve Twin	74 cid	Four-Speed	High Compression
Model 45US	Side-Valve Twin	74 cid	Four-Speed	Medium Comp./ Sidecar Gear
Model 45E	Overhead-Valve Twin	61 cid	Four-Speed	Medium Compression
Model 45EL	Overhead-Valve Twin	61 cid	Four-Speed	High Compression
Model 45ES	Overhead-Valve Twin	61 cid	Four-Speed	Medium Comp./ Sidecar Gear
Model 45F	Overhead-Valve Twin	74 cid	Four-Speed	Medium Compression
Model 45FL	Overhead-Valve Twin	74 cid	Four-Speed	High Compression
Model 45ES	Overhead-Valve Twin	74 cid	Four-Speed	Medium Comp./ Sidecar Gear
Model 45G	Side-Valve Twin	45 cid	Three-Speed w/Reverse	Tow Bar
Model 45GA	Side-Valve Twin	45 cid	Three-Speed w/Reverse	No Tow Bar

** WLA models were sold as surplus after World War II had ended.

Production and Prices

Model	Production	Price
Model 45WL	1357	$395.97
Model 45WLA	8,317	Gov't Contract
Model 45U	513	$427.25
Model 45UL	555	$427.25
Model45US	217	$427.25
Model 45E	NA	$463.67
Model 45EL	398	$463.67
Model 45ES	282	$463.67
Model 45F	NA	$465
Model 45FL	619	$465
Model 45FS	131	$465
Model 45G	26	$580.33
Model 45GA	60	$568.43

1946

As far as mechanical or cosmetic changes went, 1946 would be a lackluster year for the Harley-Davidson lineup. Most of the manufacturing world was still recovering from wartime efforts, and the Milwaukee company was no different. Its efforts taken during the war to prepare for post-war expansion would soon payoff, but for now, just getting back on track was first priority.

Sales of the military-built WLA totaled more than 15,000 before all was said and done. They could be purchased through Harley dealers as well as several other locations. Once purchased, many were customized for street use, and built to meet with the new owner's specifications and tastes.

The balance of the remaining lineup did receive a few minor upgrades, but most would happen between the middle and end of the model year. There were still deficits of raw materials in the country, and it would take awhile for some materials to be readily available again.

1946 Model Year Lineup

Model	Engine type	Displacement	Transmission	Special Feautre(s)
Model 46WL	Side-Valve Twin	45 cid	Three-Speed	—
Model 46U	Side-Valve Twin	74 cid	Four-Speed	Medium Compression
Model 46UL	Side-Valve Twin	74 cid	Four-Speed	High Compression
Model 46US	Side-Valve Twin	74 cid	Four-Speed	Medium Comp./ Sidecar Gear
Model 46E	Overhead-Valve Twin	61 cid	Four-Speed	Medium Compression
Model 46EL	Overhead-Valve Twin	61 cid	Four-Speed	High Compression
Model 46ES	Overhead-Valve Twin	61 cid	Four-Speed	Medium Comp./ Sidecar Gear
Model 46F	Overhead-Valve Twin	74 cid	Four-Speed	Medium Compression
Model 46FL	Overhead-Valve Twin	74 cid	Four-Speed	High Compression
Model 46FS	Overhead-Valve Twin	74 cid	Four-Speed	Medium Comp./ Sidecar Gear
Model 46G	Side-Valve Twin	45 cid	Three-Speed w/Reverse	Tow Bar
Model 46GA	Side-Valve Twin	45 cid	Three-Speed w/Reverse	No Tow Bar

Pre-war Harleys featured saddles filled with whipped latex for comfort. Machines built during the war would find their seats filled with horsehair—a far less comfortable, yet readily available material. The 1946 models would once again be filled with a latex material, but it was "spun" versus "whipped." We can only assume this was an improvement in the comfort department.

In about the middle of the product cycle, silver-painted tappet guides were found on every model sold by Harley. In the latter part of the model year, chrome plating would once again begin to appear on various components. The scant civilian models sold during the war were devoid of any shiny bits due to the drastic reduction in materials.

The three Big Twin models shared a few common changes. The steering head was given a new 30-degree angle to improve handling, although the bikes proved to be harder to handle than before.

Total production for the year would only increase slightly, to about 15,500 units, but all of these machines were built for public consumption, unlike the four years previous. Within a few years, Harley-Davidson would again take off, while Indian slowly disappeared into the history books.

Production and Prices

Model	Production	Price
Model 46WL	4,410	$395.97
Model 46U	670	$427.25
Model 46UL	1,800	$427.25
Model 46US	1,052	$427.25
Model 46E	NA	$463.67
Model 46EL	2,098	$463.67
Model 46ES	244	$463.67
Model 46F	NA	$465
Model 46FL	3,986	$465
Model 46FS	418	$465
Model 46G	766	$593.93
Model 46GA	678	$582.07

1947 would be the final year for the Knucklehead motor, which had distinguished itself during its 11-year run.

1947

Eager buyers were lining up around the block to get their hands on a "new" 1947 Harley, even though the machines were largely 1941 models with a few alterations. This didn't seem to matter the horde of hungry consumers with their pent-up buying power.

Foreshadowing things to come, the 1947 front fork could be fitted with a hydraulic damper in place of the friction-controlled style that had been in place for many years. Offering an increase in rider comfort, the hydraulic adaptation was well received.

The bulk of the amendments for 1947 were applied to the entire model line.

The previous "boat-tail" or "beehive" taillight housing was replaced by the now popular "tombstone" design. The latest tank emblem was plated in chrome, and was the work of Brook Stevens, the famous automotive designer. Additional bits of chrome began to return as post-war supply lines opened up. The air cleaner housing, front fender light, and horn covers were just a few of the chrome tidbits on the '47 models.

Speedometer faces were given a fresh look with larger numerals, a red indicator, and a background that faded from dark

Chrome may not get you home, but it was back in full force for the '47 models.

The tank-mounted instrument panel remained popular, and the face of the speedometer was all new for 1947.

to light closer to the center of the gauge. Mounting a spotlight on your Harley was becoming a popular practice, so a ready-to-use terminal was added to the '47s as well.

Factory accessories were beginning to become fashionable, and Harley offered an extensive catalog of everything from hardware to clothing. The first-ever "official" Harley black leather jacket made its first appearance in the catalog, and has become a staple of the riding world since then.

1947 Model Year Lineup

Model	Engine Type	Displacement	Transmission	Special Feature(s)
Model 47WL	Side-Valve Twin	45 cid	Three-Speed	—
Model 47U	Side-Valve Twin	74 cid	Four-Speed	Medium Compression
Model 47UL	Side-Valve Twin	74 cid	Four-Speed	High Compression
Model 47US	Side-Valve Twin	74 cid	Four-Speed	Medium Comp./ Sidecar Gear
Model 47E	Overhead-Valve Twin	61 cid	Four-Speed	Medium Compression
Model 47EL	Overhead-Valve Twin	61 cid	Four-Speed	High Compression
Model 47ES	Overhead-Valve Twin	61 cid	Four-Speed	Medium Comp./ Sidecar Gear
Model 47F	Overhead-Valve Twin	74 cid	Four-Speed	Medium Compression
Model 47FL	Overhead-Valve Twin	74 cid	Four-Speed	High Compression
Model 47FS	Overhead-Valve Twin	74 cid	Four-Speed	Medium Comp./ Sidecar Gear
Model 47G	Side-Valve Twin	45 cid	Three-Speed w/Reverse	Tow Bar
Model 47GA	Side-Valve Twin	45 cid	Three-Speed w/Reverse	No Tow Bar

Shift gate patterns were also modified on all models for 1947. By locating the first gear notch at the rear of the gate (except on Servi-Car), the rider had an easier starting position, even in the dark.

To meet the ever-expanding needs of the customer, Harley once again took on additional manufacturing space by purchasing the Capitol Drive plant in Milwaukee. As history would soon show, this would not be the final phase of growth for Harley-Davidson.

H-D's racing efforts were back in full force after the war's end, and the company's earlier domination continued with victories at tracks all across the U.S.

Production and Prices

Model	Production	Price
Model 47WL	3,338	$490
Model 47U	422	$545
Model 47UL	1,243	$545
Model 47US	1,267	$545
Model 47E	NA	$590
Model 47EL	4,117	$590
Model 47ES	237	$590
Model 47F	NA	$605
Model 47FL	6,893	$605
Model 47FS	401	$605
Model 47G	1,307	$710
Model 47GA	870	$695

Enter the Panhead

Probably the biggest news for 1948 was the introduction of the new OHV motor. It would earn the nickname of "Panhead" due to the configuration of the all-new aluminum-alloy cylinder heads. The new heads were designed with valve-seat inserts of aluminum-bronze, as well as valve guides formed of steel. A first for Harley was the installation of hydraulic pushrod lifters. This layout created more effective cooling for the enclosed valves. The new motor weighed in at 8 lbs. less than the Knucklehead version, but provided no boost in power. Both the 1936 EL and the 1948 EL claimed 40 hp @ 4800 rpm. The hydraulic valve train did run quieter though, and required less maintenance.

While the top end of the engine was new, the bottom end was largely the previous Knucklehead design with a few enhancements. Both the crankcase and cylinders were modified to allow for improved lubrication. Earlier OHV models were found with external oil lines, but the new motor was fed the vital lubrication internally. This improved the lubrication process, as well as the tidiness of the motor.

Other alterations changed the camshaft and exhaust ports and pipes. The intake manifold now had brazed tubing.

The new motor was a long-lasting success, considering it would remain in production until the next motor was introduced in 1966.

The new "Panhead" motor featured enclosed valves and aluminum cylinder heads.

The FL was Harley's latest OHV model for 1948, and would become an icon of the lineup.

1948

Along with new versions of H-D's overhead-valve models, a new variation was seen in company catalogs for 1948. These two major upgrades were mixed in with the usual assortment of revisions to the remaining hardware.

The newest OHV motor was mounted into a revised frame that provided extra space for the taller engine, and the front down tubes were splayed for clearance. Several small mounts were added, but would not be used until the 1949 model were introduced. A steering head lock was also added to the new frame design.

The second new face in the showrooms was the all-new S-125 model. This diminutive, single-cylinder model was based loosely on the German DKW RT125 machine. The single-cylinder two-stroke engine displaced 125 cc's and fed into a three-speed transmission. The combination claimed a mileage rating of 90 mpg. Even with only 1 3/4 gallons in the tank, a rider could go quite a distance before needing to stop for fuel.

The drive train was mounted into a rigid frame that steered with a sturdy girder-style front fork. A tiny front brake provided the stopping power on the lightweight machine.

While most Harley buyers wanted more size and power, the new S-125 found plenty of riders who longed for something more

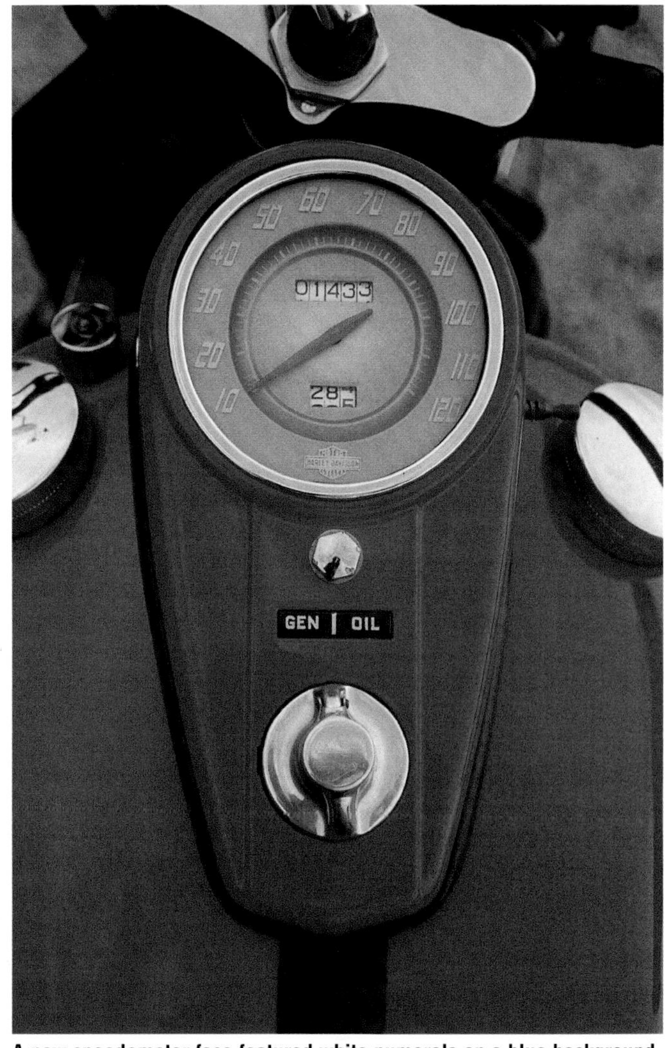

A new speedometer face featured white numerals on a blue background.

While not your typical Harley, the S-125 sold in huge numbers.

The single-cylinder engine was a two-stroke model and produced just under 2 hp.

nimble, and more than 10,000 units were assembled in the first year of production. Not even the venerable WLA was built in such quantities.

Changes to the rest of the lineup were detail-oriented as Harley-Davidson continued to improve the breed with every passing year.

1948 Model Year Lineup

Model	Engine Type	Displacement	Transmission	Special Feature(s)
Model 48S	Two-Stroke Single	125cc	Three-Speed	—
Model 48WL	Side-Valve Twin	45 cid	Three-Speed	—
Model 48U	Side-Valve Twin	74 cid	Four-Speed	Medium Compression
Model 48UL	Side-Valve Twin	74 cid	Four-Speed	High Compression
Model 48US	Side-Valve Twin	74 cid	Four-Speed	Medium Comp./ Sidecar Gear
Model 48E	Overhead-Valve Twin	61 cid	Four-Speed	Medium Compression
Model 48EL	Overhead-Valve Twin	61 cid	Four-Speed	High Compression
Model 48ES	Overhead-Valve Twin	61 cid	Four-Speed	Medium Comp./ Sidecar Gear
Model 48F	Overhead-Valve Twin	74 cid	Four-Speed	Medium Compression
Model 48FL	Overhead-Valve Twin	74 cid	Four-Speed	High Compression
Model 48FS	Overhead-Valve Twin	74 cid	Four-Speed	Medium Comp./ Sidecar Gear
Model 48G	Side-Valve Twin	45 cid	Three-Speed w/Reverse	Tow Bar
Model 48GA	Side-Valve Twin	45 cid	Three-Speed w/Reverse	No Tow Bar

The speedometer faces were again changed, and the new style featured white numerals against a pale blue background. All enameled parts were now "Bonderized" before the application of the paint. This new process provided an extra measure of durability to the painted surfaces. To improve access to the wiring, a terminal box was located under the seats.

The three Big Twin models received a few additional changes. An optional tank-mounted oil filter could be ordered along with the usual array of accessories. Models built early in the model year ran with exhaust pipes and a muffler painted matt black. The exhaust pipes changed to a silver finish later in the production run. 1948 would also be the final year of production for the 74-inch, side-valve U model.

Production and Prices

Model	Production	Prices
Model 48S	10,117	NA
Model 48WL	2,124	$535
Model 48U	401	$590
Model 48UL	970	$590
Model 48US	1,006	$590
Model 48E	NA	$635
Model 48EL	4,321	$635
Model 48ES	198	$635
Model 48F	NA	$650
Model 48FL	8,071	$650
Model 48FS	334	$650
Model 48G	1,050	$755
Model 48GA	728	$740

The girder-style fork added stability to the tiny chassis.

The 1949 E and F models were trimmed with plenty of stainless steel and a triple row of chrome strips on the rear fender.

1949

Compared to the previous year, when the Panheads and the S-125 were introduced, 1949 was quiet for H-D. The biggest news was in the suspension on the Panhead models.

Front forks were designed to provide control and comfort under a wide range of conditions. The introduction of hydraulic front forks on the '49 Panheads was a drastic improvement. The new Hydra-Glide front end was comprised of internal fork springs with hydraulic damping. The upper assembly was now enclosed in sleek steel tubes, while the lower legs were painted black. Not only did the new suspension work better, it looked a lot cleaner. Last year's front fork could still be ordered as an option, but most buyers took advantage of the new Hydra-Glide technology.

A larger front brake was also installed in 1949. The internal-expanding brake measured 8 inches in diameter, and added to the big bikes' stopping capacity. Redesigned handlebar mounts allowed for a bit of adjustment so each rider could tailor his machine to fit him best. Optional rubber-mounted bars were also available.

The rear fender on the '49 Panheads were trimmed with a triple row of chrome strips near the taillight assembly. The rear fender was also hinged to make it easier to remove the rear wheel.

The Panhead motors were assembled with several stainless-steel parts this year as well. The air-cleaner cover, rocker covers, timer cover, and generator cover were all formed from this durable material. An optional stainless-steel muffler cover was also available.

The 74-cubic inch OHV motor of the FL proved to be a popular option.

The Forty-Five-powered WL was also given the some components in stainless steel, but only the timer, generator, and air-cleaner covers were included. Rubber-mounted handlebars were also an option on the WL.

1949 Model Year Lineup

Model	Engine Type	Displacement	Transmission	Special Feature(s)
Model 49S	Two-Stroke Single	125cc	Three-Speed	—
Model 49WL	Side-Valve Twin	45 cid	Four-Speed	—
Model 49E	Overhead-Valve Twin	61 cid	Four-Speed	Medium Compression
Model 49EL	Overhead-Valve Twin	61 cid	Four-Speed	High Compression
Model 49ES	Overhead-Valve Twin	61 cid	Four-Speed	Medium Comp./ Sidecar Gear
Model 49EP	Overhead-Valve Twin	61 cid	Four-Speed	Med.Comp./ Sidecar Gear/Spr. Fork
Model 49ELP	Overhead-Valve Twin	61 cid	Four-Speed	High Comp.w/ Springer Fork
Model 49F	Overhead-Valve Twin	74 cid	Four-Speed	Medium Compression
Model 49FL	Overhead-Valve Twin	74 cid	Four-Speed	High Compression
Model 49FS	Overhead-Valve Twin	74 cid	Four-Speed	Medium Comp./ Sidecar Gear
Model 49FP	Overhead-Valve Twin	74 cid	Four-Speed	Med.Comp/ Sidecar Gear/Spr. Fork
Model 49FLP	Overhead-Valve Twin	74 cid	Four-Speed	High Comp.w/ Springer Fork
Model 49G	Side-Valve Twin	45 cid	Three-Speed w/Reverse	Tow Bar
Model 49GA	Side-Valve Twin	45 cid	Three-Speed w/Reverse	No Tow Bar

The hot new S-125 received only minor revisions for the its second year of production. The engine was now finished in "siliconized" silver paint, while the mufflers received a coating of the same paint in black. This new finish was highly heat resistant to reduce peeling and wear. The S was also available in any color the buyer wanted, as long as that color was black.

The Servi-Car soldiered on, and was also the recipient of a few upgrades. Mufflers received a coat of the "siliconized" black paint, and several bits of stainless steel were used on the motor. All else remained unchanged.

Production and Prices

Model	Production	Price
Model 49S	7,291	$325
Model 49WL	2,289	$590
Model 49E	NA	$735
Model 49EL	3,419	$735
Model 49ES	177	$735
Model 49EP	NA	NA
Model 49ELP	99	NA
Model 49F	NA	$750
Model 49FL	8,014	$750
Model 49FS	490	$750
Model 49FP	NA	NA
Model 49FLP	486	NA
Model 49G	494	$860
Model 49GA	545	$845

1950

The new decade would see even fewer changes to the lineup but, as always, alterations were made. One option removed from the order sheet was the springer front fork on the Big Twin models. The new Hydra-Glide performed so well that the older-style fork was deemed a waste of production time.

The E and F models received a boost of 10 percent more horsepower by having their cylinder heads reconfigured. Inlet ports on the newly drafted heads were given the credit for the increased power. Previous steel valve guides were now formed from bronze. The motor exhaled through a new "Sport" muffler that was available in either black or chrome. The lower fork legs were not painted black this year, but retained their natural steel look. This provided a more seamless look to the Hydra-Glide forks. The name "Hydra-Glide" was also stamped into the upper front panel of the fork enclosure.

1950 Model Year Lineup

Model	Engine Type	Displacement	Transmission	Special Feature(s)
Model 50S	Two-Stroke Single	125 cc	Three-Speed	—
Model 50WL	Side-Valve Twin	45 cid	Three-Speed	—
Model 50E	Overhead-Valve Twin	61 cid	Four-Speed	Medium Compression
Model 50EL	Overhead-Valve Twin	61 cid	Four-Speed	High Compression
Model 50ES	Overhead-Valve Twin	61 cid	Four-Speed	Medium Comp./ Sidecar Gear
Model 50F	Overhead-Valve Twin	74 cid	Four-Speed	Medium Compression
Model 50FL	Overhead-Valve Twin	74 cid	Four-Speed	High Compression
Model 50FS	Overhead-Valve Twin	74 cid	Four-Speed	Medium Comp./ Sidecar Gear
Model 50G	Side-Valve Twin	45 cid	Three-Speed w/Reverse	Tow Bar
Model 50GA	Side-Valve Twin	45 cid	Three-Speed w/Reverse	No Tow Bar

The WL model remained in the catalog, and was the recipient of a few minor changes as well. An improved carburetor featured recalibrated settings and a fixed jet. The fuel line was now encased in rubber and entered the fuel filter through a compression fitting. The Sport muffler was also offered in either black or chrome on the Side-Valve model.

The only change to the Servi-Car was the fuel line and filter arrangement found on the WL.

Sales of the S-125 continued to drop, and would only reach about half of the first year's 10,000-unit mark in 1950. Revisions were provided for the new models, but did little to enhance consumers' desire for the two-stroke cycle. A sprung saddle was added for an extra measure of comfort. The control cables were re-routed for trouble-free use, and the piston pin was enlarged.

Production and Prices

Model	Production	Price
Model 50S	4,708	$325
Model 50WL	1,108	$590
Model 50E	NA	$735
Model 50EL	2,046	$735
Model 50ES	268	$735
Model 50F	NA	$750
Model 50FL	7,407	$750
Model 50FS	544	$750
Model 50G	520	$860
Model 50GA	483	$845

1951

Changes in the Harley catalog were few and far between for the next few model years, while the usual range of detail alterations would continue. The standard E and F models were discontinued for 1951, leaving only eight models in the everyday lineup. "Have Fun in '51" was the boast printed on the front of the factory literature, and all the modern conveniences were detailed within.

The Sixty-One- and Seventy-Four-inch Hydra-Glide variants claimed a number of minute improvements for the new year. Inside the OHV motor, the pistons were fitted with chrome-plated compression rings for longer life and a better seal. Rocker arm assemblies had machined-in pushrod sockets, and the pushrod seals were of a neoprene/cork composite.

The triple row of chrome stripes on the rear fender was replaced by a single band of steel.

The "S" and "Y" exhaust pipes were now chrome plated.

Options for the Hydra-Glides included a one-piece safety guard, and a chrome "Hydra-Glide" badge for the front fender.

1951 Model Year Lineup

Model	Engine Type	Displacement	Transmission	Special Feature(s)
Model 51S	Two-Stroke Single	125cc	Three-Speed	Tele-Glide Forks
Model 51WL	Side-Valve Twin	45 cid	Four-Speed	Last Year in USA
Model 51EL	Overhead-Valve Twin	61 cid	Four-Speed	High Compression
Model 51ELS	Overhead-Valve Twin	61 cid	Four-Speed	High Comp./ Sidecar Gear
Model 51FL	Overhead-Valve Twin	74 cid	Four-Speed	High Compression
Model 51FLS	Overhead-Valve Twin	74 cid	Four-Speed	High Comp./ Sidecar Gear
Model 51G	Side-Valve Twin	45 cid	Three-Speed w/Reverse	Tow Bar
Model 51GA	Side-Valve Twin	45 cid	Three-Speed w/Reverse	No Tow Bar

The WL continued on, and featured a Linkert M-54 carburetor with a fixed jet. The pipe that connected the exhaust was also chrome plated this year. After a long run of production, the WLA was discontinued in the U.S. after 1951.

The Servi-Car continued to be improved as increased applications for the three-wheeler were created. The rear wheels were now solid discs, and were slowed by hydraulic brakes. The front binder was put into duty as the parking brake.

The G and GA were fitted with a larger muffler that ended up in a horizontal fishtail.

The S-125 received the most significant revision in 1951, but sales continued to sag. The biggest change was the installation of the Tele-Glide front fork. The latest design added a touch of "big bike" to the tiny machine, and provided vastly improved handling.

A new speedometer was located just in front of the handlebars in the top of the headlight nacelle. A larger 7-inch headlight provided an extra measure of safety for riding at night.

Some small cosmetic changes were applied to the entire line, including a new tank badge that featured the Harley-Davidson logo in script, with a straight line beneath.

Production and Prices

Model	Production	Price
Model 51S	5,101	$365
Model 51WL	1,044	$730
Model 51EL	1,532	$885
Model 51ELS	76	$885
Model 51FL	6,560	$900
Model 51FLS	135	$900
Model 51G	778	$1,095
Model 51GA	632	$1,080

The FLF variation featured the all-new foot-shift, and this example also wears the hard-to-find color-matched grips and kick-start pedal.

1952

The 1952 model year would see the loss of one model, and the introduction of another. The time-tested WL had done its duty, and was removed from the domestic catalog. To fill its shoes, an entirely new type of Harley rolled onto the scene.

The new K model would be powered by a small, side-valve, 45-cubic inch motor, but boasted a long list of new features. While still a side-valve motor, the new K featured aluminum-alloy heads, and fully enclosed valve gears. The pistons were also formed from aluminum alloy, and were designed for low expansion.

The K Model sent power to the rear wheel via four-speed transmission, but the mechanism was enclosed in the same case as the motor. Also new on the K was a hand-clutch, foot-shift layout. It was obvious that the new machine was going to take some getting used to, but it was quickly accepted among those seeking something smaller than the EL and FL models.

The K also featured coil spring/hydraulic suspension at both ends, a first for a Harley. The larger Duo-Glide would not appear for many years to come. The fuel tank held 4 1/2 gallons, as well as a small amount of reserve. Between the physical design of the machine, and the radical features, it was no wonder the K model became so popular so quickly. Its racing brethren, the KR and KRTT, also became class favorites.

Changes to the standard OHV models were minor, but the hand-clutch, foot-shift option was first offered on the '52 models. Diehards could still get their beloved hand-shift layout, but it would soon be eclipsed by the more acceptable design. When equipped with the new foot-shift, they were accompanied by a sprung clutch booster that would quickly earn the nickname "mousetrap." Anyone servicing one of these devices learned quickly where the name was derived. It aided the rider when shifting, but at the cost of some pain at repair time.

Other changes to the EL and FL models were minor. Valves were now "Parko-Lubricized" for longer life and smoother operation. The addition of "rotating" exhaust valves came in the

The spring-loaded clutch booster "mousetrap" is seen here, mounted to the front downtube of the frame.

middle of the model year. Motor mounts and brackets for the toolbox were also revised for 1952.

Sales of the 61-cubic inch EL model were waning when compared to the more robust 74-cubic inch FL, and 1952 would mark the final year for the smaller OHV model.

1952 Model Year Lineup

Model	Engine Type	Displacement	Transmission	Special Feature(s)
Model 52S	Two-Stroke Single	125 cc	Three-Speed	—
Model 52K	Side-Valve Twin	45 cid	Four-Speed	Foot-Shift/Hyd. Suspension
Model 52EL	Overhead-Valve Twin	61 cid	Four-Speed	High Compression
Model 52ELF	Overhead-Valve Twin	61 cid	Four-Speed	Hand-Clutch/ Foot-Shift
Model 52ELS	Overhead-Valve Twin	61 cid	Four-Speed	High Comp./ Sidecar Gear
Model 52FL	Overhead-Valve Twin	74 cid	Four-Speed	High Compression
Model 52FLF	Overhead-Valve Twin	74 cid	Four-Speed	Hand-Clutch/ Foot-Shift
Model 52FLS	Overhead Valve Twin	74 cid	Four-Speed	High Comp./ Sidecar Gear
Model 52G	Side-Valve Twin	45 cid	Three-Speed w/Reverse	Tow Bar
Model 52GA	Side-Valve Twin	45 cid	Three-Speed w/Reverse	No Tow Bar

The S-125 remained on the roster and was improved for the 1952. The Tele-Glide forks, introduced on the 1951 models remained, were now lubricated with oil versus the grease of the previous year. Folding footpegs and an improved Jiffy stand provided some extra value. Top speed on the speedometer was now 60 mph, and brake and clutch cables were increased in size to 1/8 inch.

With the exception of the bumpers being moved closer to the body by 2 1/2 inches, the Servi-Cars remained unaltered for 1952.

Production and Prices

Model	Production	Price
Model 52S	4,576	NA
Model 52K	1,970	$865
Model 52EL	918	$955
Model 52ELF	NA	$955
Model 53ELS	42	$955
Model 52FL	5,554	$970
Model 52FLF	NA	$970
Model 52FLS	186	$970
Model 52G	515	$1,175
Model 52GA	532	$1,160

1953

This year would mark the 50th year of operations for Harley-Davidson, while a few states away, the Indian Motorcycle brand would cease to exist. Poor planning by the Springfield, Massachusetts, company after World War II ultimately let to its demise. Oddly enough, H-D 50th anniversary badges would not appear until the 1954 models rolled out.

Only one OVH motor was offered in 1953, the 74-inch FL model. Harley had decided to discontinue the smaller EL variant after the 1952 sales year. A "Traffic" version of the FL was offered to help fill the place of the smaller machine. The Traffic model was assembled with a milder camshaft and smaller carburetor for use in parades, or other non-performance applications.

The remaining OHV engine was treated to a wide variety of upgrades to ensure a continued history of reliability. Earlier examples were built with the hydraulic lifters on top of the pushrods. The '53 models had the lifters beneath the pushrods for more consistent lubrication. The pushrods also featured a ball end at the top, and an adjustable screw-in fitting at the bottom. This allowed for much easier adjustments to the valve train.

1953 Model Year Lineup

Model	Engine Type	Displacement	Transmission	Special Feature(s)
Model 53ST	Two-Stroke Single	165 cc	Three-Speed	—
Model 53K	Side-Valve Twin	45 cid	Four-Speed	Final Year For The K
Model 53FL	Overhead-Valve Twin	74 cid	Four-Speed	Hand Shift
Model 53FLF	Overhead-Valve Twin	74 cid	Four-Speed	Hand-Clutch/ Foot-Shift
Model 53FLE	Overhead-Valve Twin	74 cid	Four-Speed	Traffic Model/ Hand-Shift
Model 53FLEF	Overhead-Valve Twin	74 cid	Four-Speed	Traffic Model/ Foot-Shift
Model 53G	Side-Valve Twin	45 cid	Three-Speed w/Reverse	Tow Bar
Model 53GA	Side-Valve Twin	45 cid	Three-Speed w/Reverse	No Tow Bar

Tappets were now drilled to allow for a bath of oil to be thrown onto the lifters. The tappet blocks were cast iron to improve durability as well. Both the right and left crankcases were altered to better feed the latest lubrication design. Oil scraper rings on the pistons were heat treated for longer life.

The K model entered into the second year of production with only minor revisions. A faster-acting throttle was joined by the now standard Solo Group of options. Plastic saddle bags and a two-place buddy seat could also be ordered for the new K. The 1953 model year would also prove to the final year for the K model, as improved versions were installed into the lineup.

The S-125 grew in displacement and became the ST-165 in 1953. The bigger motor delivered an extra measure of power while retaining its ease of operation. Alemite grease fittings were added to lubricate the 165 engine's main bearings for winter storage. Sales of the newest S-125 bikes remained at about the same level as the 1952 models.

The FLs and Servi-Cars were also fitted with refreshed speedometer faces that featured a black-and-gray background, yellow-silver numerals and hash marks, and an indicator of white. No other changes were made to the G and GA models.

Production and Prices

Model	Production	Price
Model 53ST	4,225	$405
Model 53K	1,723	$875
Model 53FL	1,986	$1,000
Model 53FLF	3,351	$1,000
Model 53FLE	NA	$1,000
Model 53FLEF	NA	$1,000
Model 53G	1,146	$1,190
Model 53GA	NA	$1,175

This 1954 FLF is complete with the "Anniversary" yellow paint and matching grips.

1954

The new models all wore medallions celebrating the 50 years of their production, despite the fact that it was H-D's 51st year. Besides the fender mounted badges, a raft of subtle revisions were made to the remaining models.

The two-stroke 165s were back again, and if the raucous power of the standard ST was too much for you, a restricted intake model—the STU—could be purchased instead. The shift lever and gate were both without serrations this year, and the lever was strengthened. A 70-mph speedometer was installed on both the ST and STU versions.

The K model was no more, replaced by a stronger-running KH variation. The new KH featured a 55-cubic inch motor that helped deliver 12 percent more power than the K had. Almost every internal component received revisions, starting with pistons that were cam ground and drilled around their lower edge for better oil dispersion. Intake valves were increased by 7/64 inch, and inlet and exhaust ports were reshaped for better flow. Valve springs styled like the performance-based KR were now found on the street-going KH. Additional strength was added to the transmission/crank case through a redesigned shape. The new clutch was comprised of seven plates, instead of the previous five.

Even the frame of the KH was modified to augment handling on the more powerful model. Brake shoes of pressed steel and superior brake linings were used to help slow the faster KH.

The F Series met with some new alterations, but none were radical. Three different frame styles were used throughout the model year with the final iteration wearing straight downtubes in

The F Models could be had in two-tone schemes, like this Pepper Red and Daytona Cream example.

The FLF speedometer face read 1 through 12, versus 10 through 120, and was new in 1953.

The KH was new for 1954 and featured the bigger 55-cubic inch motor.

place of the earlier wishbone design. The trumpet-shaped Jubilee horn took the place of the long-running circular version, and became an instant classic.

1954 Model Year Lineup

Model	Engine Type	Displacement	Transmission	Special Feature(s)
Model 54ST	Two-Stroke Single	165 cc	Three-Speed	—
Model 54STU	Two-Stroke Single	165 cc	Three-Speed	Restricted Intake
Model 54KH	Side-Valve Twin	55 cid	Four-Speed	—
Model 54FL	Overhead-Valve Twin	74 cid	Four-Speed	Hand Shift
Model 54FLF	Overhead-Valve Twin	74 cid	Four-Speed	Foot Shift
Model 54FLE	Overhead-Valve Twin	74 cid	Four-Speed	Traffic Model/ Hand Shift
Model 54FLEF	Overhead-Valve Twin	74 cid	Four-Speed	Traffic Model/ Foot Shift
Model 54G	Side-Valve Twin	45 cid	Three-Speed w/Reverse	Tow Bar
Model 54GA	Side-Valve Twin	45 cid	Three-Speed w/Reverse	No Tow Bar

More responsive throttle and spark controls were added, much like they had been on the 1953 K model. The foot-shift lever was reshaped, and could now be ordered with an optional heel-shift extension. Braking power was increased by adding the same pressed-steel shoes and improved linings found on the KH.

The G and GA models trundled on with only new pinion-shaft sealing rings to crow about.

Production and Prices

Model	Production	Price
Model 54ST	2,835	$405
Model 54STU	NA	NA
Model 54KH	1579	$925
Model 54FL	4,757	$1,015
Model 54FLF	NA	$1,015
Model 54FLE	NA	$1,015
Model 54FLEF	NA	$1,015
Model 54G	1,397	$1,240
Model 54GA	NA	$1,225

The lower-compression FLF model retained its crown among the Big-Twin offerings from Harley in 1955.

1955

The Harley-Davidson catalog for 1955 would show a few new listings, although neither of them was a completely original idea for the company. The Hummer was a 125cc two-stroke machine, and the FLH was simply an FL with added compression. Of course, the usual range of revisions was applied to the existing models as well.

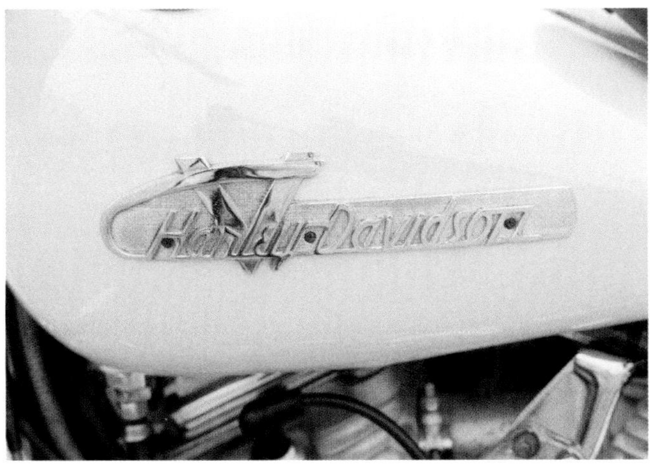

The new tank logo was applied to every model in the 1955 lineup.

There were thousands of customers who appreciated the size and power the 165cc ST model provided, but others still lamented the loss of the smaller 125cc version. The 1955 Hummer was a stripped-down S model that filled that need. Devoid of a front brake, battery-powered lighting, and a battery ignition, the Hummer was about a simple as a motorcycle could be. All the earlier chrome components were replaced by black-painted pieces as another way of cutting costs. The larger 165cc ST and STU were also available, and were largely unchanged.

Modifications to the FL line were minor, and mostly cosmetic. The standard FL motor did undergo a few changes aimed at improving oil retention and ease of maintenance. Previous examples of the OHV motor utilized hex nuts and flat seals to connect the inlet manifold to the cylinders. The 1955 method used O-rings and hose clamps, thus allowing easier removal of the carburetor. Base gaskets for the cylinders were changed to rubber-impregnated asbestos from the fiber-based versions used previously.

Minor improvements made the 1955 Panhead motor the best yet.

The bottom end of the OHV motor had tapered roller bearings and slightly larger cases. Thrust washers were no longer required on the newly designed flywheels. Outside the motor, the primary cover had a rounder profile, and was painted black.

The FLH models appeared during the model run and featured higher compression for added power. The FLH earned its extra power through the use of polished and flowed inlet ports, and higher-lift "Victory" camshafts. A boost of 10 percent in the horsepower rating was claimed by the factory literature.

Cosmetic revisions on the FL and FLH models included a newly shaped taillight and different ribbing on the panel surrounding the tops of the forks.

1955 Model Year Lineup

Model	Engine Type	Displacement	Transmission	Special Feature(s)
Model 55B	Two-Stroke Single	125cc	Three-Speed	—
Model 55ST	Two-Stroke Single	165cc	Three-Speed	—
Model 55STU	Two-Stroke Single	165cc	Three-Speed	Restricted Intake
Model 55KH	Side-Valve Twin	55 cid	Four-Speed	—
Model 55KHK	Side-Valve Twin	55 cid	Four-Speed	High Performance Model
Model 55FL	Overhead-Valve Twin	74 cid	Four-Speed	Hand Shift
Model 55FLE	Overhead-Valve Twin	74 cid	Four-Speed	Traffic Model/ Hand Shift
Model 55FLEF	Overhead-Valve Twin	74 cid	Four-Speed	Traffic Model/ Foot Shift
Model 55FLF	Overhead-Valve Twin	74 cid	Four-Speed	Foot Shift
Model 55FLH	Overhead-Valve Twin	74 cid	Four-Speed	High Comp./Hand Shift
Model 55FLHF	Overhead-Valve Twin	74 cid	Four-Speed	High Comp./Foot Shift
Model 55G	Side-Valve Twin	45 cid	Three-Speed w/Reverse	Tow Bar
Model 55GA	Side-Valve Twin	45 cid	Three-Speed w/Reverse	No Tow Bar

The KH would not escape the wheels of change, although revisions were slight. For easier access to the transmission, a door was now found on the side of the case. Better lubrication was delivered through a duct in the transmission case itself. The cylinder heads were now polished to a mirror finish, and the frame was stronger due to the use of chrome-moly steel. The rear wheel was augmented by sturdier spokes and hub.

The KHK variant would be the high-performance cousin of the KH. With the application of racing cams and polished ports (both inlet and exhaust), the KHK would become a race bike for the street. A distinctive appliqué on the oil tank told the world you were aboard the KHK model.

The side-valve motor of the Servi-Car received a pair of chrome-plated compression rings, but no other modifications were listed.

All models had the latest tank badges grafted onto their sides. An aggressive "V" was added to the Harley-Davidson script, and the entire affair was chrome plated.

Production and Prices

Model	Production	Price
Model 55B	1,040	$320
Model 55ST	2,263	$405
Model 55STU	NA	$405
Model 55KH	616	$925
Model 55KHK	449	$993
Model 55FL	953	$1,015
Model 55FLE	853	$1,015
Model 55FLEF	220	$1,015
Model 55FLF	2,013	$1,015
Model 55FLH	63	$1,083
Model 55FLHF	1,040	$1,083
Model 55G	394	$1,240
Model 55GA	647	$1,225

Factory accessories continued to grow in popularity. This well-dressed 1955 example is a rolling showroom of ups and extras.

The 1956 models sported new tank graphics that were seen for one year only.

1956

Continuous improvements were made to all models, but no new eggs were being broken in 1956.

The B Model received no changes at all, and the slightly larger ST was fitted with a new taillight and 18-inch wheels.

The KHs and KHKs were seen with several changes, but 1956 would also be the last year for these models. A new frame design, coupled with modified shocks, provided a lower saddle height for the mid-line models. A bevy of minute changes were also found on the 1956 models, most in efforts to strengthen existing assemblies. A new oval taillight was stamped from steel, and the color would match the hue of the bike.

The OHV models also benefited from numerous minor changes for '56. A change in the crankcase delivered oil to the top end via an oil-pump check valve that was spring operated. The D-rings were now cast-aluminum and featured 12 holes for screw mounting. Machines fitted with the high-compression FLH motors were decorated with colorful decals on both sides of the oil tank pronouncing the bike's prowess. The model year would mark the final appearance of the lower-powered FLE "Traffic" models.

The air cleaner cover was 7 inches in diameter, formed of stainless steel, and was mounted with a centrally located Phillips-

The 55-cubic inch side-valve motor served the K model series well.

head screw. Air cleaners formed of corrugated paper and wire mesh resided beneath the newly designed covers. The steering head lock was also fitted with a stainless-steel cover. A chrome-plated instrument panel was available for fans of the shiny stuff.

The speedometer faces would once again be altered, this time with luminescent numerals and a brighter, red indicator needle. New swoopy graphics adorned the fuel tanks of the '56 models, with colors that contrasted the base color of the chosen machine.

The Servi-Cars would find only a few modifications on the latest examples. The same air cleaner cover and paper filter on the FL was applied to the side-valve motor, and information about the air cleaner was stamped into the cover itself.

The iron cylinder heads were now tapped for use of 14mm spark plugs, and the openings for the head bolts measured 7/16 inch. The battery box was no longer in use on the three-wheeled model.

1956 Model Year Lineup

Model	Engine Type	Displacement	Transmission	Special Feature(s)
Model 56B	Two-Stroke Single	125 cc	Three-Speed	—
Model 56ST	Two-Stroke Single	165 cc	Three-Speed	—
Model 56STU	Two-Stroke Single	165 cc	Three-Speed	Restricted Intake
Model 56KH	Side-Valve Twin	55 cid	Four-Speed	—
Model 56KHK	Side-Valve Twin	55 cid	Four-Speed	High-Performance Model
Model 56FL	Overhead-Valve Twin	74 cid	Four-Speed	Hand Shift
Model 56FLE	Overhead-Valve Twin	74 cid	Four-Speed	Traffic Model/ Hand Shift
Model 56FLEF	Overhead-Valve Twin	74 cid	Four-Speed	Traffic Model/ Foot Shift
Model 56FLF	Overhead-Valve Twin	74 cid	Four-Speed	Foot Shift
Model 56FLH	Overhead-Valve Twin	74 cid	Four-Speed	High Comp./Hand Shift
Model 56FLHF	Overhead-Valve Twin	74 cid	Four-Speed	High Comp./Foot Shift
Model 56G	Side-Valve Twin	45 cid	Three-Speed w/Reverse	Tow Bar
Model 56GA	Side-Valve Twin	45 cid	Three-Speed w/Reverse	No Tow Bar

Production and Prices

Model	Production	Price
Model 56B	1,384	$320
Model 56ST	2,219	$405
Model 56STU	NA	$405
Model 56KH	539	$935
Model 56KHK	714	$1,003
Model 56FL	856	$1,055
Model 56FLE	671	$1,055
Model 56FLEF	162	$1,055
Model 56FLF	1,578	$1,055
Model 56FLH	224	$1,123
Model 56FLHF	2,315	$1,123
Model 56G	467	$1,240
Model 56GA	736	$1,225

The all-new XL model was rolled out in 1957 and was an instant favorite.

1957

The sales catalog for 1957 would once again be lacking some previous models, while gaining a new one. The KH and its siblings were eliminated at the end of the '56 model year, as were the "Traffic" models of the FL family. An all-new XL model was introduced for 1957, and would remain in the lineup until the present day.

The XL, or Sportster, was introduced to combat the rising tide of British bikes being sold in the U.S. The KH had been a good attempt, but lacked enough power to draw a large audience. The new 55-cubic inch XL would feature overhead valves, just like its bigger brother, the FL. Unlike the Panhead motor, the Sportster's engine was not the result of grafting new heads onto an existing bottom end, but was of an all-new design. A hybrid KL model was attempted, but H-D decided to go a different direction.

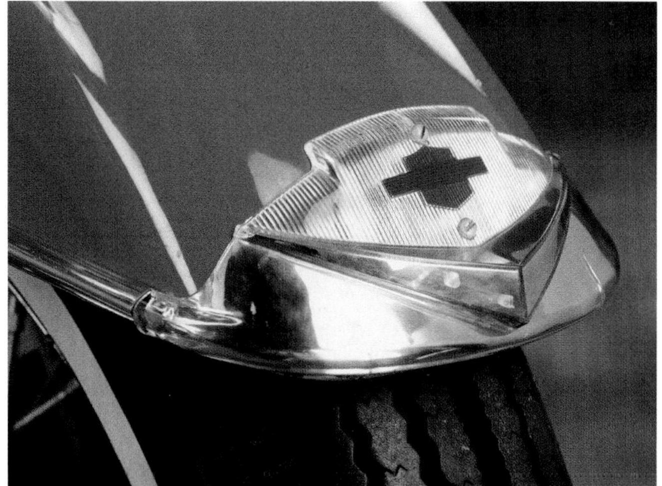

Front fender trim added another touch of color to the 1957 FLs.

Power from the new machine considered top notch, even though the first XLs were only offered in "touring" trim. Internally, the motor was packed with new techniques and materials. Within the cast-iron cylinder walls pumped aluminum pistons that were topped by hemispheric combustion chambers. The valve train was also enclosed in aluminum rocker boxes, motivated by aluminum-alloy pushrods. The entire motor breathed in through a compact

The Sportster filled the void left by the departed KH model.

The Panhead motor was largely unchanged for 1957.

The tank badge was new for 1957, and was a one-year-only version.

An instrument panel bathed in chrome was a popular feature on the big FL models.

Linkert carburetor, and exhaled through a newly designed exhaust. The four-speed transmission was housed in the same case as the motor, and was shifted by foot, using a lever mounted on the right side of the bike. This practice was common on British machines—H-D's only competition at the time. The clutch was hand operated at the handlebar.

The telescopic front forks were topped off with a steel housing that also enclosed the speedometer. Brakes on both wheels assured that the XL could stop as well as it could go. A solo seat was standard, but an optional dual saddle was available at the dealer.

Despite the terrific magazine reviews, the XL sold slowly for the first few years it was offered. It was hardly a bargain when compared to the bigger FL models, which sold for only $100 more than the new XL in 1957. It would be several years before the XL models carved out their own market among the eager buyers of Harley-Davidsons.

The Hummer remained in the catalog for 1957, and now featured a front brake, which was operated by a hand lever on the handlebars. A more durable muffler mount was the only other change besides the latest tank graphics.

The ST and STU now rode on front wheels complete with needle bearings in the hub, and also had a stronger muffler mount. A refreshed speedometer face was joined by the new tank graphic.

The FL models were virtually untouched, but a few revisions were made to the big OHVs. Both intake and exhaust valve guides of steel alloy were added to the motor's top end, and heftier valve springs joined the fray mid-year as well.

The speedometer face on the FL was also modified, and tank badges were new, and a one-year only design. This badge change affected the Servi-Cars also, but no other alterations are found.

1957 Model Year Lineup

Model	Engine Type	Displacement	Transmission	Special Feature(s)
Model 57B	Two-Stroke Single	125cc	Three-Speed	Front Brake
Model 57ST	Two-Stroke Single	165cc	Three-Speed	—
Model 57STU	Two-Stroke Single	165cc	Three-Speed	Restricted Intake
Model 57XL	Overhead-Valve Twin	55 cid	Four-Speed	First Year Sportster
Model 57FL	Overhead-Valve Twin	74 cid	Four-Speed	Hand Shift
Model 57FLF	Overhead-Valve Twin	74 cid	Four-Speed	Foot Shift
Model 57FLH	Overhead-Valve Twin	74 cid	Four-Speed	High Comp./Hand Shift
Model 57FLHF	Overhead-Valve Twin	74 cid	Four-Speed	High Comp./Foot Shift
Model 57G	Side-Valve Twin	45 cid	Three-Speed w/Reverse	Tow Bar
Model 57GA	Side-Valve Twin	45 cid	Three-Speed w/Reverse	No Tow Bar

Production and Prices

Model	Production	Price
Model 57B	1,350	$356
Model 57ST	2,401	$445
Model 57STU	NA	$445
Model 57XL	1,983	$1,103
Model 57FL	1,579	$1,167
Model 57FLF	1,259	$1,167
Model 57FLH	164	$1,243
Model 57FLHF	2,614	$1,243
Model 57G	518	$1,367
Model 57GA	674	$1,352

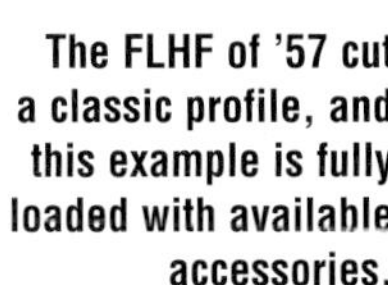

The FLHF of '57 cut a classic profile, and this example is fully loaded with available accessories.

The XL model was back in 1958, and was joined by three other Sportster models.

1958

Unlike many years in Harley-Davidson's history, 1958 was rife with changes. Between several new models in the Sportster lineup, and hydraulic rear suspension on the FL models, things were rapidly expanding within the hallowed halls of H-D.

The first Hydra-Glide appeared in 1949, and the addition of real front suspension made a big difference in comfort. By adding hydraulic dampers to the rear axle as well, an entirely new level of riding luxury to the Harley camp. A pair of chrome "Duo-Glide" badges were also applied to the front fender to show the world what you rode.

The application of the rear shocks brought about another radical alteration to an accepted H-D design. Previous rear fenders had been supported by braces that terminated at the rigid

This was the tank badge worn only by 1958 models, except for the XLC and XLCH.

The front and rear fenders on the XLCs and XLCHs were "bobbed."

frame. With a new pivoting swing arm, a new method of fender mounting was required. Two S-shaped chrome bars were used to hold the rear sheet metal in place, and have since become a Harley trademark. The new frame layout required a new oil tank to nestle within the steel tubes. The oil filter was mounted with a new bracket, and an improved oil-return line was used.

Also on the tail end, a hydraulic brake was added to the equation. Hydraulic brakes had not been used on Harley's two-wheeled models before, but had been in use on the Servi-Car since 1951. The new drum brake added an enormous amount of stopping power to the heavyweight machines.

The 74-cubic inch motors were treated to a few minor tweaks, but now exhaled through a single-pipe exhaust system. A dual-outlet system could be purchased as an accessory. The left and right crankcases, as well as the cylinder heads and gear cover, all received minor changes to accommodate the newest hardware.

The XL listings grew by three, and now included the XL, XLH, XLC, and XLCH models. The XLH variant was a high-compression version of the well-received XL of 1957. The XLC and XLCH were competition models, devoid of lighting or

The XLCH was new for 1958 and was dubbed "XL, Competition Hot."

The XLCH motor was 55 cubic inches of high-compression power.

The "H" appliqué put the world on notice that this was no ordinary XL model.

speedometer. Short, performance-oriented mufflers were unbaffled to promote maximum horsepower. Both the XLC and XLCH were also fitted with shortened, or "bobbed," fenders at both ends. Magneto ignitions were used to fire the plugs, with no battery on board. The four models equaled the number of XLs built for the 1957 model year.

The Servi-Car also rode with the Hydra-Glide front forks as part of the standard package. This included the front end, brake, axle, and headlight from the two-wheeled version.

Another new tank badge would make a one-year-only appearance. Two-tone paint options abounded, along with the usual group of solid-color options. All white or silver remained for police use only.

Production and Prices

Model	Production	Price
Model 58B	1,677	$375
Model 58ST	2,445	$465
Model 58STU	NA	$465
Model 58XL	579	$1,155
Model 58XLH	711	$1,155
Model 58XLC	NA	NA
Model 58XLCH	239	NA
Model 58FL	1,591	$1,255
Model 58FLF	1,299	$1,255
Model 58FLH	195	$1,320
Model 58FLHF	2,953	$1,320
Model 58G	283	$1,465
Model 58GA	643	$1,450

The front forks of the XLC and XLCH were stripped of headlights and speedometer.

1958 Model Year Lineup

Model	Engine Type	Displacement	Transmission	Special Feature(s)
Model 58B	Two-Stroke Single	125cc	Three-Speed	—
Model 58ST	Two-Stroke Single	165cc	Three-Speed	—
Model 58STU	Two-Stroke Single	165cc	Three-Speed	Restricted Intake
Model 58XL	Overhead-Valve Twin	55 cid	Four-Speed	—
Model 58XLH	Overhead-Valve Twin	55 cid	Four-Speed	High Compression
Model 58XLC	Overhead-Valve Twin	55 cid	Four-Speed	Competition Model
Model 58XLCH	Overhead-Valve Twin	55 cid	Four-Speed	Compet. Model/ High Comp.
Model 58FL	Overhead-Valve Twin	74 cid	Four-Speed	Hand Shift
Model 58FLF	Overhead-Valve Twin	74 cid	Four-Speed	Foot Shift
Model 58FLH	Overhead-Valve Twin	74 cid	Four-Speed	High Comp./Hand Shift
Model 58FLHF	Overhead-Valve Twin	74 cid	Four Speed	High Comp./Foot Shift
Model 58G	Side-Valve Twin	45 cid	Three-Speed w/Reverse	Tow Bar
Model 58GA	Side-Valve Twin	45 cid	Three-Speed w/Reverse	No Tow Bar

This 1959 FLF was pressed into funeral parade duty.

1959

After the introduction of the Duo-Glide and three new Sportsters in 1958, 1959 would turn out to be rather anticlimactic.

In what would be their last year of production, the B model received nothing more than a new tank logo for 1959. An optional, two-person Buddy seat was also an option this year.

The ST and STU would also vanish from the catalog for 1960, but a few changes were made to the '59s. A 5 3/4-inch-diameter headlight was found on the 165 models, and a Trip-O-Meter speedometer was placed in the upgraded Tele-Glide enclosure. The same new logo was added to the 1959 STs as well.

The standard-level XL was not selling well, and 1959 would be the last year for this version of the Sportster. The XLC was already removed from the roster after 1958. Even in its final year of production, the XL would receive several revisions.

A new wraparound nacelle would encompass the top of the forks, and house the headlight and new Trip-O-Meter speedometer. The sides of the front fenders were extended down over the tires slightly, with the look of a small skirt.

Options for the XL would include a pair of stacked mufflers, and the dual-place Buddy seat.

The high-compression XLH version would also be treated to the same revisions as the XL model, and also get high-lift intake cams and improved exhaust cams.

The small, green dome on the instrument panel was a neutral indicator lamp on foot-shift models.

The XLCH, previously a "competition-only" model, was converted for street-legal use. The additions of head and taillights, electrical system, and a horn satisfied the government requirements for a streetable machine. A speedometer completed the changes for street use, but alterations within the motor added some extra motivation.

The same high-lift intake cam and reshaped exhaust cams used on the XLH were applied to the XLCH. A high-mounted, two-into-one exhaust was attached, and a louder set of mufflers could be added. Rubber-mounted chrome handlebars topped off the changes for the XLCH.

The FLs were identified as 1959 models by only the tiniest of changes. The FLF and FLHF models now had a neutral indicator light on the instrument panel, helping to inform the rider when he was between gears. Front and rear fender tip décor was chrome plated, and of a new design. Floorboards were Parkerized and painted black.

The XLCH was not only street legal, but race ready.

The thinly disguised XLCH race bike came complete with electrics and lighting.

The Servi-Car was proving its mettle and was revised ever so slightly for 1959. A diaphragm-style fuel petcock was added beneath the saddle, and an aluminum-bodied carburetor with altered manifold and gas lines completed the list.

Every 1959 model except the XLCH was now seen with the latest "Arrow-Flite" logo on the fuel tank.

Perhaps bigger news than the changes to the Harley-Davidson line was the appearance of a "small" Japanese company touting that "You meet the nicest people on a Honda." While the ads were considered cute, the impact that Honda, and other overseas makers, would have on Harley would be dramatic.

1959 Model Year Lineup

Model	Engine Type	Displacement	Transmission	Special Feature(s)
Model 59B	Two-Stroke Single	125cc	Three-Speed	Last Year For the B
Model 59ST	Two-Stroke Single	165cc	Three-Speed	Last Year For The ST
Model 59STU	Two-Stroke Single	165cc	Three-Speed	Restrict. Int./Last Year For STU
Model 59XL	Overhead-Valve Twin	55 cid	Four-Speed	Last Year For The Standard XL
Model 59XLH	Overhead-Valve Twin	55 cid	Four-Speed	High Compression
Model 59XLCH	Overhead-Valve Twin	55 cid	Four-Speed	High Comp./Now Street Legal
Model 59FL	Overhead-Valve Twin	74 cid	Four-Speed	Hand Shift
Model 59FLF	Overhead-Valve Twin	74 cid	Four-Speed	Foot Shift
Model 59FLH	Overhead-Valve Twin	74 cid	Four-Speed	High Comp./Hand Shift
Model 59FLHF	Overhead-Valve Twin	74 cid	Four-Speed	High Comp./Foot Shift
Model 59G	Side-Valve Twin	45 cid	Three-Speed w/Reverse	Tow Bar
Model 59GA	Side-Valve Twin	45 cid	Three-Speed w/Reverse	No Tow Bar

Production and Prices

Model	Production	Prices
Model 59B	1,285	$385
Model 59ST	2,311	$475
Model 59STU	NA	$475
Model 59XL	42	$1,175
Model 59XLH	947	$1,200
Model 59XLCH	1,059	$1,285
Model 59FL	1,201	$1,280
Model 59FLF	1,222	$1,280
Model 59FLH	121	$1,345
Model 59FLHF	3,223	$1,345
Model 59G	288	$1,500
Model 59GA	524	$1,470

This 1960 FLHF is trimmed with an entire catalog of official H-D accessories.

1960

The big news for 1960 was actually the introduction of another small cycle from Harley-Davidson. With the company still convinced a certain segment of the market wanted a simple, yet nimble machine, the "Topper" was born.

While it shared the same displacement as the ST of the previous year, the A Model, or Topper, featured all-new hardware and was wrapped in a body of fiberglass. Still a two-stroke, the Topper was driven by a 165cc, single-cylinder motor. The motor was attached to the frame with rubber mounts for additional smoothness. Simple pull-starting was used to get your Topper running. A restricted intake AU model was offered to meet with the 5-hp limits in some regions. Power from the motor was put to the ground by way of a centrifugal clutch that fed power into a belt system, providing all the convenience of an "automatic" transmission. Final drive on the Topper was still delivered by chain.

With leading-link suspension out front, and variable extension springs out back, the Topper delivered a large amount of comfort in a compact package. Five-inch brakes were found on each wheel as well, providing decent stopping power. The brake lever on the left handlebar did double duty as the parking brake activator when it was squeezed and locked into place. The two-place "Buddy" seat also provided a storage compartment beneath the rear section of the saddle.

For those still wanting a bit more "cycle" in their two-wheeled transport, the BT and BTU replaced the ST and STU of 1959. Mostly unchanged, the BT did operate with a new 165cc motor that included aluminum heads and 6 hp. The restricted BTU would only produce 5 hp to meet with guidelines. The electrical system was now water resistant, and spark was delivered with the use of two, low-tension coils.

The Sportster offerings were reduced to two for 1960: the XLH and XLCH. The changes were minimal, and included recalibrated suspension damping in the shocks, and 19-inch-diameter front rim was placed up front on the XLCH.

Revisions to the FL model were also incremental for the year. The headlight nacelle was now a two-piece assembly, which required the adaptation of the windshield brackets and lower panels to fit the new surround. The handlebars were also of two-piece design, and were secured by a centrally located clamp. Spotlight mounting points also needed to be revised to work with the latest headlight nacelle.

Internal motor modifications were limited to a few components. Stellite-faced valves previously used only on the FLH were now applied to the FL models as well. Oil-control piston rings were now a rail configuration, and valve springs were enhanced for heavier duty. The gear side of the main bearing also rode on crowned rollers.

The two-place Buddy seat and dual exhaust make this example a luxury liner.

The suspension rates were recalibrated on the big FLs along with the XLs.

Servi-Car models were also fitted with the new headlight nacelle and related hardware. New versions of both the Winter and Summer windshields were available.

Even with its longstanding history behind it, Harley-Davidson was already feeling the pinch of the new Asian-built market entries. There was still no threat to Harley's Big Twin models, but even that dominance would prove to be fragile in the years to come.

1960 Model Year Lineup

Model	Engine Type	Displacement	Transmission	Special Feature(s)
Model 60A	Two-Stroke Single	165cc	Automatic	Only Year for A Model
Model 60AU	Two-Stroke Single	165cc	Automatic	Restricted Intake
Model 60BT	Two-Stroke Single	165cc	Three-Speed	—
Model 60BTU	Two-Stroke Single	165cc	Three-Speed	Restricted Intake
Model 60XLH	Overhead-Valve Twin	55 cid	Four-Speed	High Compression
Model 60XLCH	Overhead-Valve Twin	55 cid	Four-Speed	"Competition Hot"
Model 60FL	Overhead-Valve Twin	74 cid	Four-Speed	Hand Shift
Model 60FLF	Overhead-Valve Twin	74 cid	Four-Speed	Foot Shift
Model 60FLH	Overhead-Valve Twin	74 cid	Four-Speed	High Comp./Hand Shift
Model 60FLHF	Overhead-Valve Twin	74 cid	Four-Speed	High Comp./Foot Shift
Model 60G	Side-Valve Twin	45 cid	Three-Speed w/Reverse	Tow Bar
Model 60GA	Side-Valve Twin	45 cid	Three-Speed w/Reverse	No Tow Bar

Production and Prices

Model	Production	Price
Model 60A	—	$430
Model 60AU	—	$430
Total Production For All 1960 Topper Models	3,801	—
Model 60BT	—	$455
Model 60BTU	—	$455
Total Production For All 1960 Lightweight Models	2,488	—
Model 60XLH	—	$1,225
Model 60XLCH	—	$1,310
Total Production For Both 1960 Sportster Models	2,765	—
Model 60FL	—	$1,310
Model 60FLF	—	$1,310
Model 60FLH	—	$1,375
Model 60FLHF	—	$1,375
Total Production For All 1960 Duo-Glide Models	5,967	—
Model 60G	—	$1,530
Model 60GA	—	$1,500
Total Production For All 1960 Servi-Car Models	707	—

1961

More limited changes would arrive in 1961 for Harley-Davidson. Sales had been sagging across the board for the H-D lineup, and no major introductions were on the way anytime soon. However, with H-D's recent partnership with the Italian firm Aermacchi completed, one notable new entry was made to the catalogs for 1961.

The Sprint was basically an Aermacchi model renamed for Harley-Davidson, and was meant to fill the gap between the 165cc models and the larger FLs. Featuring a 250cc, single-cylinder engine, the Sprint was definitely a departure from Harley's typical design. With its single cylinder jutting out from the cases horizontally, the Sprint looked like no other Harley before it. The overhead valves were pushrod activated, and were a bit behind the times at introduction. The Japanese had already begun building far more advanced, overhead-cam motors, and were selling them on the streets of the U.S.

The Sprint appealed to the segment of the market that wanted a lightweight cycle with a bit more power. Fully loaded, the Sprint only tipped the scale at 270 lbs., and delivered more than enough punch to satisfy riders. The $700 sticker price also made sense to some buyers. While never sold in large numbers, the Sprint would stay around and find its way into several variations.

The Topper was back for another year, and the A model of 1960 was supplanted by a higher-powered AH version. Delivering 9 hp, the '61 AH brought 50 percent more motivation to the table. The restricted-intake AU was still available for those living with output limitations in their region. Both models now carried the Jiffy stand on the right side of the frame. To increase the versatility of the Topper, both a sidecar and a utility box were offered .

The next steps up in the catalog were the BT and BTU 165 CC machines. Sixteen-inch wheels were the only change applied to these cycles for the year.

The XLH and XLCH returned almost unchanged from 1960. A new "Double-Duty" saddle was included as standard equipment. A cross between the solo-saddle and the two-place Buddy seat, the newest perch provided an extra measure of versatility.

Even the star performers were little changed for the new year of sales. The FL line did receive a dual-points, dual-fire ignition system that replaced the sometimes finicky wasted-spark arrangement of previous years.

A new and improved "FLH" decal was used on the oil tanks of the appropriate models, and the FLs also received the upgraded tank badges. New tank striping was used across the model line as well. Only the Topper was delivered without the latest paint trim.

The G and GA variations had the latest tank badging.

Sales of all Harley models were faltering in 1961, and management continued to scramble to find the perfect mix of big and small machines.

1961 Model Year Lineup

Model	Engine Type	Displacement	Transmission	Special Feature(s)
Model 61AH	Two-Stroke Single	165cc	Automatic	High Compression
Model 61AU	Two-Stroke Single	165cc	Automatic	Restricted Intake
Model 61BT	Two-Stroke Single	165cc	Three-Speed	—
Model 61BTU	Two-Stroke Single	165cc	Three-Speed	Restricted Intake
Model 61C	Overhead-Valve Single	250cc	Four-Speed	—
Model 61XLH	Overhead-Valve Twin	55 cid	Four-Speed	High Compression
Model 61XLCH	Overhead-Valve Twin	55 cid	Four-Speed	—
Model 61FL	Overhead-Valve Twin	55 cid	Four-Speed	Hand Shift
Model 61FLF	Overhead-Valve Twin	55 cid	Four-Speed	Foot Shift
Model 61FLH	Overhead-Valve Twin	55 cid	Four-Speed	High Comp./Hand Shift
Model 61FLHF	Overhead-Valve Twin	55 cid	Four-Speed	High Comp./Foot Shift
Model 61G	Side-Valve Twin	45 cid	Three-Speed w/Reverse	Tow Bar
Model 61GA	Side-Valve Twin	45 cid	Three-Speed w/Reverse	No Tow Bar

Production and Prices

Model	Production	Price
Model 61AH	—	$445
Model 61AU	—	$445
Total Production For Both 1961 Topper Models	1,341	—
Model 61BT	—	$465
Model 61BTU	—	$465
Total Production For Both 1961 Lightweight Models	1,587	—
Model 61C	—	$695
Model 61XLH	—	$1,250
Model 61XLCH	—	$1,335
Total Production For 1961 Sportster Models	2,014	—
Model 61FL	—	$1,335
Model 61FLF	—	$1,335
Model 61FLH	—	$1,400
Model 61FLHF	—	$1,400
Total Production For All 1961 Duo-Glide Models	4,927	—
Model 61G	—	$1,555
Model 61GA	—	$1,525
Total Production For All 1961 Servi-Car Models	628	—

1962

The total number of units sold for the 1962 model year would remain nearly stagnant, despite the fact that several new variations were being offered. The big FL model was virtually untouched, while the new lightweight division received all the attention.

The Toppers were back for another year, but changes were minor. Newly shaped handlebars that featured revised grips appeared up front, along with fingertip ignition and a neutral lockout device.

The power-restricted BTU was unchanged, except for new paint. There were, however, a bevy of additions made to the remaining BT series. The BT of '61 was back as the Pacer, and now ran with a 175cc motor instead of the previous 165 version. Available with the two-person Buddy seat, the Pacer was more useful than before. An off-road version of the 165cc BT was the BTF Ranger. Built with high-mounted exhaust and fenders, and no lighting, it was for non-street use only. The new BTH Scat variant featured the 175cc motor, and was designed for both on- and off-road use. The combination of high-mounted fenders, upturned exhaust, buckhorn bars, and semi-knobby tires allowed for a wide variety of riding options.

The Italian-made Sprint was also back for another year and was found with redesigned tank graphics, but no other modifications. Numerous internal modifications were made to enhance durability. A new high-compression H model was also available around the middle of the model year. A larger carburetor and the higher compression added three horsepower to the H, giving it 21 hp. The standard C model had 18. The air cleaner was also larger and had a greater capacity than the H model. High-mounted exhaust, additional clearance for the front fender, and a shortened rear fender made the CH perfect for trail riding. Still equipped with lights and electrics, the CH was also at home on the street.

The same two Sportster models were available again for '62, and the addition of an aluminum upper fork brace was the only change seen.

The venerable FL models remained the best sellers of the group, but even they only received minor alterations.

In its quest to diversify, Harley-Davidson acquired the Tomahawk Boat Company, which had a proven record of producing components from fiberglass, many of which would soon be appearing on Harley's two-wheeled machines.

1962 Model Year Lineup

Model	Engine Type	Displacement	Transmission	Special Feature(s)
Model 62AH	Two-Stroke Single	165cc	Automatic	—
Model 62AU	Two-Stroke Single	165cc	Automatic	Restricted Intake
Model 62BTF	Two-Stroke Single	165cc	Three-Speed	Off-Road Model
Model 62BTU	Two-Stroke Single	165cc	Three-Speed	Restricted Intake
Model 62BT	Two-Stroke Single	175cc	Three-Speed	—
Model 62BTH	Two-Stroke Single	175cc	Three-Speed	On/Off Road Model
Model 62C	Overhead-Valve Single	250cc	Four-Speed	—
Model 62CH	Overhead-Valve Single	250cc	Four-Speed	High Compression
Model 62XLH	Overhead-Valve Twin	55 cid	Four-Speed	High Compression
Model 62XLCH	Overhead-Valve Twin	55 cid	Four-Speed	—
Model 62FL	Overhead-Valve Twin	74 cid	Four-Speed	Hand Shift
Model 62FLF	Overhead-Valve Twin	74 cid	Four-Speed	Foot Shift
Model 62FLH	Overhead-Valve Twin	74 cid	Four-Speed	High Comp./Hand Shift
Model 62FLHF	Overhead-Valve Twin	74 cid	Four-Speed	High Comp./Foot Shift
Model 62G	Side-Valve Twin	45 cid	Three-Speed w/Reverse	Tow Bar
Model 62GA	Side-Valve Twin	45 cid	Three-Speed w/Reverse	No Tow Bar

Production and Prices

Model	Production	Price
Model 62AH	—	$445
Model 62AU	—	$445
Model 62BTF	—	$440
Model 62BTU	—	$465
Model 62BT	—	$465
Model 62BTH	—	$475
Total Production For The 1962 Lightweight Models	1,983	—
Model 62C	—	$695
Model 62CH	—	$720
Model 62XLH	—	$1,250
Model 62XLCH	—	$1,335
Total Production For The All 1962 Sportster Models	1,998	—
Model 62FL	—	$1,335
Model 62FLF	—	$1,335
Model 62FLH	—	$1,400
Model 62FLHF	—	$1,400
Total Production For All 1962 Duo-Glide Models	5,184	—
Model 62G	—	$1,555
Model 62GA	—	$1,525
Total Production For All 1962 Servi-Car Models	703	—

The 1963 BTH Scat model was meant for on- or off-road riding, and sold fairly well.

1963

After several years with only minor changes, the FLs would finally be the recipient of some styling and mechanical alterations for 1963. It would be several more years before the newest motor was installed, so for now a few tweaks would have to suffice.

With the exception of a new body-mounted H-D logo and the installation of a Hypalon saddle, the AU and AH Topper models were unchanged. Sales slid slightly downward, as the novelty of the Topper was wearing off.

Positioned just above the Topper were the BT models. The 165cc BTF Ranger was not included in the 1963 offerings, leaving three models in its wake. All three of the middleweight models were now powered by the 175cc motor, but the BTU ran with a restricted intake. A more pliant rear suspension system was added to the line, complete with a pivoting swing arm. Other changes to the remaining three were minimal, including tank emblems. The BT and BTU now rode with the same handlebars as the BTH Scat, and the Scat sported an upswept rear fender.

The Sprints were back in 1963, this time with updated tanks, handlebars, and saddles. The lower-position bars had not grown as popular in the U.S. as they had in Europe, and were scrapped in favor of taller versions. The saddle was redesigned to match the new riding position, and the fuel tank was reshaped for a fresh look. The CH model added more clearance between the front wheel and fender.

Inside the C and CH, the lower end bearing was enhanced, and the tappets were now of lighter "racing" configuration. The rear-frame tubing on the C was beefed up, and a 60-watt generator was added, along with a bigger battery on both models. An improvement was made in the lubrication of the Sprints by installing a better oil filter.

The Sportsters received a few changes, starting with the newest design of tank badging on both the XLH and XLCH. The two variations continued to wear individual fuel tanks that were model-specific. Third-gear ratios were changed to bring them closer to that of fourth. Both models were delivered with a pair of short, staggered exhaust pipes replacing the two-into-one version of 1962.

A tachometer was added to the XLCH model, along with a rubber-mounted headlight assembly. The XLCH also got a better magneto, complete with an ignition key lock.

The FL models received both cosmetic and mechanical updates for 1963. Oil lines on the motor had been moved inside during the Knucklehead era, but were once again located outside the cylinders for 1963.

The larger rear chain guard was the most notable alteration, and the FL stopped with a wider rear drum brake and a matching shoe. Instead of replacing the entire brake assembly when it wore

The AH Topper was unchanged for 1963, except for the new H-D logo.

The high-compression H model proudly wore an emblem claiming its power.

With the optional sidecar, another person could join in on the riding fun.

out, the new drum could be relined. An improved hydraulic brake cylinder also reduced the foot pressure required to stop the big FL.

1963 Model Year Lineup

Model	Engine Type	Displacement	Transmission	Special Feature(s)
Model 63AH	Two-Stroke Single	165cc	Automatic	—
Model 63AU	Two-Stroke Single	165cc	Automatic	Restricted Intake
Model 63BT	Two-Stroke Single	175cc	Three-Speed	—
Model 63BTU	Two-Stroke Single	175cc	Three-Speed	Restricted Intake
Model 63BTH	Two-Stroke Single	175cc	Three-Speed	On/Off Road Model
Model 63C	Overhead-Valve Single	250cc	Four-Speed	—
Model 63CH	Overhead-Valve Single	250cc	Four-Speed	High Compression
Model 63XLH	Overhead-Valve Twin	55 cid	Four-Speed	High Compression
Model 63XLCH	Overhead-Valve Twin	55 cid	Four-Speed	—
Model 63FL	Overhead-Valve Twin	74 cid	Four-Speed	Hand Shift
Model 63FLF	Overhead-Valve Twin	74 cid	Four-Speed	Foot Shift
Model 63FLH	Overhead-Valve Twin	74 cid	Four-Speed	High Comp./Hand Shift
Model 63FLHF	Overhead-Valve Twin	74 cid	Four-Speed	High Comp./Foot Shift
Model 63G	Side-Valve Twin	45 cid	Three-Speed w/Reverse	Tow Bar
Model 63GA	Side-Valve Twin	45 cid	Three-Speed w/Reverse	No Tow Bar

The optional dual-exhaust system was available with chrome "fishtail" ends, which were becoming a hot styling trend. Another new option was the hard-sided fiberglass saddlebags. The addition of these molded items made the bikes better road trip machines, because riders could bring a change of clothes and some gear.

Front and rear turn signals were modified and now featured a convex back, with different mounting locations both front and rear.

The only change to the Servi-Car was the new tank logo.

Production and Prices

Model	Production	Price
Model 63AH	972	$460
Model 63AU	6	$460
Model 63BT	824	$485
Model 63BTU	39	$485
Model 63BTH	877	$495
Model 63C	150	NA
Model 63CH	1,416	NA
Model 63XLH	432	$1,270
Model 63XLCH	1,001	$1,355
Model 63FL	1,096	$1,360
Model 63FLF	950	$1,360
Model 63FLH	100	$1,425
Model 63FLHF	2,100	$1,425
Model 63G	NA	$1,590
Model 63GA	NA	$1,550

This 1964 FLHF is complete with windshield, fishtail exhaust, and a two-place Buddy seat.

1964

The 1964 model year was one of the quietest in H-D history. Perhaps the next year's introduction of the new Electra-Glide took all the R&D Harley-Davidson could muster, leaving only minor changes on the table. The year did see the final appearance of several models in the lineup, but this was no surprise as slow sales had predicted their demise.

The two Topper models were still offered in 1964, but the restricted-intake AU would not make the 1964 cut. Sales in '63 dropped below 10, making future production a waste of time and effort. The 1964 models did receive a rear-mounted nameplate. A reconfigured flywheel compression plate and a shield for the magneto chamber were the extent of the alterations.

The white panels on the fuel tanks were used on nearly every model for 1964.

The XLCH was seen wearing the white-sided fuel tanks for 1964, but little else was changed.

Tank graphics on the BT, BTU, and BTH were the only deviations from the 1963s, and 1964 would be the final year for the BTU version.

Both Sprint versions made the '64 catalog, and each found a few variations. For both the C and CH, the primary gears were of a wider design, providing a larger surface to smooth the action. Both models also received revised clutch linings, Stellite-faced tappets, and a higher-pressure oil pump. The C and CH were treated with the same white-sided fuel tanks as most of the '64 models. The CH was now called the Scrambler while the C remained the Sprint.

The Sportster team still retained two members, and each received minor changes. Both the XLH and XLCH were found with a full-width, die-cast aluminum front brake drum between the spokes.

Aluminum tappets were used inside the motor, and an improved polyacrylic seal was used on the clutch assembly. The white-sided fuel tanks found their way onto the Sportsters as well.

The front fork on the XLCH had last year's black lower fork bracket replaced with a chrome version of the same.

The FL would receive a radical alteration in 1965, leaving the '64 models near duplicates of the previous year's models. A two-key system was implemented, one for the fork lock and another for

A tachometer and speedometer allowed the rider to keep close tabs on his performance.

the ignition. Obviously cycle thievery must have been becoming more of an issue if extra measures were being taken to thwart would-be criminals in their tracks. The oil pressure switch was improved, along with a wider Jiffy stand. Late in the model year, a chrome, two-section rear chain guard was made available as an option. White side panels were used on the big FLs, too.

1964 Model Year Lineup

Model	Engine Type	Displacement	Transmission	Special Feature(s)
Model 64AH	Two-Stroke Single	165cc	Automatic	—
Model 64AU	Two-Stroke Single	165cc	Automatic	Final Year Of Production
Model 64BT	Two-Stroke Single	175cc	Three-Speed	—
Model 64BTU	Two-Stroke Single	175cc	Three-Speed	Final Year Of Production
Model 64BTH	Two-Stroke Single	175cc	Three-Speed	On/Off Road Model
Model 64C	Overhead-Valve Single	250cc	Four-Speed	—
Model 64CH	Overhead-Valve Single	250cc	Four-Speed	High Compression
Model 64XLH	Overhead-Valve Twin	55 cid	Four Speed	High Compression
Model 64XLCH	Overhead-Valve Twin	55 cid	Four-Speed	—
Model 64FL	Overhead-Valve Twin	74 cid	Four-Speed	Hand Shift
Model 64FLF	Overhead-Valve Twin	74 cid	Four-Speed	Foot Shift
Model 64FLH	Overhead-Valve Twin	74 cid	Four-Speed	High Comp./Hand Shift
Model 64FLHF	Overhead-Valve Twin	74 cid	Four-Speed	High Comp./Foot Shift
Model 64GE	Side-Valve Twin	45 cid	Three-Speed w/Reverse	Electric Start

The Servi-Car was only offered in the GE trim level for 1964. Although no tow bar was fitted, the first electric starter was there to fill the void. No longer would stern kick starting be required to get your three-wheeler going. The three-speed with reverse transmission was altered to meet the new requirements of the electric start motor, and a 12-volt electrical system replaced the 6-volt arrangement. The FL model would be fitted with electric starters the following year, thus enabling bikers of all sizes to more easily start their heavyweight Harleys.

Production and Prices

Model	Production	Price
Model 64AH	800	$470
Model 64AU	25	$470
Model 64BT	600	$495
Model 64BTU	50	$495
Model 64BTH	800	$505
Model 64C	230	NA
Model 64CH	1,550	NA
Model 64XLH	810	$1,295
Model 64XLCH	1950	$1,360
Model 64FL/FLF	2,775	$1,385
Model 64FLH/FLHF	2,725	$1,450
Model 64GE	725	$1,628

The big 1965 FLB started with the push of a button, bringing a new level of convenience to Harley riders.

1965

A new era of motorcycling was introduced in 1965 when Harley-Davidson added an electric starting system to its classic Big Twin models. Although the three-wheeled Servi-Car got the system in 1964, it saw little use in the civilian market. The Electra Glide was the first electric-start Harley offered to the consumer, and would eventually become the standard way of thinking. Honda had rolled out their machines several years earlier with a start button, but a Harley fan didn't consider the tiny Japanese machines to be real motorcycles.

Several related changes were made to the FL to make it start with the touch of a button. The earlier 6-volt battery was pitched so a larger 12-volt system could be installed. The much larger battery displaced the famous horseshoe oil tank, and a larger rectangular model was installed. The new oil tank was also fitted with internal oil filters, replacing the previously external location.

Both the inner and outer primary-chain covers were now cast from aluminum for greater strength. This cast assembly bolted solidly to the transmission case. This staunch assembly was required to offset the enormous torque generated when electric-starting the Big Twin motor. Previous examples had their primary chains adjusted by sliding the transmission back and forth on its mounts. With the transmission now a fixed unit, a shoe within the primary case was used to make the required adjustments.

The 3 1/2-gallon fuel tanks used on past FLs were supplanted with larger 5-gallon units. The hand-shift versions still utilized the smaller tanks for another year. While the kick-start pedal was no longer needed, it remained on the FL for two more years. Many old-school riders bemoaned the loss of their beloved kick-start models, but soon grew accustomed to the convenience of finger starting their Big Twins. The letter "B" was now applied to all FL models to designate the electric start.

Another new entry in the 1965 sales book was the tiny M-50. Powered by a little 50cc, two-stroke motor, and featuring a step-through frame, the Italian built scooter would account for over a third of production in its first model year. At a cost of only $225, it appealed to many new riders eager to get their feet wet on a two-wheeled machine.

The AH Topper would return unchanged from the previous year, and 1965 would be its final year of production.

The BT was another model that would see its last year of production in 1965. Also largely unchanged from the '64 version, the 175cc machine did wear new side panels for the final year. The on-/off-road BTH Scat was still available, but would also disappear the following model year.

The Sprints received minor alterations for 1965. The C now had folding footpegs and a wider saddle. The CH also received the new saddle and improved pegs, as well as a low-mounted exhaust and a relocated crankcase breather tube.

XLH and XLCH models remained kick-start models, but a 12-volt electrical system was added in 1965. This would prove to be useful when the electric start was added in the 1967 model year.

Every year saw more accessories being added to the FL models.

The cast-aluminum housing for the primary is seen here beneath the newest oil tank used on the 1965 Electra Glides.

The 1965 12-volt system required a new battery box, and the chrome plating added a touch of flash.

The XLH could now carry 3.7 gallons of fuel in the new tank, and a "High-fidelity" horn was added to the left side of the frame. The XLCH also received the new horn, but carried the same tank as the previous models.

1965 Model Year Lineup

Model	Engine Type	Displacement	Transmission	Special Feature(s)
Model 65M	Two-Stroke Single	50cc	Three-Speed	—
Model 65AH	Two-Stroke Single	165cc	Automatic	Final Year Of Production
Model 65BT	Two-Stroke Single	175cc	Three-Speed	Final Year Of Production
Model 65BTH	Two-Stroke Single	175cc	Three-Speed	On/Off Road Model
Model 65C	Overhead-Valve Single	250cc	Four-Speed	—
Model 65CH	Overhead-Valve Single	250cc	Four-Speed	High Compression
Model 65XLH	Overhead-Valve Twin	55 cid	Four-Speed	High Compression
Model 65XLCH	Overhead-Valve Twin	55 cid	Four-Speed	—
Model 65FLB	Overhead-Valve Twin	74 cid	Four-Speed	Hand Shift
Model 65FLFB	Overhead-Valve Twin	74 cid	Four-Speed	Foot Shift
Model 65FLHB	Overhead-Valve Twin	74 cid	Four-Speed	High Comp./Hand Shift
Model 65FLHFB	Overhead-Valve Twin	74 cid	Four-Speed	High Comp./Foot Shift
Model 65GE	Side-Valve Twin	45 cid	Three-Speed w/Reverse	—

Having electric start added in 1964 was enough for the Servi-Car, and it went unchanged for 1965.

In an effort to bolster the financials of the company, Harley-Davidson had its first stock offering in 1965. With stock available to both the public and company employees, the plan was to raise enough capital to keep the expansion moving. By 1968 it was obvious that this stock sale was not enough, and another avenue was explored.

Production and Prices

Model	Production	Price
Model 65M	9,000	$225
Model 65AH	500	NA
Model 65BT	500	NA
Model 65BTH	750	NA
Model 65C	230	NA
Model 65CH	1,550	NA
Model 65XLH	955	NA
Model 65XLCH	2,815	NA
Model 65FLB/FLFB	2,130	NA
Model 65FLHB/FLHFB	4,800	NA
Model 65GE	725	NA

Out with the Panhead, in with the Shovelhead

The Panhead motor had served Harley-Davidson well since its introduction in 1948, but H-D was not one to sit on its laurels for long. Some riders had experienced periodical leakage from their Panheads, and the Shovelhead of 1966 was designed to correct that. Along with better sealing, additional power was made available.

By adding the "power pac" aluminum heads to the existing bottom end, the new Shovelhead was born. The resulting motor ran with less noise, and delivered a 10-percent boost in horsepower. The design of the new heads reduced oil leaks dramatically, and their new shape garnered the engine the "Shovelhead" moniker. Cast in aluminum, the latest heads were a welcome improvement. Changes to the exhaust flanges were another highlight of the newest motor.

The air/fuel mixture was fed into the new motor by a new carburetor in 1966 as well. A die-cast zinc model made by Linkert was the first unit attached to the Shovelhead. The Model DC worked well, but was not easy to adjust. Other brands and models were adapted through the motor's life, but all were met with varying degrees of success and acceptance.

Additional revisions were made to the new motor as time went by, but the 1966 version proved to be a hit on the sales floor. Nearly 1,000 additional FLB and FLHB units were sold once the Shovelhead was announced.

The Shovelhead was big news for H-D in 1966.

The FLHFB was the best-selling H-D model for 1966, but more M-50S models were assembled.

1966

The new Shovelhead motor was the big news at H-D for 1966, but other modifications were seen across the line. A few models were gone from the catalog, but a few new versions of existing machines made their way onto the sales floor.

The 50cc M-50 was still available, and was joined by a sportier M-50S variant. The "S" model was attired with a fuel tank reminiscent of larger racing models, and the saddle was also flatter to mimic a more powerful racing machine.

With the Topper gone, the BTH was modified for 1966. Now called the Bobcat, it was largely an upgraded BT Pacer from 1965. Clothed in molded, ABS bodywork that enclosed both the tank and rear fender, the Bobcat offered a radical new look for the aging hardware beneath. Even this revision would not save the BT series, and it would be removed from the lineup in 1967.

The Sprint and Scrambler returned for another year, and were unchanged from the 1965 models.

Sportster models received a 15-percent boost in horsepower for 1966 through the use of improved "P" cams and a Tillotson carburetor. A patented insulator was installed to keep heat from affecting the performance of the new carburetor. The application of the now classic "ham-can" air cleaner cover was the only other change to the XLH and XLCH.

1966 Model Year Lineup				
Model	**Engine Type**	**Displacement**	**Transmission**	**Special Feature(s)**
Model 66M	Two-Stroke Single	50cc	Three-Speed	—
Model 66MS	Two-Stroke Single	50cc	Three-Speed	Sport Model
Model 66BTH	Two-Stroke Single	175cc	Three-Speed	One-Piece Molded Body
Model 66C	Overhead-Valve Single	250cc	Four-Speed	—
Model 66CH	Overhead-Valve Single	250cc	Four-Speed	High Compression
Model 66XLH	Overhead-Valve Twin	55 cid	Four-Speed	High Compression
Model 66XLCH	Overhead-Valve Twin	55 cid	Four-Speed	—
Model 66FLB	Overhead-Valve Twin	74 cid	Four-Speed	Hand Shift
Model 66FLFB	Overhead-Valve Twin	74 cid	Four-Speed	Foot Shift
Model 66FLHB	Overhead-Valve Twin	74 cid	Four-Speed	High Comp./Hand Shift
Model 66FLHFB	Overhead-Valve Twin	74 cid	Four-Speed	High Comp./Foot Shift
Model 66GE	Side-Valve Twin	45 cid	Three-Speed w/Reverse	—

The Electra Glides received little else outside of the new Shovelhead motor, although that alone was a huge step forward for the Big Twins. The "ham-can" air cleaner cover was also seen on the Electra Glides, and the left fuel tank was revised. The new version had no fuel valve on the top, but held the petcock beneath.

The GE air cleaner was now capable of having the Tillotson carburetor mounted on it, and a Delco alternator was fitted with a rectifier.

Production and Prices		
Model	**Production**	**Price**
Model 66M	5,700	$225
Model 66MS	10,500	$275
Model 66BTH	1,150	$515
Model 66C	600	NA
Model 66CH	4,700	NA
Model 66XLH	900	$1,415
Model 66XLCH	3,900	NA
Model 66FLB/FLFB	2,175	$1,545
Model 66FLHB/FLHFB	5,625	$1,610
Model 66GE	625	NA

This 1966 FL is fully loaded with the two-tone buddy seat, a pair of hard saddlebags, and the color-keyed windscreen.

The rear passenger of this 1967 XLH had a stout back support as well as a comfortable perch beneath.

1967

If we are to believe Harley-Davidson's claim for the 1967 model year, it was "electrifying." Of course, that boast was referring to the electric starter being added to the XLH Sportster, but the other changes to the existing models could be considered radical.

With the demise of the BTH Bobcat, the only remaining lightweights were the M and MS. These machines were both bumped up to 65cc in an effort to rekindle interest in them. After

The XLH model received electric starting in 1967 and the Sportster world was forever changed.

more than 15,000 50cc units were built for 1966, many were still sitting at the dealer with no buyers in sight. The boost in displacement did little to enhance sales, and both variations were removed from the listings for 1968.

The Sprint and Scrambler (H) received additional modifications, and the previous C was now the SS model. This designation was applied to the "Street Scrambler," while the H remained the same. Both models received new motors featuring shorter strokes and longer bores. The heads and cylinders were now of an alloy material. The SS gained some ground clearance and its headlight was designed for easy removal. The H was seen with a fresh fuel tank for 1967.

1967 Model Year Lineup

Model	Engine Type	Displacement	Transmission	Special Feature(s)
Model 67M	Two-Stroke Single	65cc	Three-Speed	—
Model 67MS	Two-Stroke Single	65cc	Three-Speed	Sport Model
Model 67SS	Overhead-Valve Single	250cc	Four-Speed	Was "C" in 1966
Model 67CH	Overhead-Valve Single	250cc	Four-Speed	High Compression
Model 67XLH	Overhead-Valve Twin	55 cid	Four-Speed	Electric Start
Model 67XLCH	Overhead-Valve Twin	55 cid	Four-Speed	High Compression
Model 67FLB	Overhead-Valve Twin	74 cid	Four-Speed	Hand Shift
Model 67FLFB	Overhead-Valve Twin	74 cid	Four-Speed	Foot Shift
Model 67FLHB	Overhead-Valve Twin	74 cid	Four-Speed	High Comp./Hand Shift
Model 67FLHFB	Overhead-Valve Twin	74 cid	Four-Speed	High Comp./Foot Shift
Model 67GE	Side-Valve Twin	45 cid	Three-Speed w/Reverse	—

The XLH was fitted with an electric starter, just like its big brother, the FL. The XLCH shared the same humped case, but received no starter within. Modifications to the rear shocks were the only other changes for 1967.

The FLBs breathed through the Tillotson carbs installed on the Sportsters the previous year, but it seemed to cause more trouble than the change was worth. Despite the difficulties, the Tillotson would remain as the standard carb until the 1970 model year. At the rear end, the brake drum, axle, and related spacer were modified. Wheel hubs at both ends were now sealed, ball-bearing units. Fender tips were found with a square profile, and optional "turnout" mufflers were a new option.

Late in the production run, GEs were assembled using boxes formed of fiberglass. Harley-Davidson's investment in the Tomahawk Company was beginning to pay off with the use of fiberglass accessories and components.

Production and Prices

Model	Production	Price
Model 67M	2,000	$230
Model 67MS	3,267	$265
Model 67SS	7,000	NA
Model 67CH	2,000	NA
Model 67XLH	2,000	$1,650
Model 67XLCH	2,500	$1,600
Model 67FLB/FLFB	2,150	$1,735
Model 67FLHB/FLHFB	5,600	$1,800
Model 67GE	600	$1,930

The 55-cid XLH carried a sticker price of $1,650.

The XLCH remained a potent performer in 1968, even when faced with competitive machines from across the pond.

1968

By the end of 1968, Harley-Davidson found itself in an awkward position that no one, not even the company itself, had predicted. Being THE dominant builder and seller of motorcycles in the early '50s, it was hard to imagine that The Motor Company would need outside help to survive. The initial stock sale in 1965 had helped, but had not gone far enough to save the ailing manufacturer. The truth of the matter was that Honda was outselling Harley by almost a 3-to-1 ratio. Seems you could meet a lot of the nicest people on Hondas.

During 1967 and the early part of 1968, Harley management deemed that growth without a corporate partner was impossible. Mere survival was even questioned without some deep pockets to keep the wheels rolling. The decision was made to seek a partner capable of providing guidance and financial stability to the existing company. An initial attempt at a hostile takeover was made by the Bangor Punta Company. American Machine and Foundry (AMF) then joined the contest for the chance to own the Milwaukee firm. After a painful and drawn-out battle for ownership, AMF was declared the winner.

The 1968 XLH wore its badge on the oil tank.

The move that should have, and perhaps did, save The Motor Company from extinction, almost proved to be fatal initially. Between opening up plants outside of Milwaukee, and increasing production without maintaining quality standards, the AMF period machines were some of the worst in Harley-Davidson's history. The eventual increase in production was made at the sacrifice of quality, and both riders and the company suffered.

The only addition to the 1968 lineup was the 125cc Rapido. Another Aermacchi-built Italian model, it featured a two-stroke engine with a four-speed transmission. Power was limited, and handling was considered minimal on the road.

1968 Model Year Lineup

Model	Engine Type	Displacement	Transmission	Special Feature(s)
Model 68M	Two-Stroke Single	65cc	Three-Speed	—
Model 68MS	Two-Stroke Single	65cc	Three-Speed	Sport Model
Model 68ML	Two-Stroke Single	125cc	Three-Speed	Rapido Model
Model 68SS	Overhead-Valve Single	250cc	Four-Speed	—
Model 68CH	Overhead-Valve Single	250cc	Four-Speed	High Compression
Model 68XLH	Overhead-Valve Twin	55 cid	Four-Speed	No Kick-Start Pedal
Model 68XLCH	Overhead-Valve Twin	55 cid	Four-Speed	—
Model 68FLB	Overhead-Valve Twin	74 cid	Four-Speed	Hand Shift
Model 68FLFB	Overhead-Valve Twin	74 cid	Four-Speed	Foot Shift
Model FLHB	Overhead-Valve Twin	74 cid	Four-Speed	High Comp./Hand Shift
Model 68FLHFB	Overhead-Valve Twin	74 cid	Four-Speed	High Comp./Foot Shift
Model 68GE	Side-Valve Twin	45 cid	Three-Speed w/Reverse	—

The M-65 and M-65S returned with no changes, and even fewer sales. The M's would remain on the roster for several more years, but had to be just about given away at the dealers.

The SS and CH Sprints also returned for another year with no modifications.

The Sportster department was not exactly bristling with changes, either, but a few items were revised. The kick-start pedal was removed from the XLH, and the smaller peanut tank of the XLCH could be ordered as an option. Both the XLH and XLCH had their forks improved with better damping and an additional inch of travel.

The FLBs claimed an oil pump with an aluminum body and a new instrument panel. Indicator lights were now rectangular and arranged in a single row. Clutch use was simplified by the application of wet plates and an improved set of springs. Sidecar bodies were now molded in fiberglass.

The GE models were untouched for 1968, and continued to sell at about the same pace as years before.

Production and Prices

Model	Production	Price
Model 68M	1,200	$235
Model 68MS	1,700	$265
Model 68ML	5,000	NA
Model 68SS	4,150	NA
Model 68CH	NA	NA
Model 68XLH	1,975	$1,650
Model 68XLCH	4,900	$1,600
Model 68FLB/FLFB	1,650	$1,735
Model FLHB/FLHFB	5,300	$1,800
Model 68GE	600	$1,930

1969

With The Motor Company now under the wing of its new parent AMF, it would take awhile for things to change. The '69 models were mostly duplicates of the 1968 lineup.

The slow-moving and even slower-selling M-65 and M-65S were still in force, but mostly sold at highly discounted prices. People wanted more than the tiny machine could deliver, or bought similar Japanese cycles.

The Rapido street model was joined by an off-road version, the MLS. The S, or scrambler version, quickly became more popular, and the street variant was removed from the catalog at the end of the 1969 model year.

The Sprints were boosted by 100cc to become the SS and ERS. The SS was meant for street use, while the ERS headed for the trails. The new level of power was welcomed, but sales remained slow for the Sprints.

The Sportsters both received a modified exhaust as the standard setup. The head pipes were joined by a balancing tube, and the dual mufflers were stacked. A new shape for the taillight lens was the only other variation seen for 1969.

The Electra Glides benefited from a few minor alterations for 1969, and shared some of them with the Servi-Car. On the FLB models, the front brake was relocated to the right side of the wheel, and an operating cam was installed as well. 1969 would mark the final year for the ribbed exhaust down tubes, along with the flat-sided cam cover. This would be the last year for generator-equipped models as well.

The wiring harness was improved on the FLB and GE models to include spade-tipped terminals for use with the hydraulic brake light switch. Both models also received the latest in taillight lenses.

The large, white saddlebags on the FLBs could be accessorized with a matching Tour-Pak and front fairing. The Tour-Pak provided an enormous amount of storage space, and the fairing helped keep the wind and rain off the rider and his passenger. All the components were molded in white fiberglass.

1969 Model Year Lineup

Model	Engine Type	Displacement	Transmission	Special Feature(s)
Model 69M	Two-Stroke Single	65cc	Three-Speed	—
Model 69MS	Two-Stroke Single	65cc	Three-Speed	Sport Model
Model 69ML	Two-Stroke Single	125cc	Three-Speed	Rapido Street Model
Model 69MLS	Two-Stroke Single	125cc	Three-Speed	Rapido Scrambler
Model 69SS	Overhead-Valve Single	350cc	Four-Speed	Sprint Street Model
Model 69ERS	Overhead-Valve Single	350cc	Four-Speed	Off-Road Sprint
Model 69XLH	Overhead-Valve Twin	55 cid	Four-Speed	—
Model 69XLCH	Overhead-Valve Twin	55 cid	Four-Speed	—
Model 69FLB	Overhead-Valve Twin	74 cid	Four-Speed	Hand Shift
Model 69FLFB	Overhead-Valve Twin	74 cid	Four-Speed	Foot Shift
Model 69FLHB	Overhead-Valve Twin	74 cid	Four-Speed	High Comp./Hand Shift
Model 69FLHFB	Overhead-Valve Twin	74 cid	Four-Speed	High Comp./Foot Shift
Model 69GE	Side-Valve Twin	45 cid	Three-Speed w/Reverse	—

Production and Prices

Model	Production	Price
Model 69M	950	NA
Model 69MS	1,750	NA
Model 69ML	1,000	NA
Model 69MLS	3,275	NA
Model 69SS	4,575	NA
Model 69ERS	250	NA
Model 69XLH	2,700	$1,765
Model 69XLCH	5,100	$1,698
Model 69FLB/FLFB	1,800	$1,885
Model 69FLHB/FLHFB	5,500	$1,900
Model 69GE	475	$2,065

The XLH received an improved ignition system in 1970, as did the FLB models.

1970

Harley-Davidson was still getting its sea legs under the big top that was AMF, and history would eventually show the effect of having a corporate "partner" that wasn't initially involved with motorcycles. At least the financial aspects looked better, and H-D toiled on with several substantial changes for the 1970 models.

The base M-65 was no longer a part of the game, but the M-65S trundled along with a minimum of sales. No changes were made to the small machine.

The staggered dual exhaust pipes on the 1970 XLH were complete with "bullet" tips.

XLH instrumentation was complete with tachometer and speedometer.

Another addition to the family was the lightweight Leggero, which was powered by a 65cc, two-stroke motor. The Leggero only weighed 122 lbs., and could, in theory, be carried almost anywhere. It was shifted with a three-speed gearbox.

With the absence of the Rapids street model, the Scrambler remained to take the reins. No alterations to it either.

There was another new small bike rolled out for 1970. The Baja 100 was named for the grueling off-road race, and was built for heavy riding on rough terrain. Powered by a 100cc motor, the Baja was full of high-performance tricks. With an 11.5:1 compression ratio, ported cylinders, and expansion chamber, the Baja squeezed out 12 hp—two more than the larger Rapido. Shifting was through with a five-speed gearbox that was available with either close or wide ratios. Though small in size, the Baja still achieved a high number of victories in races around the U.S.

1970 Model Year Lineup

Model	Engine Type	Displacement	Transmission	Special Feature(s)
Model 70MS	Two-Stroke Single	65cc	Three-Speed	Sport Model
Model 70MSR	Two-Stroke Single	100cc	Five-Speed	High-Performance/Off-Road
Model 70MLS	Two-Stroke Single	125cc	Three-Speed	Off-Road Model
Model 70SS	Overhead-Valve Single	350cc	Four-Speed	Street Model
Model 70ERS	Overhead-Valve Single	350cc	Four-Speed	Off-Road Model
Model 70XLH	Overhead-Valve Twin	55 cid	Four-Speed	Optional Boat Tail Fender
Model 70XLCH	Overhead-Valve Twin	55 cid	Four-Speed	—
Model 70FLB	Overhead-Valve Twin	74 cid	Four-Speed	Hand Shift
Model 70FLBF	Overhead-Valve Twin	74 cid	Four-Speed	Foot Shift
Model 70FLHB	Overhead-Valve Twin	74 cid	Four-Speed	High-Comp./Hand Shift
Model 70FLHFB	Overhead-Valve Twin	74 cid	Four-Speed	High-Comp./Foot Shift
Model 70GE	Side-Valve Twin	45 cid	Three-Speed w/Reverse	—

The SS and ERS Sprints continued their lives with Harley-Davidson, but were not altered.

As was the case with most of the bikes in H-D's 1970 brochures, the XLH and XLCH received a new ignition, complete with a coil and points. The previous generator was now gone from the scene. A new option was available for the XLH as well. An extended "boat tail" fender and seat module could be ordered to add an entirely new look to the Sportster. Its popularity was not great, but it did make for an interesting piece of rolling art.

The FLB models lost their generators in 1970, and were now sparked by an alternator. The points and coil route proved to be an important move to correct earlier ignition woes. This change in the ignition system required an entirely new set of crankcases. In addition to the new cases, a revised timing cover was implemented. Gone was the flat-sided unit of 1969, and in came the conical housing. Carburetors were Tillotson, and were well received, but would only be used through 1971. The oil tank was also reconfigured, and was complete with its own level-checking dipstick. The ribbed exhaust covers were replaced by a pair of smooth, chrome exhaust pipes.

Those purchasing the fiberglass saddlebags found a heavier-duty hinge, a locking hook, and a key-operated lock.

Production and Prices

Model	Production	Prices
Model 70MS	2,080	NA
Model 70MSR	1,427	NA
Model 70MLS	4,059	NA
Model 70SS	4,513	NA
Model 70ERS	102	NA
Model 70XLH	3,033	NA
Model 70XLCH	5,527	NA
Model 70FLB/FLFB	1,706	NA
Model 70FLHB/FLHFB	5,909	NA
Model 70GE	494	NA

The FX was an all-new model for 1971, and filled the gap between the FL and XLH.

1971

The merger with AMF was still causing some dissention, but new models were being rolled out for 1971 despite the tension at the management level.

For several years there was a gap in the lineup between the smaller Sportsters and the much larger FLs. To fill this gap, and new model, the FX, debuted for 1971. Built on the frame of an FL, with the forks from the XL, the FX did fulfill many riders' needs.

The "boat tail" rear fender assembly added some flair, but was not well received.

The Super Glide weighed in at 70 lbs. less than the big FL, and handling was far more nimble around town. To combat some ills found on earlier XL forks, the FX units had seals that prevented leakage. While more nimble than the big FLs, the less substantial front end did lead to some problems. Power for the FX still came from the 74-cubic inch Shovelhead, so power output was the same.

Power was provided by the 74-cubic inch Shovelhead motor of the 1971 FLP.

The shift lever faced backwards on the 1971 FX.

The 3 1/2-gallon tanks of the FX were adorned with an instrument panel and the AMF #1.

Four-speed transmissions were also the same as used on the FL models, but the shift lever was mounted in a reverse fashion. Foot pegs were used in place of the larger footboards found on the FL.

Drum brakes were used at both ends of the FX, at least for now. Riding on a 16-inch rear wheel, and a 19-inch front wheel, the Super Glides had a whole new stance. The FX was also kick-start-only model, and the lack of electrics may have helped to save a few pounds.

1971 Model year Lineup

Model	Engine Type	Displacement	Transmission	Special Feature(s)
Model 71MS	Two-Stroke Single	65cc	Three-Speed	—
Model 71MSR	Two-Stroke Single	100cc	Five-Speed	Baja Model
Model 71MLS	Two-Stroke Single	125cc	Three-Speed	Rapido Model
Model 71SS	Overhead-Valve Single	350cc	Four-Speed	Street Sprint
Model 71SX	Overhead-Valve Single	350cc	Four-Speed	On-/Off-Road Sprint
Model 71ERS	Overhead-Valve Single	350cc	Four-Speed	Off-Road Only Sprint
Model 71XLH	Overhead-Valve Twin	55 cid	Four-Speed	Wet Clutch
Model 71XLCH	Overhead-Valve Twin	55 cid	Four-Speed	—
Model 71FX	Overhead-Valve Twin	74 cid	Four-Speed	Boat Tail Rear Fender
Model 71FLP	Overhead-Valve Twin	74 cid	Four-Speed	Super-Sport/ Hand Shift
Model 71FLPF	Overhead-Valve Twin	74 cid	Four-Speed	Super-Sport/Foot Shift
Model 71FLH	Overhead-Valve Twin	74 cid	Four-Speed	High Comp./Hand Shift
Model 71FLHF	Overhead-Valve Twin	74 cid	Four-Speed	High Comp./Foot Shift
Model 71GE	Side-Valve Twin	45 cid	Three-Speed w/Reverse	—

The "boat tail" rear fender was applied to the FX as well, but remained unpopular. The fuel tanks held 3 1/2 gallons, and featured the tank-mounted instrument panel found on the FLs.

The FL line now breathed in through Bendix carburetors, but H-D would soon replace them in its search for the perfect mix.

Sportsters had their points and condenser moved to a new location. The new home behind a removeable plate on the timing cover made a world of difference when service was required. A wet clutch with a single spring replaced the dry version used previously.

The Sprint collection now included an on-/off-road version called the SX-350. Wearing lights, high fenders and exhaust, the SX could take on street or trail.

In an effort to upgrade assembly, the decision was made to relocate the final assembly plant to a facility in York, Pennsylvania. Engines and transmissions were built in the Capital Drive plant in Wisconsin. All the 1971 models wore a new nameplate that touted both Harley-Davidson and AMF branding.

Production and Prices

Model	Production	Price
Model 71MS	3,100	NA
Model 71MSR	1,200	NA
Model 71MLS	5,200	NA
Model 71SS	1,500	NA
Model 71SX	3,920	NA
Model 71ERS	50	NA
Model 71XLH	3,950	NA
Model 71XLCH	6,825	NA
Model 71FX	4,700	NA
Model 71FLP/FLPF	1,200	NA
Model FLH/FLHF	5,475	NA
Model 71GE	500	NA

The Shortster was the newest addition to the Harley family in 1972, and appealed to the younger riders eager to get their two-wheeled activities started.

1972

The 1972 model year would bring a new machine, as well as numerous modifications, to the existing catalog.

The newest model was the 65cc Shortster. Powered by another variation of an Aermacchi single-cylinder two-stroke, the Shortster had a three-speed transmission and was intended to introduce younger riders to the world of motorcycles.

While the Shortster was the new small model, the existing XLH and XLCH received a bump in displacement to 61 cubic inches, or 1000 cc's. The increase in displacement improved horsepower and performance while not adversely affecting reliability or mileage.

The FX, introduced for 1971 was fitted with a more conventional rear fender in place of the fiberglass boat tail. While not as dramatic looking as the previous variation, it was more widely accepted by the buying public. The altered rear fender also resulted in the saddle taking a new shape that consisted of two-place seating versus the flat, single surface from 1971.

1972 Model Year Lineup

Model	Engine Type	Displacement	Transmission	Special Feature(s)
Model 72MC	Two-Stroke Single	65cc	Three-Speed	Shortster Model
Model 72MS	Two-Stroke Single	65cc	Three-Speed	Sport Model
Model 72MSR	Two-Stroke Single	100cc	Five-Speed	Baja 100
Model 72MLS	Two-Stroke Single	125cc	Three-Speed	Rapido
Model 72SS	Overhead-Valve Single	350cc	Four-Speed	Street Sprint
Model 72SX	Overhead-Valve Single	350cc	Four-Speed	On-/Off-Road Sprint
Model 72ERS	Overhead-Valve Single	350cc	Four-Speed	Off-Road-Only Sprint
Model 72XLH	Overhead-Valve Twin	61 cid	Four-Speed	Bigger Motor For '72
Model 72XLCH	Overhead-Valve Twin	61 cid	Four-Speed	Bigger Motor For '72
Model 72FX	Overhead-Valve Twin	74 cid	Four-Speed	New Rear Fender
Model 72FLP	Overhead-Valve Twin	74 cid	Four-Speed	Hand Shift
Model 72FLPF	Overhead-Valve Twin	74 cid	Four-Speed	Foot Shift
Model 72FLH	Overhead-Valve Twin	74 cid	Four-Speed	High-Comp./Hand Shift
Model 72FLHF	Overhead-Valve Twin	74 cid	Four-Speed	High-Comp./Foot Shift
Model 72GE	Side-Valve Twin	45 cid	Three-Speed w/Reverse	—

Perhaps the biggest news for the '72 models was the addition of a disc brake on the front wheel of the FL models. Slowing down the 700-plus-lbs. machines had been a chore with only two drum brakes, and the single, 10-inch disc reduced stopping distances dramatically. Efforts to incorporate lighter materials into the heavyweight FL led to plastic switch housings on the handlebars. These housings also incorporated self-canceling turn signals for the first time.

Total production was up by nearly 20,000 units for 1972. While the increased production helped to satisfy eager buyers, the quality was dropping at an alarming pace. Even longtime dealers were worried. Honda's 750-four machine was making high-speed inroads on previous Harley devotees, and a change would need to be made quickly to staunch the flow of lost sales to the Asian-built cycles.

Production and Prices

Model	Production	Price
Model 72MC	8,000	NA
Model 72MS	3,708	NA
Model 72MSR	1,200	NA
Model 72MLS	6,000	NA
Model 72SS	3,775	NA
Model 72SX	2,525	NA
Model 72ERS	50	NA
Model 72XLH	7,500	NA
Model 72XLCH	10,450	NA
Model 72FX	6,500	NA
Model 72FLP/FLPF	1,600	NA
Model 72FLH/FLHF	8,100	NA
Model 72GE	400	NA

Ready to hit the open road, this 1972 FL had every box on the options sheet checked before it was built.

The big 1973 FL was now stopped with two disc brakes, and was only shifted by foot.

1973

There was a flurry of activity for the latest models, most of which were considered to be improvements. A few more new alpha-numeric designations showed up on the '73 roster as well.

The Shortster reappeared as the X-90 for 1973 and, as the name implies, it was fitted with a larger motor than the 65cc engine used in the '72s.

The Rapido was gone in name only, and was reincarnated as the TX-125. It was mostly unchanged except for the new moniker. The TX did include the latest in oil injection, eliminating the need to pre-mix your fuel and oil. A smaller version was also introduced, and its title was the Z-90.

The Baja 100 was back for what would prove to be its final year of sale.

The Sprint models were down to two, the SS-350 and the SX-350. Both now started with the touch of a button, but it was too little, too late as the Sprint would also disappear from the catalog at the end of the following model year.

The Sportsters were now assembled using front forks from a Japanese manufacturer, Kayaba. The new forks were also treated to a single disc brake for the first time. Plastic control housings on the handlebars added the self-canceling turn signals found on the FLs of 1972.

The 1973 FX rode with the front disc brake and a new fuel tank. The latest tank was actually transplanted from the old Sprint model, but added a bit of grace to the mid-level model. The new tank did, however, force the speedometer to be relocated to the handlebars from the previous tank-mounted instrument panel. Plastic switch housings with self-canceling signals were also used on the FX. A revised foot-brake lever and master cylinder location made their way onto the FX as well.

The Big Twin FL models received a second disc brake, this one on the rear wheel. Fitted with a pair of steel discs, the machine was easier to halt. The kick-start pedal and its related hardware were also removed for the first time. Fans of shifting by hand would be forced into foot shifting with the elimination of the

Fitted with the accessory Buddy seat and hard bags, the FL made a terrific long-haul machine.

hand-shift models. The conical gear cover was still in place, but featured a new profile, as did the taillight lens.

The three-wheeled Servi-Car would only remain in the lineup until the end of the 1973 model year. Introduced for the 1932 model year, it had proven to be a machine that filled the needs of a small percentage of the market, but with sales falling below 500 units annually, it was time to say good-bye.

The GE did receive disc brakes on the rear wheels late in the model year.

The decision to move final assembly to York, Pennsylvania had been made in 1971, and 1973 would be the first year that production was completed at the East Coast facility.

1973 Model Year Lineup

Model	Engine Type	Displacement	Transmission	Special Feature(s)
Model 73X	Two-Stroke Single	90cc	Three-Speed	Replaced The Shortster
Model 73Z	Two-Stroke Single	90cc	Three-Speed	Smaller Version Of The TX-125
Model 73MSR	Two-Stroke Single	100cc	Five-Speed	Final Year Of Sale
Model 73TX	Two-Stroke Single	125cc	Five-Speed	Replaced The Rapido
Model 73SS	Overhead-Valve Single	350cc	Four-Speed	Electric Start
Model 73SX	Overhead-Valve Single	350cc	Four-Speed	Electric Start
Model 73XLH	Overhead-Valve Twin	61 cid	Four-Speed	Front Disc Brake
Model 73XLCH	Overhead-Valve Twin	61 cid	Four-Speed	Front Disc Brake
Model 73FX	Overhead-Valve Twin	74 cid	Four-Speed	Front Disk Brake
Model 73FL	Overhead-Valve Twin	74 cid	Four-Speed	Rear Disc Brake
Model 73FLH	Overhead-Valve Twin	74 cid	Four-Speed	High Comp./Rear Disc
Model 73GE	Side-Valve Twin	45 cid	Three-Speed	Last Year

Production and Prices

Model	Production	Price
Model 73X	8,250	NA
Model 73Z	8,250	NA
Model 73MSR	986	NA
Model 73TX	9,225	NA
Model 73SS	4,137	NA
Model 73SX	2,431	NA
Model 73XLH	9,875	NA
Model 73XLCH	10,825	NA
Model 73FX	7,625	NA
Model 73FL	1,025	NA
Model 73FLH	7,750	NA
Model 73GE	425	NA

1974

After the raft of changes for 1973 models, the 1974s were mostly carryovers. A few existing models would soon be gone from the family, but a few new faces were added.

Both the X-90 and Z-90 returned for another year, and neither received any alterations. The Baja 100, previously known as the MSR, was now the SR, but would fade from the veldt after the 1974 model year.

The newly introduced TX-125 was renamed the SX-125, and was joined by a larger SX-175 playmate.

Even with electric starters installed, the SS-350 and SX-350 sold poorly, and they would also be removed from the mix after the 1974 model year.

1974 Model Year Lineup

Model	Engine Type	Displacement	Transmission	Special Feature(s)
Model 74X	Two-Stroke Single	90cc	Three-Speed	—
Model 74Z	Two-Stroke Single	90cc	Three-Speed	—
Model 74SR	Two-Stroke Single	100cc	Five-Speed	Final Year Of Sale
Model 74SX	Two-Stroke Single	125cc	Five-Speed	Was TX-125
Model 74SX	Two-Stroke Single	175cc	Five-Speed	New Model For 1974
Model 74SS	Overhead-Valve Single	350cc	Four-Speed	Final Year Of Sale
Model 74SX	Overhead-Valve Single	350cc	Four-Speed	Final Year Of Sale
Model 74XLH	Overhead-Valve Twin	61 cid	Four-Speed	Throttle Return Spring
Model 74XLCH	Overhead-Valve Twin	61 cid	Four-Speed	Throttle Return Spring
Model 74FX	Overhead-Valve Twin	74 cid	Four-Speed	—
Model 74FXE	Overhead-Valve Twin	74 cid	Four-Speed	Electric Start FX
Model 74FLH	Overhead-Valve Twin	74 cid	Four-Speed	—
Model 74FLHF	Overhead-Valve Twin	74 cid	Four-Speed	—
Model 74FLP	Overhead-Valve Twin	74 cid	Four-Speed	Police Model

In response to a new government mandate, the XLH and XLCH throttles now functioned with a return spring. This prevented the rider from removing both hands from the bars without a sudden slowdown of his machine.

The FX Super Glide was back, and it also featured the spring-loaded throttle. The shift lever was repositioned to reach forward instead of backwards, as in previous years. The first-gear ratio was increased, and improvements were made for second gear as well.

Another new entry was the FXE. It was basically an FX with an electric starter. Now you could choose between the two options. In its first year, the FXE outsold the FX by a 2-to-1 margin, and that ratio would grow even larger the following year. It was obvious that people liked the convenience of electric starting. The FXE's starter system was made up of the starter from the FLH with a battery from the XLH. Changes made to the FX were carried over to the FX.

The FLH variants now drew breath through a Keihin carburetor. The saddle was reconfigured for more comfort, and the Big Twins now came complete with alarm systems. The FLHF was again available, as was an FL Police model. The FLP featured lower compression to handle the long hours of idling and running during an 8-hour shift.

Production

Model	Production
Model 74X	7,019
Model 74Z	7,168
Model 74SR	1,396
Model 74SX-125	4,000
Model 74SX-175	3,612
Model 74SS	2,500
Model 74SX-350	2,085
Model 74XLH	13,295
Model 74XLCH	10,535
Model 74FX	3,034
Model 74FXE	6,199
Model 74FLH	5,166
Model 74FLHF	1,310
Model 74FLP	791

1975

As far as headlines for the new year, it was a slow day in the Harley-Davidson news room. The new catalog was largely a carryover from the previous year, with only a few modifications. The entire lineup was touted as "The Great American Freedom Machines" for 1975.

The 90cc "mini-bikes," the X and Z, returned with no alterations except colors. This would, however, be their last year of production.

The slightly larger SX-125 of '74 became the SXT-125. Its bigger sibling, the SX-175, retained the same moniker and was also unchanged. Two new variations were found in the SS-250 and SX-250. Basically the same machine as the smaller versions with a slightly bigger motor, the SS was a street-going variant of the on-/off-road SX gang. All four versions featured five-speed transmissions and Dell 'Orto carburetors. The 250cc versions were included to soften the blow of losing the Sprints for 1975.

1975 Model Year Lineup

Model	Engine Type	Displacement	Transmission	Special Feature(s)
Model 75X	Two-Stroke Single	90cc	Three-Speed	Final Year Of Sale
Model 75Z	Two-Stroke Single	90cc	Three-Speed	Final Year Of Sale
Model 75SXT	Two-Stroke Single	125cc	Five-Speed	Was The SX In 1974
Model 75SX	Two-Stroke Single	175cc	Five-Speed	On/Off Road Model
Model 75SX	Two-Stroke Single	250cc	Five-Speed	On/Off Road Model
Model 75SS	Two-Stroke Single	250cc	Five-Speed	Street Model
Model 75XLH	Overhead-Valve Twin	61 cid	Four-Speed	Left-Side Shift Pedal
Model 75XLCH	Overhead-Valve Twin	61 cid	Four-Speed	Left-Side Shift Pedal
Model 75FX	Overhead-Valve Twin	74 cid	Four-Speed	Kick-Start Model
Model 75FXE	Overhead-Valve Twin	74 cid	Four-Speed	Electric Start Model
Model 75FLH	Overhead-Valve Twin	74 cid	Four-Speed	—
Model 75FLHF	Overhead-Valve Twin	74 cid	Four-Speed	—
Model 75FLP	Overhead-Valve Twin	74 Cid	Four-Speed	Police Model

In response to more government mandates, the XLH and XLCH now had their shift levers moved to the left side of the frame, with the brake pedal on the right. This was to ensure a common layout on all U.S.-bound cycles.

The FX and FXE both stopped more confidently with the addition of rear disc brakes. Just like the bigger FL models, the middle model now featured hydraulic disc braking at both ends. The new rotor stopped the FXs better and kept more competitive with the Japanese-built machines.

Like most of the rest of the models in the catalog, the FL models were now fitted with dual return springs on the throttle.

Production

Model	Production
Model 75X	1,586
Model 75Z	2,562
Model 75SXT	2,500
Model 75SX-175	8,500
Model 75SS-250	3,000
Model 75SX-250	11,000
Model 75XLH	13,515
Model 75XLCH	5,895
Model 75FX	3,060
Model 75FXE	9,350
Model 75FLH	1,200
Model 75FLHF	1,535
Model 75FLP	900

1976

With the exception of a few SS models being added to the mix, and a line of "Liberty Edition" models, 1976 was strictly a carryover year. The Liberty Edition machines were finished in metallic black paint, and were trimmed with red, white and blue badges to mark the country's 200th birthday. The top of the fuel tanks of the Super Glides were also adorned with a graphic panel, including the spread-winged eagle, and the bar-and-shield logo.

1976 Model Year Lineup

Model	Engine Type	Displacement	Transmission	Special Feature(s)
Model 76SS	Two-Stroke Single	125cc	Five-Speed	Street Model
Model 76SXT	Two-Stroke Single	125cc	Five-Speed	On/Off Road Model
Model 76SS	Two-Stroke Single	175cc	Five-Speed	Street Model
Model 76SX	Two-Stroke Single	175cc	Five-Speed	On/off Road Model
Model 76SS	Two-Stroke Single	250cc	Five-Speed	Street Model
Model 76SX	Two-Stroke Single	250cc	Five-Speed	On/Off Road Model
Model 76XLH	Overhead-Valve Twin	61 cid	Four-Speed	—
Model 76XLCH	Overhead-Valve Twin	61 cid	Four-Speed	—
Model 76FX	Overhead-Valve Twin	74 cid	Four-Speed	—
Model 76FXE	Overhead-Valve Twin	74 cid	Four-Speed	—
Model 76FLH	Overhead-Valve Twin 74 cid	74 cid	Four-Speed	—

With the X-90 and Z-90 removed from the balance, the SXT-125 was now the smallest model sold by Harley-Davidson. All three versions of the two-stroke singles were now available in SX and SS trim. The SX variations were for on- and off-road applications, while the SS models were street trim only.

Sportsters were available in the new Liberty Edition, but no other modifications were found on the '76 models.

Super Glides were also unaltered for the new year, but could be purchased in the Liberty Edition livery.

Liberty Edition Electra Glides had the carryover hardware. The FLHF and FLP models were eliminated.

Production

Model	Production
Model 76SS-125	1,560
Model 76SXT-125	6,056
Model 76SS-175	1,461
Model 76SX-175	NA
Model 76SS-250	1,416
Model 76SX-250	3,125
Model 76XLH	12,844
Model 76XLCH	5,238
Model 76FX	3,857
Model 76FXE	13,838
Model 76FLH	11,891

The 1977 XLCR was an all-new bike for Harley, but it was not a terrific seller.

1977

Following two years of little or no change, 1977 would turn out to be a blockbuster of new models and variations of existing machines.

Sales of the single-cylinder models were lagging badly, and dealer incentives were used to move the remaining units. The SX-175 was not offered for 1977, and it would be the final year for all the two-stroke models except the SS-250, which would last through the '78 model year. No alterations were listed for the Italian models.

The Sportster family was to be joined by two new iterations. The XLT was a touring model of the XLH, and the XLCR was a new direction for Harley-Davidson. The XLT featured a more heavily padded saddle, larger fuel tanks borrowed from the FX, and molded saddlebags from the FLH. The higher handlebars rode behind a clear windshield, and provided a comfortable riding environment for those seeking longer days on the road.

The XLCR was a radical departure from the rest of Harley's laid-back "cruisers." The XLCR wore a fuel tank and tail section with angular shapes never before seen on a Big Twin. The triangular side covers accented the new look. The small bikini-style fairing was another first for Harley, and added another measure of "performance" to the mix. All the body parts were coated in glossy black paint for a more ominous appearance.

The exhaust pipes were "Siamesed" and finished in flat black paint. The 61-cubic inch motor was also dipped in flat black paint to complete the package. The wheels were cast versus spoked, and were mounted with a trio of 10-inch disc brakes. White-letter tires finished off the appearance package.

The XLCR was the first-ever factory custom, but was not well received. Most Harley buyers preferred the more relaxed riding posture offered by the other models in the catalog. In contrast to

Nestled behind the bikini fairing were the instruments and indicator lights on the 1977 XLCR.

A pair of 10-inch disc brakes on the front wheel added real stopping power to the XLCR.

the initially poor sales and short lifespan, the XLCR has grown to be coveted by collectors.

The XLH and XLCH were assembled with new cases that were more conducive to the recently introduced left-side shift. An alteration to the frame allowed the oil pump to be removed without taking the motor out of the frame.

The FX lineage was expanded with the addition of the FXS "Low Rider." Based on the kick-start FX model, the FXS rode on shortened rear suspension that placed the saddle a scant 27 inches from the ground. The seat height of the Sportster was 31 1/2 inches. The same front Showa forks and cast wheels used on the new XLCR were also in place on the FXS. The drag-style, flat handlebars reached back to the rider with curved risers. The two-place saddle was deeply sculpted for comfort and lower ride height. Finished in a metallic gray paint with red tank graphics, the FXS appealed to many riders for many reasons. The forward controls and highway pegs made the FXS a terrific choice for long days in the saddle, as well as for quick jaunts around town.

The FX and FXE now steered with Showa front forks as well. A cast rear wheel could be ordered as an option on both models.

The FLHS was a one-year-only model that featured an extra measure of comfort delivered by its sprung seat. The FLHS was trimmed with brown metallic paint and a tan saddle. The FLH and FLHS were both recipients of revised transmissions that included caged bearings for the main drive gear and countershaft. The scavenger/breather valve was also revised on the big FLH and FLHS models.

1977 Model Year Lineup

Model	Engine Type	Displacement	Transmission	Special Feature(s)
Model 77SS	Two-Stroke Single	125cc	Five-Speed	Final Year Of Sale
Model 77SXT	Two-Stroke Single	125cc	Five-Speed	Final Year Of Sale
Model 77SS	Two-Stroke Single	175cc	Five-Speed	Final Year Of Sale
Model 77SS	Two-Stroke Single	250cc	Five-Speed	—
Model 77SX	Two-Stroke Single	250cc	Five-Speed	Final Year Of Sale
Model 77XLH	Overhead-Valve Twin	61 cid	Four-Speed	—
Model 77XLT	Overhead-Valve Twin	61 cid	Four-Speed	Touring Model
Model 77XLCH	Overhead-Valve Twin	61 cid	Four-Speed	—
Model 77XLCR	Overhead-Valve Twin	61 cid	Four-Speed	Café Racer Model
Model 77FX	Overhead-Valve Twin	74 cid	Four-Speed	—
Model 77FXE	Overhead-Valve Twin	74 cid	Four-Speed	—
Model 77FXS	Overhead-Valve Twin	74 cid	Four-Speed	Low Rider
Model 77FLH	Overhead-Valve Twin	74 cid	Four-Speed	—
Model 77FLHS	Overhead-Valve Twin	74 cid	Four-Speed	Special Paint And Seat

Production

Model	Production
Model 77SS-125	488
Model 77SXT-125	48
Model 77SS-175	110
Model 77SS-250	1,416
Model 77SX-250	558
Model 77XLH	12,742
Model 77XLT	1,099
Model 77XLCH	4,074
Model 77XLCR	1,923
Model 77FX	2,049
Model 77FXE	9,400
Model 77FXS	3,742
Model 77FLH	8,691
Model 77FLHS	535

The 75th Anniversary Edition of the XL was loaded with special features to celebrate Harley-Davidson's birthday in 1978.

1978

To help celebrate its 75th year of production, Harley-Davidson added a few new twists to the lineup, a well as offering a few models to commemorate the occasion.

The only single-cylinder model remaining was the SS-250, and it, too, would be gone at the end of the 1978 production run. People wanting small, two-stroke machines were turning to the Japanese dealers, so H-D decided to concentrate on this segment of the market.

The XL models were now fired by electronic ignitions, and exhaled through the same Siamese exhaust pipes used on the XLCR. All XL models were also based on the same frame

The dual disc brakes were mounted to a special gold-colored wheel on the anniversary model.

design as the previous XLCR. The oil tanks and batteries for all four variations were mounted inboard on the frame in 1978. Cast wheels like those found on the XLCR could be ordered with any of the Sportsters, and the XLCH could have a two-place saddle. Neither the XLT or XLCR gained in sales, and both were dropped for the following model year.

The XLH Anniversary model wore gleaming black paint with gold pinstripes, gold-tone cast wheels, and a seat covered in leather, instead of vinyl.

The FX, FXE, and FXS changed little for 1978. All three were also sparked via an electronic ignition. The FXS could be delivered in silver paint with black side panels as an option. All three also changed in the middle of the year to include valve guides of cast iron, harder valve stems, and revisions to the intake manifold. Flat O-rings were also implemented on the manifolds.

The FLHs also received electronic ignitions for the new year, and there was another significant change to the Shovelhead motor. Up until now, the 74-cid motor was the only choice a buyer had when purchasing his new FLH. To offset changes dictated by the government, a bigger 80-cid motor was available. While making the same power as the 74, it ran quieter and cleaner—something the government was demanding.

The new 80-cubic-inch models featured an enormous air cleaner cover that housed the improved airbox beneath. The cylinders of the 80-cid models also had only nine cooling fins, compared to the 10 found on the 74s. The new FLH-80 was sold in an exclusive black-cherry paint with cast wheels.

The FLH was also available in 75th Anniversary trim, complete with the black and gold finish and leather saddle. The clutch cover was emblazoned with a golden eagle as well.

1978 model Year Lineup

Model	Engine Type	Displacement	Transmission	Special Feature(s)
Model 78SS	Two-Stroke Single	250cc	Five-Speed	Final Year Of Sale
Model 78XLH	Overhead-Valve Twin	61 cid	Four-Speed	—
Model 78XLH Anniv.	Overhead-Valve Twin	61 cid	Four-Speed	75th Anniversary Trim
Model 78XLT	Overhead-Valve Twin	61 cid	Four-Speed	Final Year Of Sale
Model 78XLCH	Overhead-Valve Twin	61 cid	Four-Speed	—
Model 78XLCR	Overhead-Valve Twin	61 cid	Four-Speed	Final Year Of Sale
Model 78FX	Overhead-Valve Twin	74 cid	Four-Speed	—
Model 78FXE	Overhead-Valve Twin	74 cid	Four-Speed	—
Model 78FXS	Overhead-Valve Twin	74 cid	Four-Speed	—
Model 78FLH	Overhead-Valve Twin	74 cid	Four-Speed	—
Model 78FLH Anniv.	Overhead-Valve Twin	74 cid	Four-Speed	75th Anniversary Trim
Model 78FLH-80	Overhead-Valve Twin	80 cid	Four-Speed	—

Production

Model	Production
Model 78SS	479
Model 78XLH	11,271
Model 78XLH Anniversary	2,323
Model 78XLT	6
Model 78XLCH	2,758
Model 78XLCR	1,201
Model 78FX	1,774
Model 78FXE	8,314
Model 78FXS	9,787
Model 78FLH	4,761
Model 78FLH Anniversary	2,120
Model 78FLH-80	2,525

The saddle of the 1978 Anniversary model was covered in real leather.

The FXS was back for another year in 1978, and was turning out to be a favorite with buyers.

The 1978 black paint was accented by gold stripes and graphics.

1979

The 1979 offerings from Harley-Davidson would vary slightly from the previous year, and a few new faces could be seen in the family catalog photos.

With all of the Italian lightweights removed from the game, the Sportster was now the smallest cycle built by Harley. The XLH and XLCH had a kick-starter only as an option. A new braking system and master cylinder resided where the kick-start mechanism had been. This would also be the final year of production for the XLCH. Thanks to the popularity of the FXS Low Rider, the XLS was introduced for 1979. Later to become the Roadster, the XLS was an XLH fitted with extended front forks, flat drag bars on risers, and a "sissy bar" out back. A leather storage pouch, two-tone paint, and highway pegs completed the package.

1979 Model Year Lineup

Model	Engine Type	Displacement	Transmission	Special Feature(s)
Model 79XLH	Overhead-Valve Twin	61 cid	Four-Speed	—
Model 79XLS	Overhead-Valve Twin	61 cid	Four-Speed	Roadster Model
Model 79XLCH	Overhead-Valve Twin	61 cid	Four-Speed	Final Year Of Sale
Model 79FXE	Overhead-Valve Twin	74 cid	Four-Speed	—
Model 79FXS-74	Overhead-Valve Twin	74 cid	Four-Speed	—
Model 79FXS-80	Overhead-Valve Twin	80 cid	Four-Speed	—
Model 79FXEF-80	Overhead-Valve Twin	74 cid	Four-Speed	Fat Bob Model
Model 79FXEF-74	Overhead-Valve Twin	80 cid	Four-Speed	Fat Bob Model
Model 79FLH-74	Overhead-Valve Twin	74 cid	Four-Speed	—
Model 79FLH-80	Overhead-Valve Twin	80 cid	Four-Speed	—
Model 79FLHC	Overhead-Valve Twin	80 cid	Four-Speed	Limited Edition Model
Model 79FLHCE	Overhead-Valve Twin	80 cid	Four-Speed	Sidecar Model
Model 79FLHP-74	Overhead-Valve Twin	74 cid	Four-Speed	Police Model
Model 79FLHP-80	Overhead-Valve Twin	80 cid	Four-Speed	Police Model

The FX group was also upgraded, and a few new names were added to the list. All the FX-based models received the electronic ignition system for 1979, and the FXS continued to be a best seller. Another first for 1979 was the availability of the 80-cubic-inch motor in the FX line late in the model year.

To further strengthen the FX series, the Fat Bob version was also introduced. The Fat Bob models came with high handlebars and wire wheels in place of the cast ones used on the FX, FXE, and FXS. The Fat Bobs could be ordered in either 74- or 80-cid variations.

The 80-cid motor was once again offered as an option in the FLH models, and a Limited Edition version was another choice. Finished in tan and crème paint, the Limited Edition came complete with cast wheels, frame-mounted fairing, saddle bags, rear-mounted storage box, and chrome case guards. The catalog would later offer an official sidecar model to complete the lineup. The CLE was equipped with lower gearing and greater angle on the steering head. This allowed for better handling of the three-wheeled rig.

Production

Model	Production
Model 79XLH	6,525
Model 79XLS	5,123
Model 79XLCH	141
Model 79FXE	3,117
Model 79FXS-74	3,827
Model 79FXS-80	9,433
Model 79FXEF-74	4,678
Model 79FXEF-80	5,264
Model 79FLH-74	2,612
Model 79FLH-80	3,429
Model 79FLHC	4,368
Model 79FLHCE	353
Model 79FLHP-74	596
Model 79FLHP-80	84

The FXWG was an all-new model for 1980 and captured the essence of "custom" in a factory-built motorcycle.

1980

The new decade would bring a host of changes to the Harley-Davidson production lines in a time when falling sales were the trend. The economy was heading into a recession, and AMF/Harley had decided to concentrate on its biggest, most-expensive models. Competition from the Japanese manufacturers grew stronger with every passing month, and big changes would be needed soon to save AMF/H-D from extinction.

Along with minor alterations to the returning models, three new additions were made.

There were only two Sportsters left in the catalog, the XLH and XLS. The XLH was now known as the "Hugger" due to its lower seat height, while the XLS was named the "Roadster." Both names were selected after the company held a contest to find the best monikers.

The FX line featured a few of the previous entrants, as well as two new faces. The three returning models were the Super Glide, Low Rider, and the Fat Bob. Only the FXS Low Rider was offered in both 74- and 80-cubic inch varieties. The Super Glide and Fat Bob were now 80-cid-only models. New to the entire FX lineup was an improved electronic ignition system. The Low Riders also received two-into-one exhaust.

The FXB Sturgis was the first new model, and featured two belt drives—one for the primary and one for the final. This was a first for a Harley, but would by no means be the last. Based largely on the FXS Low Rider, the FXB was easy to distinguish. The blacked-out theme with red accents caused the FXB to stand out in a crowd. The forks were extended by 2 inches for a more rakish appearance, and drag bars steered the machine. Forward-mounted highway pegs completed the new look.

To accommodate the new final belt drive, the rear swing arm was widened and a rubber block compensator sprocket helped to absorb shock and vibration.

The second new member of the FX family was the FXWG. The Wide Glide's appearance was achieved by spreading the fork's downtubes further apart and extending the fork by 2 inches. Rolling on the wider front axle was a 21-inch-diameter spoked front wheel. The 5-gallon fuel tank was split in two, and joined by a center console. Painted with red flames on a black base, the FXWG had no equals in the "factory custom" race.

Powered by the 80-cubic inch Shovelhead motor, the FXWG exhaled through a pair of truncated exhaust pipes. The curved buckhorn bars were mounted on risers, which brought them within comfortable reach of the rider. Forward-mounted controls added the final touch of "custom" to the new model.

The FLH models received the same improved electronic ignition as the FXs. A new addition to the FL group was also made for the 1980 model year.

The FLT was far more than an upgraded FLH, and rode on a new frame that was complete with a new system of engine isolation. The engine and transmission cases were a solid unit on the FLT, and attached to the new frame using synthetic, compressible mounts. These new mounts helped to isolate the rider from the usual level of vibration, and were a welcome relief. The new frame was more rigid than previous efforts, and extended beyond the steering head to accommodate the hard mounting of the new fairing. Enclosed in the fairing were dual headlights behind a clear dome. Larger saddlebags and the rear-mounted storage box were all part of the standard package.

The widely spaced forks and 21-inch front wheel lent an entirely new look to the FXWG.

The dual tanks held a total of 5 gallons of fuel, and were topped off by the center-mounted console.

The dual-place saddle featured a padded "sissy bar."

A new angle was used on the forks, and they were mounted behind the steering head for more agile handling. The final drive chain was enclosed in a housing that provided constant lubrication, and the transmission featured five-speed gearing. An easier-to-service spin-on oil filter was added to the 80-cubic inch motor. The disc brakes were increased in size to help slow the 725-lb. (dry) FLT.

1980 Model Year Lineup

Model	Engine Type	Displacement	Transmission	Special Feature(s)
Model 80XLH	Overhead-Valve Twin	61 cid	Four-Speed	The "Hugger"
Model 80XLS	Overhead-Valve Twin	61 cid	Four-Speed	The "Roadster"
Model 80FXB	Overhead-Valve Twin	80 cid	Four-Speed	Dual Belt Drives/ "Sturgis"
Model 80FXE	Overhead-Valve Twin	74 cid	Four-Speed	Super Glide
Model 80FXEF	Overhead-Valve Twin	80 cid	Four-Speed	Fat Bob
Model 80FXS	Overhead-Valve Twin	74 cid	Four-Speed	Low Rider
Model 80FXS	Overhead-Valve Twin	80 cid	Four-Speed	Low Rider
Model 80FXWG	Overhead-Valve Twin	80 cid	Four-Speed	Wide Glide
Model 80FLH-74	Overhead-Valve Twin	74 cid	Four-Speed	Electra Glide
Model 80FLH-80	Overhead-Valve Twin	80 cid	Four-Speed	Electra Glide
Model 80FLHC	Overhead-Valve Twin	80 cid	Four-Speed	Electra Glide Classic
Model 80FLHCE	Overhead-Valve Twin	80 cid	Four-Speed	Electra Glide Classic w/Sidecar
Model 80FLHP-74	Overhead-Valve Twin	74 cid	Four-Speed	Police Model
Model 80FLHP-80	Overhead-Valve Twin	80 cid	Four-Speed	Police Model
Model 80FLT	Overhead-Valve Twin	80 cid	Five-Speed	Tour Glide

Production

Model	Production
Model 80XLH	11,841
Model 80XLS	2,926
Model 80FXB	1,470
Model 80FXE	3,169
Model 80FXEF	4,773
Model 80FXS-74	3
Model 80FXS-80	5,922
Model 80FXWG	6,085
Model 80FLH-74	1,111
Model 80FLH-80	1,625
Model 80FLHC	2,480
Model 80FLHCE	463
Model 80FLHP-74	528
Model 80FLHP-80	391
Model 80FLT	4,480

The 1981 FLT came equipped with everything the long-distance rider needed.

1981

Harley-Davidson's merger with AMF in 1969 had more than likely kept the company afloat and able to expand. Corporate infighting, as well as a huge loss in quality, gave a group of private parties the idea of taking the company private again. With Vaughn Beals at the reins, the group purchased the required stock from AMF in June of 1981, thus regaining control. After completion of the buy back, Beals inserted a gold dipstick into the first post-AMF bike to roll off of the assembly line in York, Pennsylvania.

The eagle had become the standard symbol for freedom at Harley-Davidson, and liberal applications of the feathered beast were found across the board.

The 80-cubic inch Shovelhead motor powered all 1981 Harley-Davidson models, except the Sportsters.

Changes in the model lineup were not drastic, but notable anyway.

With the introduction of the 1981 models, the Shovelhead motor was only offered in the 80-cubic inch variety. Sales of the 74-cid models had been dwindling, so the move made sense.

The XLH and XLS were still sold, and either model could be had with a variety of component options. The standard XLH came with the 3.3-gallon tank, but the 2.2-gallon version could be selected from the options sheet. Cast or wire wheels with a 16- or 18-inch rear wheel were also choices to be made. The forks on the XLH were shortened to help bring the saddle lower.

The XLS in basic trim came with buckhorn bars, and truncated dual exhaust pipes. The standard 3.3-gallon tank could be swapped for the 2.2-gallon model, and the rear wheel was available in 16- or 18-inch diameters. As with the XLH, either cast or spoke wheels were available.

With the elimination of the 74-cid Shovelhead motor, the 80-incher received a few minor tweaks that applied to all the remaining models carrying it in their frames. To accommodate the poor-quality fuels of the era, the compression ratio was lowered to 7.4:1. This prevented engine knock and detonation, regardless of what fuel was being burned. Additional changes included the V-Fire II electronic ignition, and new drain lines from the rocker boxes. Valve guide seals were revamped, and the valve guides were increased in length.

The FXWG was now available with either the flamed fuel tanks or a pair of pinstriped metallic silver units. The balance of the FX offerings remained carryover models. 1981 was the last year of production for the Fat Bob models.

The FLH was now available as a Heritage model, complete with orange and olive green paint, fringed saddlebags, a sprung saddle, windshield, and case guards.

The FLT breathed through a revised exhaust system, and a Classic version carried special paint and appliqués.

1981 Model Year Lineup

Model	Engine Type	Displacement	Transmission	Special Feature(s)
Model 81XLH	Overhead-Valve Twin	61 cid	Four-Speed	Shorter Front Forks
Model 81XLS	Overhead-Valve Twin	61 cid	Four-Speed	—
Model 81FXB	Overhead-Valve Twin	80 cid	Four-Speed	Sturgis
Model 81FXE	Overhead-Valve Twin	80 cid	Four-Speed	Super Glide
Model 81FXEF	Overhead-Valve Twin	80 cid	Four-Speed	Fat Bob/Final Year Of Sale
Model 81FXWG	Overhead-Valve Twin	80 cid	Four-Speed	Wide Glide
Model 81FLH	Overhead-Valve Twin	80 cid	Four-Speed	Electra Glide
Model 81FLH Heritage	Overhead-Valve Twin	80 cid	Four-Speed	Electra Glide Heritage
Model 81FLHC	Overhead-Valve Twin	80 cid	Four-Speed	Electra Glide Classic
Model 81FLHCE	Overhead-Valve Twin	80 cid	Four-Speed	Electra Glide Classic w/Sidecar
Model 81FLHP	Overhead-Valve Twin	80 cid	Four-Speed	Police Model
Model 81FLT	Overhead-Valve Twin	80 cid	Five-Speed	Tour Glide
Model 81FLTC	Overhead-Valve Twin	80 cid	Five-Speed	Tour Glide Classic

Production

Model	Production
Model 81XLH	8,442
Model 81XLS	1,660
Model 81FXB	3,543
Model 81FXE	3,085
Model 81FXEF	3,691
Model 81FXWG	5,166
Model 81FLH	2,131
Model 81FLH Heritage	784
Model 81FLHC	1,472
Model 81FLHCE	152
Model81FLHP	402
Model 81FLT	1,636
Model 81FLTC	1,157

Behind the frame-mounted fairing of the FLT lived the enclosed instruments.

It was the final year for the FXB Sturgis model in 1982, but it would reappear in the '90s.

1982

Despite its newfound freedom from its corporate owners, Harley-Davidson found itself in a world of trouble by 1982. Not only did it need to make great strides in improving its motorcycles, the Japanese models were dominating the market H-D once dominated.

Late in 1982, Harley-Davidson approached the U.S. government requesting that tariffs be placed on Japanese machines larger than 700cc. The company hoped this financial burden would help it gain enough breathing space to regain its footing in the market. In addition to these sanctions, new models and enhanced designs would assist the American builder to recover from disaster. Heavy layoffs at the factory cut the workforce to about half what it was the year before.

The Sportsters both received new frames for 1982. The stamped and welded assemblies replaced those with heavy iron junctions used previously to join sections of frame together. The new design produced frames that were both lighter and stronger than ever before. New batteries required less maintenance, and improved generators delivered more spark. The battery and oil tank were also repositioned for better weight distribution.

Since 1982 marked the 25th anniversary of the Sportster, two special models were sold to celebrate. The XLHA and XLSA came to your door wearing special paint and graphics. Historical paperwork signed by Vaughn Beals and other H-D management made the models truly official.

Most of the FX models remained unaltered for 1982. They did receive plastic housings for the switchgear on the handlebars. It would be the final year for the FXB Sturgis model, and it came dressed with gold wheels and higher handlebars.

Joining the ranks were two new models: the FXR and FXRS. By combining the frame and engine isolation features of the FLT with the low-slung layout of the FXS, a new star was born. Both models rowed a five-speed transmission. The isolated engine made for one of the smoothest Harley's ever, and the plush seats only added to the comfort level. Both new machines rode on 16-inch rear and 19-inch front wheels with a wheelbase of 64.7 inches. The FXS came with spoke wheels, while the FXRS featured cast wheels. The FXR was finished in single colors, while the FXRS wore two-toned trim.

The FLH variants carried over from 1981, but the FLTs received some new items. Lower floorboards and modified handlebars provided a more natural seating position for the rider. The seat was also changed to further the latest in comfort. The saddlebags and rear box were fitted with better seals and improved locks. The primary chain oiler was also improved, and the alternator produced higher output with less required maintenance.

1982 Model Year Lineup

Model	Engine Type	Displacement	Transmission	Special Feature(s)
Model 82XLH	Overhead-Valve Twin	61 cid	Four-Speed	New Frame Design
Model 82XLHA	Overhead-Valve Twin	61 cid	Four-Speed	Anniversary Model
Model 82XLS	Overhead-Valve Twin	61 cid	Four-Speed	New Frame Design
Model 82XLSA	Overhead-Valve Twin	61 cid	Four-Speed	Anniversary Model
Model 82FXB	Overhead-Valve Twin	80 cid	Four-Speed	Sturgis/Final Year Of Sale
Model 82FXE	Overhead-Valve Twin	80 cid	Four-Speed	Super Glide
Model 82FXR	Overhead-Valve Twin	80 cid	Five-Speed	Super Glide II /Standard Model
Model 82FXRS	Overhead-Valve Twin	80 cid	Five-Speed	Super Glide II
Model 82FXS	Overhead-Valve Twin	80 cid	Four-Speed	Low Rider/Final Year Of Sale
Model 82FXWG	Overhead-Valve Twin	80 cid	Four-Speed	Wide Glide
Model 82FLH	Overhead-Valve Twin	80 cid	Four-Speed	Electra Glide
Model 82FLHC	Overhead-Valve Twin	80 cid	Four-Speed	Electra Glide Classic
Model 82FLT	Overhead-Valve Twin	80 cid	Five-Speed	Tour Glide
Model 82FLTC	Overhead-Valve Twin	80 cid	Five-Speed	Tour Glide Classic

Production

Model	Production
Model 82XLH	5,015
Model 82XLHA	932
Model 82XLS	1261
Model 82XLSA	778
Model 82FXB	1,833
Model 82FXE	1,617
Model 82FXR	3,065
Model 82FXRS	3,190
Model 82FXS	1,816
Model 82FXWG	2,348
Model 82FLH	1,491
Model 82FLHC	1,284
Model 82FLT	1,196
Model 82FLTC	833

1983

The government saw Harley-Davidson's way of thinking in 1983, and enacted the proposed tariffs on import machines greater than 700cc in displacement. This tariff would stay in effect until 1988.

The 1983 H-D lineup was a true mix of new and old, and very few models went untouched as the company attempted to reinvigorate buyers.

To draw riders into the Harley fold for the first time, a new Sportster was introduced. The XLX was equipped with a minimum of flash, but offered riders a ticket into the Harley family they could afford. A solo seat, 2.2-gallon peanut tank, low handlebars, and staggered, shorty exhaust pipes made for an appealing package. A speedometer was the only gauge included on the base model, but other trinkets could easily be added. The tires were mounted on nine-spoke cast-aluminum rims. At only $3,995, it was considered a steal.

The second new Sportster was the XR-1000. Harley-Davidson needed a small model that offered a higher level of performance to those who took their machines to the track to do more than watch. By combining the lower end of the current XL, new iron cylinders, and alloy heads from the XR-750, a performance model was born. It was fed fuel through a pair of carburetors mounted on the right side of the motor. A sweeping pair of blacked-out exhaust pipes on the left helped with performance and appeal. The rest of the machine was largely a new XLX, which may have caused the lack of interest on the showroom floor. It was also listed at a price nearly $2,000 higher than the XLH, which caused some sticker shock.

XLHs retained last year's features, but now had higher handlebars, a vacuum advance ignition, and a less-restrictive exhaust. A revised saddle capped the changes.

The XLS also had the new vacuum advance ignition, as well as a fuel tank that mimicked the bigger FXR, complete with center-mounted dash.

The FXE, FXR, FXRS, and FXWG were still available, but were joined by several new models and variations. The middleweight class seemed to be gaining the most sales for H-D, so it received the most attention.

The FXRT was designed as a smaller touring machine, and was well equipped. A frame-mounted, aerodynamic fairing was installed to shield the rider from the elements, and a pair of slick, frame-mounted saddlebags helped keep gear safe as well. The FXRT had an all-new, anti-dive front suspension that provided an unprecedented amount of control. The air suspension system also allowed for adjustment in ride stiffness. The seat of the FXRT was wider and was stuffed with thicker foam, and the low-rise handlebars made for a perfect riding posture. Options like a large touring box, am/fm cassette radio, and a full array of touring gauges let buyers order their machine to fit their needs more exactly.

A new version of the FXS was the FXSB. The big difference was the use of a belt rear drive in place of the FXS's chain. A 21-inch tire up front added some attitude.

Another variation on the FXWG Wide Glide was the FXDG Disc Glide. The name was derived from the use of a solid rear wheel in place of the cast spoke wheel on the FXWG. The FXDG was also propelled with a final drive belt, instead of a chain. The exhaust pipes were short, and finished in flat black.

The FLH models were also fitted with final drive belts in 1983.

The FLT and FLTC touted newly shaped saddles that brought the rider 1 1/2 inches closer to the ground, and their suspension was tightened up.

The final new model was the FLHT Electra Glide. By combining the chassis of the FLT with the fairing from the FLH, the FLHT was born. Rear wheels were now 16 inches in diameter, and the saddlebags held 15 percent more gear. The lids of the saddlebags were now hinged, and remained attached to the bags. Placing the battery under the seat helped to lower the center of gravity on the big machines.

Overall sales continued to fall, but Harley-Davidson had plans for a new motor that would bring customers back into the stores.

1983 Model Year Lineup

Model	Engine Type	Displacement	Transmission	Special Feature(s)
Model 83XLH	Overhead-Valve Twin	61 cid	Four-Speed	Hugger
Model 83XLS	Overhead-Valve Twin	61 cid	Four-Speed	Roadster
Model 83XLX	Overhead-Valve Twin	61 cid	Four-Speed	$3,995 Retail Price
Model 83XR	Overhead-Valve Twin	61 cid	Four-Speed	XR-750 Heads/ High Perfor.
Model 83FXE	Overhead-Valve Twin	80 cid	Four-Speed	Super Glide
Model 83FXR	Overhead-Valve Twin	80 cid	Five-Speed	Super Glide II
Model 83FXRS	Overhead-Valve Twin	80 cid	Five-Speed	Super Glide II
Model 83FXRT	Overhead-Valve Twin	80 cid	Five-Speed	Super Glide II Touring
Model 83FXSB	Overhead-Valve Twin	80 cid	Four-Speed	Low Rider/Belt Drive
Model 83FXDG	Overhead-Valve Twin	80 cid	Four-Speed	Solid Rear Disc Wheel
Model 83FXWG	Overhead-Valve Twin	80 cid	Four-Speed	Wide Glide
Model 83FLH	Overhead-Valve Twin	80 cid	Four-Speed	—
Model 83FLHT	Overhead-Valve Twin	80 cid	Five-Speed	FLT Frame/FLH Fairing
Model 83FLHTC	Overhead-Valve Twin	80 cid	Five-Speed	FLHT Classic
Model 83FLT	Overhead-Valve Twin	80 cid	Five-Speed	Tour Glide
Model 83FLTC	Overhead-valve Twin	80 cid	Five-Speed	Tour Glide Classic

Production

Model	Production
Model 83XLH	2,230
Model 83XLS	1,616
Model 83XLX	4,892
Model 83XR-1000	1,018
Model 83FXE	1,215
Model 83FXR	1,069
Model 83FXRS	1,413
Model 83FXRT	1,458
Model 83FXSB	3,277
Model 83FXDG	810
Model 83FXWG	2,873
Model 83FLH	1,272
Model 83FLHT	1,426
Model 83FLHTC	1,302
Model 83FLT	565
Model 83FLTC	475

The Year Of The Blockhead

The Shovelhead had been introduced in the 1966 models, and had served the company well. Regardless of the effectiveness of the previous variation of the V-twin, a new standard was needed after an 18-year run. The new V2 Evolution motor would help Harley get back into the market and to gain on the Asian competition.

The new-for-1984 V2 motor brought a whole new set of rules to the table, and made Harley-Davidsons faster and more reliable than ever.

The new motor was just that, all new. Besides the basic layout of overhead-valve, v-twin, the Evo incorporated new materials, and vastly improved sealing at crucial locations. The new motor didn't leak, ran strong on poor quality fuel, and even impressed the media of the day. That alone was a major accomplishment for The Motor Company.

The cylinders were now formed from an alloy, and added longevity through the use of iron liners within. The cylinder heads, now cast in aluminum were designed with valves set at a narrower angle, allowing a straighter route for the gases. The shape of the combustion chamber was also flatter which provided higher compression, but operated with the lower octane fuel of the period.

Firing the newly compressed flow was an improved electronic ignition that featured dual advance curves to meet with varying riding circumstances. Duration, lift, and timing were all under the watchful eye of an improved computer.

Overall, the new Evolution, or "Blockhead," ran cleaner, provided more horsepower and didn't leak as previous variations had. It seemed as if Harley-Davidson was ready to offer machines powered by a motor worthy of its heritage once again.

The XR-1000 was rolled out in 1983, and delivered high performance in a compact package.

1984

As if the introduction of an all-new motor—the Blockhead—wasn't enough for one year, 1984 would bring numerous additions to the existing Harley-Davidson lineup. Combinations of previous models, as well as the application of the new motor, made the catalog more appealing than ever.

Of all the models, the Sportsters received the fewest changes, and would not get the new Evo motor for two more years. The XLH, XLS, and XLX lost one of their front disc brakes for 1984, but received alternator ignitions and diaphragm-spring clutches later in the year. The XL-1000 had better brakes installed, and could be purchased in black and orange, as well as the steel gray of 1983.

The 1983 XR breathed in through a pair of Dell 'Orto carburetors.

The only 1984 Big Twins to retain the Shovelhead motor for 1984 were the FLH and FLHX, which was a special model trimmed to trumpet the final fling of the Shovel motor. The Last Edition FLHX was complete with a full compliment of touring gear, wire wheels, and black or white paint trimmed with gold

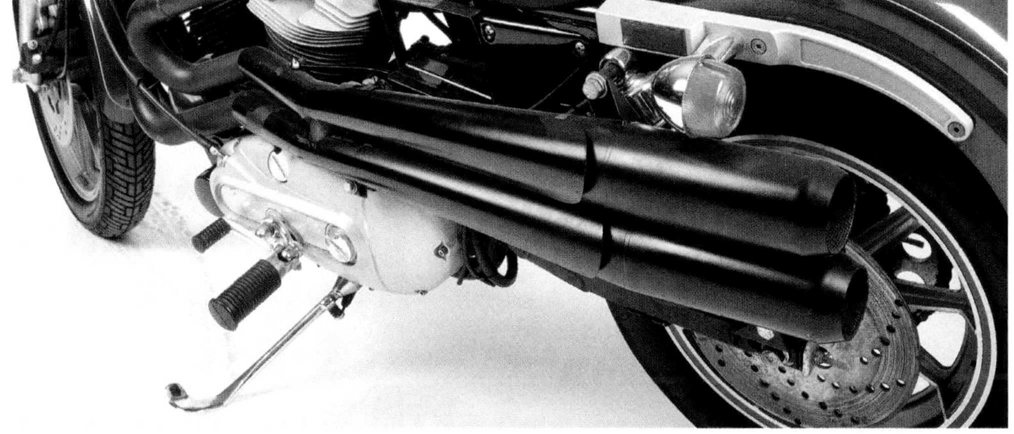

The high-mounted dual exhaust added to the performance and appearance of the XR-1000.

and red stripes. These three models also received staggered dual exhausts and forward controls for 1984.

Early examples of the FXE and FXSB were also still using the Shovelhead motor, but that would change before the production run would end. 1984 was the last time the FXE and FXSB would be offered. It also appears that the FXWG was powered by the Shovelhead engine early in the production cycle, but would have the new V2 variation later.

Besides the use of the new motor in the balance of the lineup, changes were numerous, and affected nearly every model available.

The FXRS was built with lower springs and shorter forks, providing an even lower seat height than previous models. The new diaphragm-spring clutch was installed, and one of the front brake rotors was removed. The FXRT had the new clutch type, but no other modifications.

Two new entrants in the FXR family were the FXRDG and XRP. The FXRP was a police-only version, while the FXRDG was a new combo model using bits from other machines. Built around the FXRS, the FXRDG featured the solid rear-wheel disc of the FXDG from 1983. It ran with a chain final drive, and rolled with a wire wheel up front. A "Genuine Harley-Davidson" appliqué was used on the fuel tanks, and the bikes also had the new clutch.

While H-D had been using rear suspension every year since 1949, there were some who missed the clean look of the unsprung "hard tail" models of old. To satisfy riders who yearned for the past, the Soft Tail was created. There were no visible coil springs on the rear of the machine, but the swing arm used twin dampers mounted beneath the frame to provide a smooth ride. The combination proved to a popular choice, and remains in the catalog today.

The FXST was the first model to feature the new suspension layout, and claimed a long list of features. The new motor was rigidly mounted into the frame, and the bike offered a low 27.5-inch seat height. A 21-inch wire wheel up front was mated to a single 11.5-inch brake disc. The 16-inch rear wheel was also spoked. The rear fender was the popular "bobbed" variety, and the oil tank was plated in chrome. The pullback buckhorn bars reached over a pair of fuel tanks that held 5.2 gallons of petrol.

The FLTC and FLHTC shared the same set of alterations for the new year, as well as a few individual tweaks. Both had tool kits included as part of the standard equipment, as well as the new clutch design and enhanced wiring.

The FLTC delivered its power with a final belt drive, and shifted with a five-speed transmission. Locks on the hard bags were also improved. The FLHTC came with air shocks in back, and air-assisted forks with anti-dive control up front. The cast wheels had 16 spokes each.

1984 Model Year Lineup

Model	Engine Type	Displacement	Transmission	Special Feature(s)
Model 84XLH	Overhead-Valve Twin	61 cid	Four-Speed	Single Front Disc Brake
Model 84XLS	Overhead-Valve Twin	61 cid	Four-Speed	Single Front Disc Brake
Model 84XLX	Overhead-Valve Twin	61 cid	Four-Speed	Single Front Disc Brake
Model 84XR-1000	Overhead-Valve Twin	61 cid	Four-Speed	—
Model 84FXE	Overhead-Valve Twin	80 cid	Four-Speed	Super Glide
Model 84FXSB	Overhead-Valve Twin	80 cid	Four-Speed	Low Rider
Model 84FXST	Overhead-Valve Twin	80 cid	Four-Speed	Soft Tail
Model 84FXRS	Overhead-Valve Twin	80 cid	Five-Speed	Low Glide
Model 84FXRT	Overhead-Valve Twin	80 cid	Five-Speed	Sport Glide
Model 84FXRP	Overhead-Valve Twin	80 cid	Five-Speed	Police Model
Model 84FXWG	Overhead-Valve Twin	80 cid	Four-Speed	Wide Glide
Model 84FXRDG	Overhead-Valve Twin	80 cid	Five-Speed	Disc Glide
Model 84FLH	Overhead-Valve Twin	80 cid	Four-Speed	Electra Glide
Model 84FLHX	Overhead-Valve Twin	80 cid	Four-Speed	Last Edition
Model 84FLHTC	Overhead-Valve Twin	80 cid	Five-Speed	Electra Glide Classic
Model 84FLTC	Overhead-Valve Twin	80 cid	Five-Speed	Tour Glide Classic

The FXRT model was introduced in 1983, and fitted with the all-new Evolution motor in 1984.

Production

Model	Production
Model 84XLH	2,278
Model 84XLS	678
Model 84XLX	2,165
Model 84XR-1000	759
Model 84FXE	2,606
Model 84FXSB	NA
Model 84FXST	2,110
Model 84FXRS	2,227
Model 84FXRT	2,030
Model 84FXRP	820
Model 84FXWG	2,227
Model 84FXRDG	853
Model 84FLH	1,983
Model 84FLHX	1,258
Model 84FLHTC	2,491
Model 84FLTC	1,301

1985

Since Harley-Davidson introduced a new motor and several new models the previous year, 1985 would be quiet by comparison. Even with the new motor in place, some modifications were made on the 1985s.

The Sportsters each received minor cosmetic mutations for the newest year. The XLH wore blacked-out cylinders, chrome pipes, and spoked wheels at both ends. The XLS now resembled its bigger brethren with the application of a larger tank and center-mounted console. Cast wheels both front and rear, along with the same darkened engine cylinders completed the list. The XLX sported black exhaust sprouting from the blacked-out cylinders, cast wheels, and the solo seat. The XR-1000 was removed from the catalog for the latest year of sales.

1985 Model Year Lineup

Model	Engine Type	Displacement	Transmission	Special Feature(s)
Model 85XLH	Overhead-Valve Twin	61 cid	Four-Speed	—
Model 85XLS	Overhead-Valve Twin	61 cid	Four-Speed	—
Model 85XLX	Overhead-Valve Twin	61 cid	Four-Speed	—
Model 85FXEF	Overhead-Valve Twin	80 cid	Five-Speed	Fat Bob
Model 85FXRC	Overhead-Valve Twin	80 cid	Five-Speed	Custom Model
Model 85FXRP	Overhead-Valve Twin	80 cid	Five-Speed	Police Model
Model 85FXRS	Overhead-Valve Twin	80 cid	Five-Speed	Low Glide
Model 85FXRT	Overhead-Valve Twin	80 cid	Five-Speed	Sport Glide
Model 85FXSB	Overhead-Valve Twin	80 cid	Four-Speed	Low Rider
Model 85FXST	Overhead-Valve Twin	80 cid	Five-Speed	Softail
Model 85FXWG	Overhead-Valve Twin	80 cid	Four-Speed	Wide Glide
Model 85FLTC	Overhead-Valve Twin	80 cid	Five-Speed	Tour Glide Classic
Model 85FLHTC	Overhead-Valve Twin	80 cid	Five-Speed	Electra Glide Classic

The entire 1985 FX series would be the recipient of final belt drives, bringing the belt to the forefront of preferred power delivery. The FXRT once again featured dual disc brakes on the front wheel. The FXRT saddle was amended, and featured a larger passenger section as well as a taller backrest. A new starter relay on the series eliminated an occasional problem experienced on the previous models.

The FXRC Low Glide Custom was new model added to the FX family. The FXRC was dipped in two-tone, candy orange and root beer paint, and was highlighted by a dozen of its engine covers plated in chrome. Wire wheels at both ends rolled beneath the FXRC, and the front wheel used the fender taken from the XR-1000. Less than 1,100 copies of the FXRC were built.

The FXRP was once again sold to police departments, and was largely an FXRT devoid of a rear seat. In place of the rear pillion was another storage box.

For 1985, the big FL models also found themselves being driven by final belt drives. Minor changes to the wiring and graphics rounded out the alterations for the '85s.

Production

Model	Production
Model 85XLH	4,074
Model 85XLS	616
Model 85XLX	1,824
Model 85FXEF	2,324
Model 85FXRC	1,084
Model 85FXRP	474
Model 85FXRS	3,476
Model 85FXRT	1,252
Model 85FXSB	2,359
Model 85FXST	4,529
Model 85FXWG	4,171
Model 85FLTC	1,807
Model 85FLHTC	4,007

The XLH-1100 was the larger of the two all-new Sportsters in 1986.

1986

While the majority of the Big Twin models had received the all-new Evo motor for the 1984 model year, the Sportsters had to wait until now. Not only did the Sportster finally get the new motors, but two sizes were offered. In addition to the newly powered XL models, a short run of Liberty Edition machines were built. A total of only 1,750 Liberty models were built, and $100 from each sale went to the restoration of the Statue of Liberty.

The first new Sportster to be introduced was the XLH-883. The XLH, XLS, and XLX monikers were no longer being used. Shortly after the 883cc version came the XLH-1100. It shared the same frame and running gear, but carried a bigger motor. The motor on both versions combined many new features with the classic H-D V-twin design.

The cylinders were of alloy construction, and used iron sleeves within. The new rocker boxes housed hydraulic valve lifters, and the majority of the cases were not interchangeable with the old. The latest power plant brought the latest Sportsters up to date, especially when compared to the rest of the H-D lineup. The 1100 produced 63 hp, while the smaller 883 put out 53. Practical limitations kept the new XLH models with only four-speed transmissions.

The XLH-883 was priced at $3,995 and was designed to lure new riders into Harley-Davidson showrooms. Assembled using the solo seat, peanut tank, and low-rise bars, it was an entry-level model. The 1100 listed for about $1,200 more, but also had a more luxurious saddle, higher handlebars, and more colors choices. There was also more bric-a-brac to be added to the bigger model.

The federal government had begun cracking down on motorcycle restrictions, forcing several changes across the board.

To reduce noise, both the intake and exhaust systems were modified for the 1986 models. Turn signals up front now glowed constantly, and so did the headlight.

The button controlling the turn indicators could be held down until you wanted the flashing to stop, or would continue blinking until cancelled by the rider.

A new/old model reintroduced for 1986 was the FXR Super Glide. The FXR's seat was an inch lower than the FXRS's, and the bike was driven by a chain instead of a belt. The FXRS suspension settings were firmer and it was now called the Low Rider. The FXRT could be purchased in the FXRD livery, which provided the buyer with the same fairing and saddlebags of the FXRT, but also included a rear trunk and 40-watt stereo as standard equipment. The exhaust system was also a two-into-one instead of the staggered pipes found on the FXRT. Both passenger and rider found generous floorboards for their boots, and the tanks and engine were protected by stout, chrome tubular guards.

Yet another new variant for 1986 was the FLST Heritage model. By combining the FL frame and softtail suspension, bigger tires, and wide bars, the FLST did a decent job of cloning the Hydra-Glides born in a previous decade. The front forks were cloaked in tapered shrouds to further enhance the vintage look. The round air cleaner was being applied to all the big FL models for 1986.

About the only revisions to the FLT and FLHT were the updated turn signal controls and the circular air cleaners.

1986 Model Year Lineup

Model	Engine Type	Displacement	Transmission	Special Feature(s)
Model 86XLH883	Overhead-Valve Twin	883cc	Four-Speed	$3,995 MSRP
Model 86XLH1100	Overhead-Valve Twin	1100cc	Four-Speed	—
Model 86FXR	Overhead-Valve Twin	80 cid	Five-Speed	Chain Final Drive
Model 86FXRP	Overhead-Valve Twin	80 cid	Five-Speed	Police Model
Model 86FXRS	Overhead-Valve Twin	80 cid	Five-Speed	Low Rider
Model 86FXRT	Overhead-Valve Twin	80 cid	Five-Speed	Sport Glide
Model 86FXRD	Overhead-Valve Twin	80 cid	Five-Speed	Sport Glide Deluxe
Model 86FXST	Overhead-Valve Twin	80 cid	Five-Speed	Softail
Model 86FXSTC	Overhead-Valve Twin	80 cid	Five-Speed	Softail Custom
Model 86FLST	Overhead-Valve Twin	80 cid	Five-Speed	Softail Heritage
Model 86FLTC	Overhead-Valve Twin	80 cid	Five-Speed	Tour Glide
Model 86FHLT	Overhead-Valve Twin	80 cid	Five-Speed	Electra Glide
Model 86FLHTC	Overhead-Valve Twin	80 cid	Five-Speed	Electra Glide Classic

Dual instruments and pullback bars helped differentiate the 1986 1100 from its smaller sibling.

Production

Model	Production
Model 86XLH-883	8,026
Model 86XLH-1100	3,077
Model 86FXR	2,038
Model 86FXRP	2,52
Model 86FXRS	1,846
Model 86FXRT	591
Model 86FXRD	1,000
Model 86FXST	2,402
Model 86FXSTC	3,782
Model 86FLST	2,510
Model 86FLTC	1,039
Model 86FLHT	711
Model 86FLHTC	411

The all-alloy motor produced 63 hp, and shifted through a four-speed gearbox.

1987

Harley-Davidson would make several exciting announcements during the 1987 model year. Along with introducing even more new models, they would call for an end to the tariffs that were to run until the end of 1988. This earlier than planned escape from the help of the governments protective ruling signaled the Milwaukee company's return to health.

The new Evolution-powered Sportsters were mostly unchanged, but the XLH-883 was offered in a configuration that provided an even lower seat height. With trimmed suspension and a seat with less padding, the Hugger appealed to those who found the tall saddle heights daunting.

The XLH-1100 was unchanged, but was sold in a 30th-anniversary guise along with the other models. Birthday graphics on the tank and front fender commemorated the date. Black and orange paint was also applied to the anniversary model, along with the now-popular black and chrome engine treatment.

1987 Model Year Lineup

Model	Engine Type	Displacement	Transmission	Feature(s)
Model 87XLH883	Overhead-Valve Twin	883cc	Four-Speed	—
Model 87XLH1100	Overhead-Valve Twin	1100cc	Four-Speed	—
Model 87XLH1100*	Overhead-Valve Twin	1100cc	Four-Speed	*30th Anniversary
Model 87FXR	Overhead-Valve Twin	80 cid	Five-Speed	Belt Drive
Model 87FXRS	Overhead-Valve Twin	80 cid	Five-Speed	Low Rider
Model 87FXRS-SP	Overhead-Valve Twin	80 cid	Five-Speed	Low Rider Sport
Model 87FXLR	Overhead-Valve Twin	80 cid	Five-Speed	Low Rider Custom
Model 87FXLR*	Overhead-Valve Twin	80 cid	Five-Speed	*10th Anniversary
Model 87FXRP	Overhead-Valve Twin	80 cid	Five-Speed	Police Model
Model 87FXRT	Overhead-Valve Twin	80 cid	Five-Speed	Sport Glide
Model 87FXST	Overhead-Valve Twin	80 cid	Five-Speed	Softail
Model 87FXSTC	Overhead-Valve Twin	80 cid	Five-Speed	Softail Custom
Model 87FLST	Overhead-Valve Twin	80 cid	Five-Speed	Heritage Softail
Model 87FLSTC	Overhead-Valve Twin	80 cid	Five-Speed	Heritage Softail Special
Model 87FLHS	Overhead-Valve Twin	80 cid	Five-Speed	Electra Glide Sport
Model 87FLHTC	Overhead-Valve Twin	80 cid	Five-Speed	Electra Glide Classic
Model 87FLTC	Overhead-Valve Twin	80 cid	Five-Speed	Tour Glide

The base model in the FX family was still the FXR, and it remained available. Alongside it was the newest version, the FXLR. The Low Rider Custom and the FXR were fitted with a belt final drive, instead of the chain used on the previous FXR. It had been 10 years since the first Low Rider had been introduced, and special anniversary models for the FXR and FXLR were also offered. Unique handlebars and gas tank were found only on this anniversary variation, as was a specially stamped leather grab strap across the seat. The FXLR also ran with a 21-inch laced wheel up front, and an Austrian-made solid disc on the rear. The FXR continued with cast spoke wheels at both ends. The FXLR stopped with a disc brake at each end, and the speedometer was mounted between the handlebars.

The FXRS received better-tuned suspension and a smaller front fender, just like that of the FXR. The FXRT's sound system was upgraded, but no other changes were made.

For fans of the bigger touring models, two new choices were available. The FLSTC Heritage Classic had mostly cosmetic differences, but it offered a lot of shine. The motor and transmission were given the black-and-chrome motif, and two-tone paint reminiscent of the '50s models was also applied. A large windshield and leather saddlebags made longer journeys more convenient, and the two-piece seat with backrest made them more comfortable. Finishing touches included wire wheels and floorboards.

The FLHS Electra Glide Sport was another new offering for 1987. Many riders liked the big feel of the FLHs, but wished for a less-oppressive fairing up front. The Sport model came equipped with a Lexan windshield that was height adjustable by 3 inches, providing almost any rider with the airflow he or she required. The windshield was also easily removed for those who desired an occasional day of wind-in-your-face riding. Equipped with only saddlebags but no rear box, the Sport could handle a fair amount of amenities.

Production

Model	Production
Model 87XLH-883	4,990
Model 87XLH-1100	4,018
Model 87XLH-1100 Anniversary	600
Model 87FXR	1265
Model 87FXRS	784
Model 87FXRS-Sport	1,142
Model 87FXLR	3221
Model 87FXLR Anniversary	736
Model 87FXRP	416
Model 87FXRT	287
Model 87FXST	2,024
Model 87FXSTC	5,264
Model 87FLST	2,794
Model 87FLSTC	NA
Model 87FLHS	1,054
Model 87FLHTC	699
Model 87FLTC	NA

The 1988 FXSTS Softail Springer was a new model rolled out to help celebrate the 85th birthday of The Motor Company.

1988

The 1988 model year would herald 85 years of production for The Motor Company, and between several new models, and some with anniversary trim, it would be another exciting year.

The Sportster lineup was bolstered by new variations, as well as a bump in displacement for the XLH-1100. The XLH-883 was now available in one of three formats. There was the standard issue, the Hugger, and the Deluxe. While largely the same machines, each was designed to meet with certain needs of the market. The standard remained the bargain model, while the Hugger provided a lower seat height for those who needed better access to terra firma. The Deluxe level came equipped with two-tone paint, pullback bars, dual saddle, wire wheels, extra chrome, and a tachometer. Even as well equipped as it was, the Deluxe model was only about $400 more than the $3,995 standard edition.

Last year's XLH-1100 was increased in displacement to 1,200, making it the biggest Sportster ever built. The bigger power plant boasted a 12-percent increase in horsepower and 10 percent more torque than the 1987 1,100 version. All the Sportsters had front forks measuring 39mm in diameter—an increase of 4mm over the previous versions.

The FXR Low Rider also received some revisions, including a Fat Bob fuel tank complete with twin caps and a built-in fuel gauge.

1988 Model Year Lineup

Model	Engine Type	Displacement	Transmission	Feature(s)
Model 88XLH883	Overhead-Valve Twin	883cc	Four-Speed	Standard Model
Model 88XLH883	Overhead-Valve Twin	883cc	Four-Speed	Hugger Model
Model 88XLH883	Overhead-Valve Twin	883cc	Four-Speed	Deluxe Model
Model 88XLH1200	Overhead-Valve Twin	1,200cc	Four-Speed	—
Model 88FXR	Overhead-Valve Twin	80 cid	Five-Speed	Super Glide
Model 88FXRP	Overhead-Valve Twin	80 cid	Five-Speed	Police Model
Model 88FXRS	Overhead-Valve Twin	80 cid	Five-Speed	Low Rider
Model 88FXRS-SP	Overhead-Valve Twin	80 cid	Five-Speed	Low Rider Sport
Model 88FXRS	Overhead-Valve Twin	80 cid	Five-Speed	85th Anniversary Edition
Model 88FXRT	Overhead-Valve Twin	80 cid	Five-Speed	Sport Glide
Model 88FXLR	Overhead-Valve Twin	80 cid	Five Speed	Low Rider Custom
Model 88FXST	Overhead-Valve Twin	80 cid	Five-Speed	Softail
Model 88FXSTC	Overhead-Valve Twin	80 cid	Five-Speed	Softail Custom
Model 88FXSTS	Overhead-Valve Twin	80 cid	Five-Speed	85th Anniversary Edition
Model 88FLST	Overhead-Valve Twin	80 cid	Five-Speed	Heritage Softail
Model 88FLSTC	Overhead-Valve Twin	80 cid	Five-Speed	Heritage Softail Classic
Model 88FLHS	Overhead-Valve Twin	80 cid	Five-Speed	Electra Glide Sport
Model 88FLHTC	Overhead-Valve Twin	80 cid	Five-Speed	Electra Glide Classic
Model 88FLHTC	Overhead-Valve Twin	80 cid	Five-Speed	85th Anniversary Edition
Model 88FLTC	Overhead-Valve Twin	80 cid	Five-Speed	Tour Glide
Model 88FLTC	Overhead-Valve Twin	80 cid	Five-Speed	85th Anniversary Edition

Among the four models built in the 85th-anniversary trim was a new entry to the Softail family. The FXSTS rode with a front fork featuring chromed coil springs reminiscent of the earlier models. Although looking old was OK, the design was accomplished using the latest in high-tech CAD techniques. The Softail Springer featured a sculpted saddle, high, pullback bars, and laced wheels at both ends. The front fender rode high above the tire to allow for movement of the suspension. The entire FX series also received the stauncher 39mm front forks for 1988.

The FL lineup was a carryover from the 1987 model year.

Production

Model	Production
Model 88XLH-883 Standard	5,387
Model 88XLH-883 Hugger	4,501
Model 88XLH-883 Deluxe	1,893
Model 88XLH-1200	4,752
Model 88FXR	1,205
Model 88FXRP	565
Model 88FXRS	2,637
Model 88FXRS Sport	818
Model 88FXRS Anniversary	519
Model 88FXRT	243
Model 88FXLR	902
Model 88FXST	1,467
Model 88FXSTC	6,621
Model 88FXSTS Anniversary	1,356
Model 88FLST	2,209
Model 88FLSTC	3,755
Model 88FLHS	1,677
Model 88FLHTC	3,958
Model 88FLHTC Anniversary	715
Model 88FLTC	745
Model 88FLTC Anniversary	50

The FXSTS fuel tank wore the large winged-anniversary appliqués, and another piece of art was used on the 1988 Springer's front fender.

Numerous applications of anniversary badging were present on the 1988 FLSTS, as well as the other three specially marked models.

The 1989 FXRP was pressed into duty in police departments all across the U.S.

1989

The last year of the 1980s would prove to be one of incremental changes made across most of the Harley-Davidson lineup. A few new variations on existing machines would also show up at the local dealers.

All four versions of the Sportster would receive a few minor tweaks to help improve the breed. Internally, the pistons were fitted with offset piston pins. Beneath the chrome air cleaner cover, the air cleaner had an improved element. The intake manifold was aluminum, and all 1989 Harleys, including the Sportsters, had their positive battery cables coated for protection and longevity.

A new version of the FXRS was offered, and the Convertible model provided a windshield and saddlebags that could be quickly removed and replaced to fit the rider's daily needs. Forward-mounted pegs and a rear sissy bar completed the new package.

All FX models were given updated starters, a right-side flywheel that was integral to the one-piece pinion shaft, and the same coated battery lead as on the XLs. The FXR received these modifications and a new 32-amp alternator.

The entire line of FLs also ran with the newer 32-amp alternators and single-piece pinion shaft/flywheel used on the FX series. A first for the big bikes was the application of computer-controlled, self-canceling turn signals.

Two new Ultra variations were available for the FLTC and FLHT groups. The upgraded Ultra machines provided the rider and passenger with an unprecedented array of electronic options. Cruise control, CB radio, person-to-person intercoms, and rear mounted speakers with their own volume controls were all part of the enhanced FL models. Lower fairing extensions and unique graphics set the new touring machines apart from the crowd.

Basic radio and speaker mounting resided on the top of the fuel tank.

1989 Model Year Lineup

Model	Engine Type	Displacement	Transmission	Feature(s)
Model 89XLH883	Overhead-Valve Twin	883cc	Four-Speed	Standard Model
Model 89XLH883	Overhead-Valve Twin	883cc	Four-Speed	Hugger Model
Model 89XLH883	Overhead-Valve Twin	883cc	Four-Speed	Deluxe Model
Model 89XLH1200	Overhead-Valve Twin	1200cc	Four-Speed	—
Model 89FXR	Overhead-Valve Twin	80 cid	Five-Speed	Super Glide
Model 89FXRP	Overhead-Valve Twin	80 cid	Five-Speed	Police Model
Model 89FXRS	Overhead-Valve Twin	80 cid	Five-Speed	Low Rider
Model 89FXRS-Conv.	Overhead-Valve Twin	80 cid	Five-Speed	Convertible Model
Model 89FXRS-Sport	Overhead-Valve Twin	80 cid	Five-Speed	Low Rider Sport
Model 89FXRT	Overhead-Valve Twin	80 cid	Five-Speed	Sport Glide
Model 89FXLR	Overhead-Valve Twin	80 cid	Five-Speed	Low Rider Custom
Model 89FXST	Overhead-Valve Twin	80 cid	Five-Speed	Softail
Model 89FXSTC	Overhead-Valve Twin	80 cid	Five-Speed	Softail Custom
Model 89FXSTS	Overhead-Valve Twin	80 cid	Five-Speed	Springer Softail
Model 89FLST	Overhead-Valve Twin	80 cid	Five-Speed	Heritage Softail
Model 89FLSTC	Overhead-Valve Twin	80 cid	Five-Speed	Heritage Softail Custom
Model 89FLHS	Overhead-Valve Twin	80 cid	Five-Speed	Electra Glide Sport
Model 89FLHTC	Overhead-Valve Twin	80 cid	Five-Speed	Electra Glide Classic
Model 89FLHTCU	Overhead-Valve Twin	80 cid	Five-Speed	Electra Glide Classic Ultra
Model 89FLTC	Overhead-Valve Twin	80 cid	Five-Speed	Tour Glide Classic
Model 89FLTCU	Overhead-Valve Twin	80 cid	Five-Speed	Tour Glide Classic Ultra

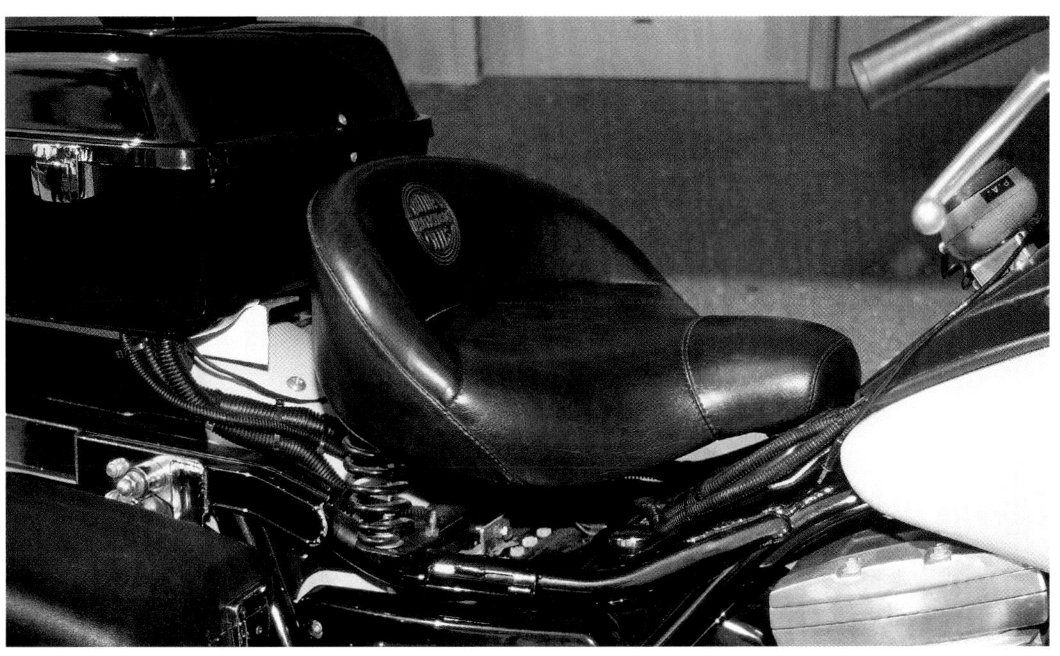

The 1989 FXRP solo pillion was a comfortable place from which to patrol the streets, and left room for the rear-mounted storage box.

Production

Model	Production
Model 89XLH-883 Standard	6,142
Model 89XLH-883 Hugger	4,467
Model 89XLH-883 Deluxe	1,812
Model 89XLH-1200	4,546
Model 89FXR	1,821
Model 89FXRP	780
Model 89FXRS	2,096
Model 89FXRS-Convertible	292
Model 89FXRS-SP	755
Model 89FXRT	255
Model 89FXLR	1,016
Model 89FXST	1,130
Model 89FXSTC	6,523
Model 89FXSTS	5,387
Model 89FLST	1,506
Model 89FLSTC	5,210
Model 89FLHS	2,330
Model 89FLHTC	3,969
Model 89FLHTCU	2,653
Model 89FLTC	588
Model 89FLTCU	530

Certified speedometers made for accurate readings on the FXRP, and "Police Special" was printed on the face of these gauges.

The Fat Boy was an all-new model for 1990 and was an immediate success.

1990

For yet another year, the majority of the catalog would receive minor modifications, but there was also another new face added to the family portrait, and it would become a favorite for many years to come.

The newest was another brainchild of Willie G. Davidson, Harley's master designer, and a descendent of the original founders. Based on a model from the Softail catalog, the new model would feature a long list of styling clues never before joined together. The name chosen was almost as outlandish as the machine: Fat Boy. Only the likes of a Harley-Davidson could carry off a title like that, while backing it up with a machine worthy of the moniker.

The FLSTF "Fat Boy" turned on a pair of solid disc wheels that were slid into 16-inch tires both fore and aft. The front fender was made of steel, and all new for the Fat Boy. The dual exhausts were arranged shotgun-style, and were dipped in chrome. The seat featured a leather insert that was textured differently than the rest of the saddle, and was paired up to a laced grab-strap and valance. The monochromatic silver paint was offset by a series of seven yellow accent stripes. Rumors of the origin for the colors and striping remain unfounded to this day.

Every motor in the fleet received several upgrades for 1990. The 40mm Keihn carburetors fitted with accelerator pumps provided seamless fuel delivery at any rpm. All models above the XL received clutch revisions that used seven plates to enhance power during take-offs and make the hand lever easier to operate.

Sportsters were now breathing through a paper filter element, and the rear fender bolts were fitted with copper washers. Additional paint selections made for greater variety at ordering time.

1990 Model Year Lineup

Model	Engine Type	Displacement	Transmission	Feature(s)
Model 90XLH883	Overhead-Valve Twin	883cc	Four-Speed	Standard Model
Model 90XLH883	Overhead-Valve Twin	883cc	Four-Speed	Hugger Model
Model 90XLH883	Overhead-Valve Twin	883cc	Four-Speed	Deluxe Model
Model 90XLH1200	Overhead-Valve Twin	1200cc	Five-Speed	—
Model 90FXR	Overhead-Valve Twin	80 cid	Five-Speed	Super Glide
Model 90FXRP	Overhead-Valve Twin	80 cid	Five-Speed	Police Model
Model 90FXRS	Overhead-Valve Twin	80 cid	Five-Speed	Low Rider
Model 90FXRS-Conv.	Overhead-Valve Twin	80 cid	Five-Speed	Low Rider Convertible
Model 90FXRS-SP	Overhead-Valve Twin	80 cid	Five-Speed	Low Rider Sport
Model 90FXRT	Overhead-Valve Twin	80 cid	Five-Speed	Sport Glide
Model 90FXLR	Overhead-Valve Twin	80 cid	Five-Speed	Low Rider Custom
Model 90FXST	Overhead-Valve Twin	80 cid	Five-Speed	Softail
Model 90FXSTC	Overhead-Valve Twin	80 cid	Five-Speed	Softail Custom
Model 90FXSTS	Overhead-Valve Twin	80 cid	Five-Speed	Springer Softail
Model 90FLST	Overhead-Valve Twin	80 cid	Five-Speed	Heritage Softail
Model 90FLSTC	Overhead-Valve Twin	80 cid	Five-Speed	Heritage Softail Custom
Model 90FLSTF	Overhead-Valve Twin	80 cid	Five-Speed	Fat Boy
Model 90FLHS	Overhead-Valve Twin	80 cid	Five-Speed	Electra Glide Sport
Model 90FLHTC	Overhead-Valve Twin	80 cid	Five-Speed	Electra Glide Classic
Model 90FLHTCU	Overhead-Valve Twin	80 cid	Five-Speed	Electra Glide Classic Ultra
Model 90FLTC	Overhead-Valve Twin	80 cid	Five-Speed	Tour Glide Classic
Model 90FLTCU	Overhead-Valve Twin	80 cid	Five-Speed	Tour Glide Classic Ultra

Seven stripes of yellow accented the silver paint scheme of the FLSTF.

FX models gained speedometers with improved lighting, and the Softails had leather saddlebags available that were styled to rekindle the 1950s look.

Ultra touring models featured an enhanced voice actuation system for the CB and intercom, as well as a cruise control with "resume" and "accelerate" options.

Production

Model	Production
Model 90XLH-883 Standard	5,227
Model 90XLH-883 Hugger	4,040
Model 90XLH-883 Deluxe	1,298
Model 90XLH-1200	4,598
Model 90FXR	1,819
Model 90FXRP	808
Model 90FXRS	2,615
Model 90FXRS Convertible	989
Model 90FXRS-SP	762
Model 90FXRT	304
Model 90FXLR	1,143
Model 90FXST	1,601
Model 90FXSTC	6,795
Model 90FXSTS	4,252
Model 90FLST	1,567
Model 90FLSTC	5,483
Model 90FLSTF	4,440
Model 90FLHS	2,410
Model 90FLHTC	3,497
Model 90FLHTCU	3,082
Model 90FLTC	476
Model 90FLTCU	575

Two of the many styling touches on the Fat Boy were the solid disc front wheel and all-steel front fender.

The FXDB Sturgis was back for another round in 1991, and was better than ever.

1991

Tradition and progress were the key words for 1991 as most of the models were improved, and yet another one was added to the roster. A few of last year's faces fell off the order sheets, but had been outsold by their "Classic" contemporaries anyway.

Big news on the Sportster front was the addition of a fifth gear in the transmission. The smaller cases had, for many years, proved too small to cram in another set of gears, but that was changed for the 1991 models. Another step forward was the application of belt drive on the standard and Deluxe XLs. The Hugger would be the last holdout to be driven by chain. In addition to these monumental alterations, smaller changes abounded on the Sportsters.

Inside the 883 and 1,200 cc motors, tappet blocks, the rear motor mount, and the oil filter mount were all integrated into the cases. The alternator's location was moved to the crankshaft, and one-piece pushrod tubes were used. Easier access was gained by the installation of the newly designed primary cover, and fluid capacity

The new frame design allowed for the use of only two rubber mounts, but provided plenty of stiffness.

The new frame also allowed the oil tank and pump to be integrated and mounted low beneath the transmission.

of the primary and transmission was brought to 40 ounces. Adjustment of the primary chain was also made easier.

Rubber-mounted passenger footpegs and self-canceling turn signals added comfort and safety to the entry-level machines.

The ever-expanding line of FX based machines grew by one, and it brought a whole new level of technology to the table. The FXDB Dyna Glide Sturgis was a kissing cousin to the first edition Sturgis, at least in looks. Designed entirely with the help of the latest CAD technology, the FXDB set the bar much higher for subsequent machines.

The balance of the FX family used a set of three rubber mounting points for the Evo motor, but the newly designed frame of the FXDB only needed two. The stiffness of the rectangular backbone allowed for more concise mounting points, thus eliminating one of the rubber mounts. The engine itself was similar to the other power plants from Harley-Davidson, but was different for the FXDB. The primary case casting was changed to alter the mounting angle of the motor by 4 degrees. This tilt of the V-twin allowed the assembly to be moved closer to the front of the frame. The long, low look of the FXDB was achieved by moving several components to new locations. The oil tank was located beneath the transmission and run with an internal pump. The new location also rid the machine of the unsightly oil lines running between tank and pump.

The rear forks were mounted in a new location to meet with the new frame design, and the front forks were mounted in a 32-degree rake. Both the 19-inch front wheel and 16-inch rear wheel received a brake disc of their own. The fuel tank had two filler caps, but only one was functional. The speedometer resided in the tank-mounted console. The all-black motif with hints of red striping remain classic to this day.

The entire Harley lineup, except for the XLs, received an assortment of upgrades for 1991. To enhance engine sealing, Kevlar base gaskets and Graphite head gaskets were employed. Gas cap gaskets were also improved. Self-canceling turn signals were finally included on every model. To facilitate easier mounting, dowel pins were added to the transmission cover and the support blocks.

The two Ultra models now featured an amplifier cutoff that was activated when using the CB or intercom. The FLTC and FLHTC also had relays installed into their brake lamp circuits.

1991 Model Year Lineup

Model	Engine Type	Displacement	Transmission	Feature(s)
Model 91XLH883	Overhead-Valve Twin	883cc	Five-Speed	Standard Model
Model 91XLH883	Overhead-Valve Twin	883cc	Five-Speed	Hugger Model
Model 91XLH883	Overhead-Valve Twin	883cc	Five-Speed	Deluxe model
Model 91XLH1200	Overhead-Valve Twin	1200cc	Five-Speed	—
Model 91FXR	Overhead-Valve Twin	80 cid	Five-Speed	Super Glide
Model 91FXRP	Overhead-Valve Twin	80 cid	Five-Speed	Police Model
Model 91FXRS	Overhead-Valve Twin	80 cid	Five-Speed	Low Rider
Model 91FXRS Conv.	Overhead-Valve Twin	80 cid	Five-Speed	Low Rider Convertible
Model 91FXRS-SP	Overhead-Valve Twin	80 cid	Five-Speed	Low Rider Sport
Model 91FXRT	Overhead-Valve Twin	80 cid	Five-Speed	Sport Glide
Model 91FXLR	Overhead-Valve Twin	80 cid	Five-Speed	Low Rider Custom
Model 91FXDB	Overhead-Valve Twin	80 cid	Five-Speed	Sturgis
Model 91FXSTC	Overhead-Valve Twin	80 cid	Five-Speed	Softail Custom
Model 91FXSTS	Overhead-Valve Twin	80 cid	Five-Speed	Springer Softail
Model 91FLSTC	Overhead-Valve Twin	80 cid	Five-Speed	Heritage Softail Custom
Model 91FLSTF	Overhead-Valve Twin	80 cid	Five-Speed	Fat Boy
Model 91FLHS	Overhead-Valve Twin	80 cid	Five-Speed	Electra Glide Sport
Model 91FLHTC	Overhead-Valve Twin	80 cid	Five-Speed	Electra Glide Classic
Model 91FLHTCU	Overhead-Valve Twin	80 cid	Five-Speed	Electra Glide Classic Ultra
Model 91FLTC	Overhead-Valve Twin	80 cid	Five-Speed	Tour Glide Classic
Model 91FLTCU	Overhead-Valve Twin	80 cid	Five-Speed	Tour Glide Classic Ultra

Production

Model	Production
Model 91XLH-883 Standard	4,922
Model 91XLH-883 Hugger	3,487
Model 91XLH-883 Deluxe	3,034
Model 91XLH-1200	6,282
Model 91FXR	272
Model 91FXRP	732
Model 91FXRS	2,183
Model 91FXRS-Convertible	1,721
Model 91FXRS-Sport	683
Model 91FXRT	NA
Model 91FXLR	1,197
Model 91FXDB	1,546
Model 91FXSTC	7,525
Model 91FXSTS	4,265
Model 91FLSTC	8,950
Model 91FLSTF	5,581
Model 91FLHS	2,383
Model 91FLHTC	90
Model 91FLHTCU	3,204
Model 91FLTC	250
Model 91FLTCU	458

The 1992 FXDB was back, but came in Daytona trim to celebrate the 50th year of the Florida rally.

1992

Harley-Davidson was fast approaching its 90th anniversary, but still provided the market with two new models for the year before the big party. As was typical, the balance of the catalog received minor advancements as well.

In the Sportster camp, the Hugger had its rear suspension truncated again, that, along with thinner padding in the seat, resulted in the lowest Hugger ever. The rest of the alterations affected all of the XLs. Many of the changes were also seen on the other models. Brake pad material was improved, and grease fittings made required maintenance an easier chore. The new grease fittings were applied across the entire catalog. A halogen headlight resided in a modified housing. All Sportsters now shared common hand controls. A new horn was installed on most models, Sportsters included. Fuel tanks were vented continuously, and this also applied to the remainder of the 1992 models.

The two new models were in the FX family, and based on the previous year's high-tech Sturgis. The FXDB was now done in a Daytona motif to mark 50 years of the annual Florida rally. Indigo blue metallic paint was contrasted by gold pearlglo, and the cast wheels and rear belt sprocket were finished in gold tone. The Daytona braked with a matching pair of discs up front and a third on the rear wheel. All brake pads were of the newest composition.

1992 Model Year Lineup

Model	Engine Type	Displacement	Transmission	Feature(s)
Model 92XLH883	Overhead-Valve Twin	883cc	Five-Speed	Standard
Model 92XLH883	Overhead-Valve Twin	883cc	Five-Speed	Hugger
Model 92XLH883	Overhead-Valve Twin	883cc	Five-Speed	Deluxe
Model 92XLH1200	Overhead-Valve Twin	1,200cc	Five-Speed	—
Model 92FXR	Overhead-Valve Twin	80 cid	Five-Speed	Super Glide
Model 92FXRP	Overhead-Valve Twin	80 cid	Five-Speed	Police Model
Model 92FXRS-Conv.	Overhead-Valve Twin	80 cid	Five-Speed	Low Rider Convertible
Model 92FXRS-SP	Overhead-Valve Twin	80 cid	Five-Speed	Low Rider Sport
Model 92FXRT	Overhead-Valve Twin	80 cid	Five-Speed	Sport Glide
Model 92FXLR	Overhead-Valve Twin	80 cid	Five-Speed	Low Rider Custom
Model 92FXDB	Overhead-Valve Twin	80 cid	Five-Speed	Daytona
Model 92FXDC	Overhead-Valve Twin	80 cid	Five-Speed	Super Dyna Glide Custom
Model 92FXSTC	Overhead-Valve Twin	80 cid	Five-Speed	Softail Custom
Model 92FXSTS	Overhead-Valve Twin	80 cid	Five-Speed	Springer Softail
Model 92FLSTC	Overhead-Valve Twin	80 cid	Five-Speed	Heritage Softail Classic
Model 92FLSTF	Overhead-Valve Twin	80 cid	Five-Speed	Fat Boy
Model 92FLHS	Overhead-Valve Twin	80 cid	Five-Speed	Electra Glide Sport
Model 92FLHTC	Overhead-Valve Twin	80 cid	Five-Speed	Electra Glide Classic
Model 92FLHTCU	Overhead-Valve Twin	80 cid	Five-Speed	Electra Glide Classic Ultra
Model 92FLTC	Overhead-Valve Twin	80 cid	Five-Speed	Tour Glide Classic
Model 92FLTCU	Overhead-Valve Twin	80 cid	Five-Speed	Tour Glide Classic Ultra

Only 1,700 copies of FXDB were assembled, making it a rare model.

The second new face in the FX clan was the FXDC. Its hardware was the same as the FXDB, but the color scheme was radically different. The frame was powder coated in silver to match the silver and black paint of the sheet metal. The engine and transmission were left in their raw aluminum state, but were fitted with a number of chromed covers. The brakes was the same as on the FXDB, including the improved pad material. The halogen headlight was applied to the FXDC as well. 1992 was the only year the FXDC was built, making it another difficult find.

The following changes were made to all the FX and Softail models for 1992. Camshaft bearings now had caged-needle style, and the neutral switch held a harder plunger. The grease fittings were found in numerous locations, and the louder horn was also installed. With the exception of the Fat Boy, all FX and ST models received the halogen headlight.

The FLHS rode with a saddle lower to the ground and was given new seals on the saddlebags.

FLTC and FLHTC variants sported glossy finishes inside their-rear mounted trunks, and also had the enhanced saddlebag seals. As with the FXs and STs, the FLs had caged needle bearings at the camshaft, new grease fittings, and more audible horns.

Production

(Production numbers for individual models are not available)

Sportster	17,623
FX and ST	48,177
Touring	10,695

Only 1,700 of the FXDBs were built for 1992, and the tank art told the story.

The 1993 FLSTN was unofficially named the "Cow Glide" due to the creative use of bovine inserts on the seat and saddlebags. It was officially known as the "Nostalgia."

1993

Harley-Davidson celebrated its 90th year of uninterrupted production in 1993. A series of anniversary models were rolled out along with two new versions built on the Dyna Glide chassis.

For the first time, the Hugger was driven by belt, just like its siblings had been since 1991. The only other change to the Sportsters was the use of the new "low-profile" clutch and brake hand levers. These new levers were applied to every model for 1993. The XLH-1200 was also available in the 90th Anniversary trim, which included silver and metallic gray paint, along with anniversary badges on several locations.

The first new model for 1993 was the FXDWG, or Dyna Wide Glide. Based on the revolutionary Dyna chassis, the new Wide Glide was assembled with a vast array of custom touches. The 21-inch front wheel was spoked, and rode between widely spaced fork downtubes. A single brake disc was in place to help slow the new model. The 16-inch rear wheel was also spoked, and had its own disc brake. The rear fender was bobbed, and contained a partially concealed taillight. The factory-installed "Ape Hanger" bars reached back over an enlarged Fat Bob fuel tank. The two-place seat offered plenty of comfort for long days in the saddle. The FXDWG was available in several color schemes, as well as in the special 90th Anniversary trim.

The second new variation on the Dyna theme was the FXDL Dyna Low Rider. Utilizing the same chassis as the FXDWG, the

1993 Model Year Lineup

Model	Engine Type	Displacement	Transmission	Feature(s)
Model 93XLH883	Overhead-Valve Twin	883cc	Five-Speed	Standard
Model 93XLH883	Overhead-Valve Twin	883cc	Five-Speed	Hugger/Final Belt Drive
Model 93XLH883	Overhead-Valve Twin	883cc	Five-Speed	Deluxe
Model 93XLH1200	Overhead-Valve Twin	1200cc	Five-Speed	—
Model 93FXR	Overhead-Valve Twin	80 cid	Five-Speed	Super Glide
Model 93FXLR	Overhead-Valve Twin	80 cid	Five-Speed	Low Rider Custom
Model 93FXRP	Overhead-Valve Twin	80 cid	Five-Speed	Police Model
Model 93FXRS-SP	Overhead-Valve Twin	80 cid	Five-Speed	Low Rider Sport
Model 93FXRS-Conv.	Overhead-Valve Twin	80 cid	Five-Speed	Low Rider Convertible
Model 93FXDWG	Overhead-Valve Twin	80 cid	Five-Speed	Dyna Wide Glide
Model 93FXDL	Overhead-Valve Twin	80 cid	Five-Speed	Dyna Low Rider
Model 93FXSTC	Overhead-Valve Twin	80 cid	Five-Speed	Softail Custom
Model 93FXSTS	Overhead-Valve Twin	80 cid	Five-Speed	Springer Softail
Model 93FLSTF	Overhead-Valve Twin	80 cid	Five-Speed	Fat Boy
Model 93FLSTC	Overhead-Valve Twin	80 cid	Five-Speed	Heritage Softail Classic
Model 93FLSTN	Overhead-Valve Twin	80 cid	Five-Speed	Heritage Softail Nostalgia
Model 93FLHS	Overhead-Valve Twin	80 cid	Five-Speed	Electra Glide Sport
Model 93FLHTC	Overhead-Valve Twin	80 cid	Five-Speed	Electra Glide Classic
Model 93FLHTCU	Overhead-valve Twin	80 cid	Five-Speed	Electra Glide Classic Ultra
Model 93FLTCU	Overhead-Valve Twin	80 cid	Five-Speed	Tour Glide Classic Ultra

DL featured a traditional front fork with cast wheels at both ends. Dual discs up front and a single on the rear wheel insured stopping power. The rear section of the seat could be easily removed for one-up riding, and the engine was brightly polished.

The remaining FX series received the new low-profile hand levers, but otherwise remained the same. The FXLR was also available in the 90th Anniversary trim.

Minor changes were also found in the Softail line. The low-profile levers were used on each model, and the FLSTS received a floating front fender. This allowed the fender to be mounted closer to the tire, since it moved in unison with the wheel. The Heritage was offered in a Nostalgia edition, which delivered black and white paint with matching "cow" inserts on the seat and saddlebags: The "Cow Glide" was born.

The three FL models shared the same list of enhancements. Low-profile hand levers were applied, and the battery was relocated beneath the seat. A remote oil reservoir was located beneath the engine and transmission. Saddlebag capacity was increased by 15 percent, and the lids were now hinged. The FLTCU, FLHTC, and FLHTCU were also offered in a variety of colors, as well as the 90th Anniversary livery.

More than 100,000 riders attended the big anniversary party thrown in Milwaukee, and it would not be the last time a gathering of this nature would occur.

Production

Sportsters	22,247
FX and ST	49,004
Touring	10,445

This 1993 "Cowglide" seems right at home grazing at a roadside rest stop.

The 1994 FLHTCU was the flagship of the Harley-Davidson lineup, and provided enough amenities to carry a rider and a passenger in comfort and style.

1994

One year after its big 90th birthday bash, The Motor Company continued its ceaseless pace in bringing new and improved models to the sales floor.

Every model except the Sportsters received a smaller sprocket at the clutch basket and a larger sprocket at the engine. A catalog-wide modification was the use of an interference-fit, carburetor float-pin pedestal.

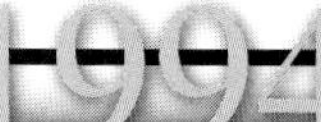

At the heart of every modern Harley is the thundering V-Twin power plant, and this big bagger is no exception.

1994 Model Year Lineup				
Model	**Engine Type**	**Displacement**	**Transmission**	**Feature(s)**
Model 94XLH883	Overhead-Valve Twin	883cc	Five-Speed	Standard
Model 94XLH883	Overhead-Valve Twin	883cc	Five-Speed	Hugger
Model 94XLH883	Overhead-Valve Twin	883cc	Five-Speed	Deluxe
Model 94XLH1200	Overhead-Valve Twin	1200cc	Five-Speed	—
Model 94FXR	Overhead-Valve Twin	80 cid	Five-Speed	Super Glide
Model 94FXLR	Overhead-Valve Twin	80 cid	Five-Speed	Low Rider Custom
Model 94FXRP	Overhead-Valve Twin	80 cid	Five-Speed	Police Model
Model 94FXDS-Conv.	Overhead-Valve Twin	80 cid	Five-Speed	Low Rider Convertible
Model 94FXDWG	Overhead-Valve Twin	80 cid	Five-Speed	Dyna Wide Glide
Model 94FXDL	Overhead-Valve Twin	80 cid	Five-Speed	Dyne Low Rider
Model 94FXSTC	Overhead-Valve Twin	80 cid	Five-Speed	Softail Custom
Model 94FXSTS	Overhead-Valve Twin	80 cid	Five-Speed	Springer Softail
Model 94FLSTF	Overhead-Valve Twin	80 cid	Five-Speed	Fat Boy
Model 94FLSTC	Overhead-Valve Twin	80 cid	Five-Speed	Heritage Softail Classic
Model 94FLSTN	Overhead-Valve Twin	80 cid	Five-Speed	Heritage Softail Nostalgia
Model 94FLHR	Overhead-Valve Twin	80 cid	Five-Speed	Road King
Model 94FLHTC	Overhead-Valve Twin	80 cid	Five-Speed	Electra Glide Classic
Model 94FLHTCU	Overhead-Valve Twin	80 cid	Five-Speed	Electra Glide Classic Ultra
Model 94FLTCU	Overhead-Valve Twin	80 cid	Five-Speed	Tour Glide Classic Ultra

The FXRS Sport was discontinued, as was the FXRS Convertible. In place of the FXRS Convertible came the FXDS Convertible. The DS was built on the latest Dyna chassis, but the remaining features were the same as the previous model.

The FLSTN "Cow Glide" was back, but trimmed in different paint and "skin." The latest version wore white and silver paint with all-black "heifer" inserts.

The FLHS Electra Glide Sport was superceded by a new entrant—the Road King. The FLHR was built using many of the same design elements as the Sport, but further details set it apart. Up front, an enormous nacelle housed the headlight assembly. The suspension was adjustable with the use of the on-board air system, and the rear section of the saddle could be easily removed. A trio of disc brakes stopped the Road King, and 16-inch cast spoke wheels were used at both ends.

The Ultra touring machines now had their "set/resume" cruise control switches sealed for improved wet-weather durability.

Production	
Sportsters	26,466
FX and ST	52,046
Touring	17,299

The Bad Boy was a new model for 1995, and was based on the Springer Softail.

1995

For the 1995 models, all the previous variations on the FXR theme were now FXD based, as the Dyna chassis moved into a more permanent home. Another new Softail was added to the sales sheets as well, along with an anniversary touring model.

The only change to the Sportsters was the addition of an electronic speedometer with a re-setable tripmeter. This new gauge would also find its way onto the FXD and FLHR models as well.

The FXR was supplanted by the FXD, which used the Dyna chassis. The staggered exhaust and nine-spoke cast wheels were the only other modifications besides the electronic speedometer. The FXRS-Convertible also became the FXDS-Convertible, with no other changes.

The new Dyna model to make the grade was the FXSTSB Bad Boy. Based on the FXSTS, the Bad Boy was cloaked in black, starting at the steel springer forks. The staggered shorty exhaust added a touch of attitude, as did the contrasting-scallop tank graphics. The front wheel was spoked, while the rear hoop was a slotted disc. A pair of floating rotor disc brakes brought the Bad Boy into the future, as well as to a safe stop.

The FLSTN Nostalgia was replaced with the FLSTN Heritage Softail Special. The FLSTN was longer trimmed with animal skin, but still wrapped in two-tone paint and highlighted with "Fat Boy" style badges.

The front Springer forks were blacked out, giving the Bad Boy an ominous appearance.

1995 Model Year Lineup				
Model	**Engine Type**	**Displacement**	**Transmission**	**Feature(s)**
Model 95XLH883	Overhead-Valve Twin	883cc	Five-Speed	Standard
Model 95XLH883	Overhead-Valve Twin	883cc	Five-Speed	Hugger
Model 95XLH883	Overhead-Valve Twin	883cc	Five-Speed	Deluxe
Model 95XLH1200	Overhead-Valve Twin	1200cc	Five-Speed	—
Model 95FXD	Overhead-Valve Twin	80 cid	Five-Speed	Dyna Super Glide
Model 95FXDS-Conv.	Overhead-Valve Twin	80 cid	Five-Speed	Dyna Convertible
Model 95FXDWG	Overhead-Valve Twin	80 cid	Five-Speed	Dyna Wide Glide
Model 95FXDL	Overhead-Valve Twin	80 cid	Five-Speed	Dyna Low Rider
Model 95FXSTC	Overhead-Valve Twin	80 cid	Five-Speed	Softail Custom
Model 95FXSTS	Overhead-Valve Twin	80 cid	Five-Speed	Springer Softail
Model 95FXSTSB	Overhead-Valve Twin	80 cid	Five-Speed	Bad Boy
Model 95FLSTF	Overhead-Valve Twin	80 cid	Five-Speed	Fat Boy
Model 95FLSTC	Overhead-Valve Twin	80 cid	Five-Speed	Heritage Softail Classic
Model 95FLSTN	Overhead-Valve Twin	80 cid	Five-Speed	Heritage Softail Special
Model 95FLHR	Overhead-Valve Twin	80 cid	Five-Speed	Road King
Model 95FLHT	Overhead-Valve Twin	80 cid	Five-Speed	Electra Glide Standard
Model 95FLHTC	Overhead-Valve Twin	80 cid	Five-Speed	Electra Glide Classic
Model 95FLHTCU	Overhead-Valve Twin	80 cid	Five-Speed	Electra Glide Classic Ultra
Model 95FLHTCUI	Overhead-Valve Twin	80 cid	Five-Speed	Electra Glide Classic Ultra w/ Fuel Inj.
Model 95FLTCU	Overhead-Valve Twin	80 cid	Five-Speed	Tour Glide Classic Ultra

The black paint was accented by red scallops and a cloisonné badge on the 1995 Bad Boy.

The FLHT Electra Glide Standard was again offered, but was complete with more conveniences than before. A full array of instrumentation included tripmeter, tachometer, fuel gauge, voltmeter, and an oil-pressure indicator. Air-adjustable suspension and the fork-mounted fairing helped to keep both rider and passenger comfortable. The hard-sided saddlebags were secured with barrel-type locks for extra safety. An accessory plug made the use of radar detectors or other devices far more convenient.

To mark the passing of 30 years since its inception, another Electra Glide hit the streets. The FLHTCUI was based on the flagship Ultra, but had sequential port fuel injection in place of the carburetor. This was a first for Harley-Davidson, and would begin. The "I" also wore commemorative badges and a special "Vivid Black" and "Burgundy Pearl" paint scheme.

Production	
Sportsters	29,625
FXD and ST	54,456
Touring	21,023

The slotted rear disc wheel was mated to a floating rotor brake—another first for Harley.

1996

1996 Model Year Lineup

Model	Engine Type	Displacement	Transmission	Feature(s)
Model 96XLH883	Overhead-Valve Twin	883cc	Five-Speed	Standard
Model 96XLH883	Overhead-Valve Twin	883cc	Five-Speed	Hugger
Model 96XLH1200	Overhead-Valve Twin	1200cc	Five-Speed	Standard
Model 96XLH1200C	Overhead-Valve Twin	1200cc	Five-Speed	Custom
Model 96XLH1200S	Overhead-Valve Twin	1200cc	Five-Speed	Sport
Model 96FXD	Overhead-Valve Twin	80 cid	Five-Speed	Dyna Super Glide
Model 96FXDS-Conv.	Overhead-Valve Twin	80 cid	Five-Speed	Dyna Convertible
Model 96FXDWG	Overhead-Valve Twin	80 cid	Five-Speed	Dyna Wide Glide
Model 96FXDL	Overhead-Valve Twin	80 cid	Five-Speed	Dyna Low Rider
Model 96FXSTC	Overhead-Valve Twin	80 cid	Five-Speed	Softail Custom
Model 96FXSTS	Overhead-Valve Twin	80 cid	Five-Speed	Springer Softail
Model 96FXSTSB	Overhead-Valve Twin	80 cid	Five-Speed	Bad Boy
Model 96FLSTF	Overhead-Valve Twin	80 cid	Five-Speed	Fat Boy
Model 96FLSTC	Overhead-Valve Twin	80 cid	Five-Speed	Heritage Softail Classic
Model 96FLSTN	Overhead-Vlave Twin	80 cid	Five-Speed	Heritage Softail Special
Model 96FLHT	Overhead-Valve Twin	80 cid	Five-Speed	Electra Glide Standard
Model 96FLHR	Overhead-Valve Twin	80 cid	Five-Speed	Road King
Model 96FLHRI	Overhead-Valve Twin	80 cid	Five-Speed	Road King w/Fuel Injection
Model 96FLHTC	Overhead-Valve Twin	80 cid	Five-Speed	Electra Glide Classic
Model 96FLHTCI	Overhead-Valve Twin	80 cid	Five-Speed	Electra Glide Classic w/Fuel Injection
Model 96FLHTCU	Overhead-Valve Twin	80 cid	Five-Speed	Electra Glide Classic Ultra
Model 96FLHTCUI	Overhead-Valve Twin	80 cid	Five-Speed	Electra Glide Classic Ultra w/Fuel Injec.
Model 96FLTCUI	Overhead-Valve Twin	80 cid	Five-Speed	Tour Glide Classic w/Fuel Injection

In terms of actual model changes for 1996, there were few, but previous offerings were expanded upon and improved.

The XL collection would lose one listing, and gain two in its stead. The XLH-883 Deluxe was no longer available, but two more versions of the XLH-1200 fell into place.

The 1200 Custom featured many details previously found on larger models. The rear wheel was a slotted disc, and both front and rear brakes were floating rotor discs. The 1200C flaunted a lower seat height, a newly shaped fuel tank complete with cloisonné badges, and a crinkle black and chrome engine package.

The 1200 Sport model featured cast, 13-spoke wheels, a triple set of floating rotor brakes, and fully adjustable suspension at both ends. The "flat track" handlebars and two-position seat finished off the list of exclusive features.

The base XLH-1200 was still available, and was unchanged.

All machines that didn't receive the electronic speedometers last year were fitted with them this year. This included the Softail and Springer models.

With the exception of the FLTCUI, every touring machine in the lineup could now be purchased with a carburetor or the latest sequential port fuel injection system. There were many who opted for the trouble-free injection system, while others preferred the old school method of fuel delivery.

Production

Sportsters	31,173
FXD and ST	63,198
Touring	24,400

The Ol' Boy was introduced for 1997, and was reminiscent of the '40s Harleys.

1997

With the loss of two models, and the introduction of another, it was a quiet year for the catalog. Minor advances were made throughout the lineup.

Sportsters were all fitted with the larger 3.3-gallon tank for 1997, and the 883 versions received new tank graphics. A maintenance-free battery provided some extra starting power. Reduced restriction on the exhaust systems provided better

The Ol' Boy pillion and saddlebags were complete with fringe, sconces, and tooling.

The valanced front fender rode above the spoked wheel and whitewall tire, adding another touch of yesteryear.

1997 Model Year Lineup				
Model	**Engine Type**	**Displacement**	**Transmission**	**Feature(s)**
Model 97XLH883	Overhead-Valve Twin	883cc	Five-Speed	Standard
Model 97XLH883	Overhead-Valve Twin	883cc	Five-Speed	Hugger
Model 97XLH1200	Overhead-Valve Twin	1200cc	Five-Speed	Standard
Model 97XLH1200C	Overhead-Valve Twin	1200cc	Five-Speed	Custom
Model 97XLH1200S	Overhead-Valve Twin	1200cc	Five-Speed	Sport
Model 97FXD	Overhead-Valve Twin	80 cid	Five-Speed	Dyna Super Glide
Model 97FXDS-Conv.	Overhead-Valve Twin	80 cid	Five-Speed	Dyna Convertible
Model 97FXDWG	Overhead-Valve Twin	80 cid	Five-Speed	Dyna Wide Glide
Model 97FXDL	Overhead-Valve Twin	80 cid	Five-Speed	Dyna Low Rider
Model 97FXSTC	Overhead-Valve Twin	80 cid	Five-Speed	Softail Custom
Model 97FXSTS	Overhead-Valve Twin	80 cid	Five-Speed	Springer Softail
Model 97FXSTSB	Overhead-Valve Twin	80 cid	Five-Speed	Bad Boy
Model 97FLSTF	Overhead-Valve Twin	80 cid	Five-Speed	Fat Boy
Model 97FLSTC	Overhead-Valve Twin	80 cid	Five-Speed	Heritage Softail Classic
Model 97FLSTS	Overhead-Valve Twin	80 cid	Five-Speed	Heritage Springer/Ol' Boy
Model 97FLHT	Overhead-Valve Twin	80 cid	Five-Speed	Electra Glide Standard
Model 97FLHR	Overhead-Valve Twin	80 cid	Five-Speed	Road King
Model 97FLHRI	Overhead-Valve Twin	80 cid	Five-Speed	Road King w/Fuel Inj.
Model 97FLHTC	Overhead-Valve Twin	80 cid	Five-Speed	Electra Glide Classic
Model 97FLHTCI	Overhead-Valve Twin	80 cid	Five-Speed	Electra Glide Classic w/Fuel Inj.
Model 97FLHTCU	Overhead-Valve Twin	80 cid	Five-Speed	Electra Glide Classic Ultra
Model 97FLHTCUI	Overhead-Valve Twin	80 cid	Five-Speed	Electra Glide Classic Ultra w/Fuel Inj.

breathing. The standard 1200 Sportster received a two-piece saddle with a rear section that was easily removed for solo riding.

The only change to the Dyna models was the addition of the same sealed, maintenance-free battery used on the Sportsters.

The Springer lineup was joined by a new model that harkened back to the early days of Harley history. The FLSTS Heritage Springer was nicknamed the "Ol' Boy" and the style seemed to fit the name. The front wheel was protected by a heavily valanced fender, and was adorned with a light-up ornament. Both wire wheels were teamed up with wide-whitewall tires. The seat and saddlebags were covered in tooled leather and trimmed with fringe and sconces. The piping used matches the stripe on the fuel tank, in either red or blue. The cross-over, dual exhaust pipes were finished off with fishtail outlets. A tombstone taillight completed the trip down memory lane.

The FLHT and FLHR models rode on new frames that delivered a lower saddle height, but were otherwise unchanged. The FLHTCU now claimed a cruise control complete with "tap-up-tap-down" speed control, and an am/fm/cassette radio that also included a weather band. Dual antennas rounded up the features list on the latest heavy hitter. The FLTCU was no longer offered.

Production	
Sportsters	31,453
FXD and ST	70,724
Touring	30,108

The FLTR was a new model based on an old model, but boasted a host of upgraded features.

1998

The 1998 model year would represent the 95th year of production for Harley-Davidson, and in typical fashion, anniversary models were made available along with the customary offerings. Due to the pending enormous change that was pending in the motor department, very few alterations were made to the '98 models.

The 1200S Sportster was treated to several enhancements, both in cosmetics and performance. The cylinder heads of the '98 1200S were fitted with dual spark plugs for an improved burn pattern of the compressed air/fuel mixture. The new design also allowed for a higher compression ration of 10.0:1, compared to the standard 9.0:1 of the other 1200 Sportys. The dual spark heads and higher compression also boosted the torque rating to 78.0 @ 4000 rpm—an increase of 7.0.

Cosmetically, the 1200S was cloaked in an almost completely black ensemble, with the exception of various engine parts that were powder coated in silver. The cast wheels of the Sport model were shod with soft-compound tires for an extra measure of performance on the street. Floating-rotor brakes assisted in slowing the high-performance S.

Based on the Tour Glide, which had taken its final bow a few years before, the new FLTR Road Glide featured a similar frame-mounted fairing for the long-distance riders. Leading the way was a new pair of elliptical headlights that were housed beneath a shroud of curved Plexiglass. Behind the fairing sat a wraparound instrument panel that housed a full bank of gauges. If purchased with a stereo, the rider got new and improved controls to allow for easier adjustments while on the road. The Road Glide was available in either carbureted or fuel-injected versions.

The FLHR Road King was dolled up, and available in Classic trim, along with the standard Road King model. The FLHRCI was only delivered with fuel injection, but the list of standard equipment included spoked wheels, wide whitewall tires, and leather, hard-sided saddlebags.

Muffler tips were cut at the same angle as the rakish bags. Tooling on the leather surfaces helped to set the Classic model apart from the other Road Kings. The fuel tank, fenders, and seat valance also wore metal emblems cast in 3-D. The FLHRCI was offered in factory colors, or the 95th anniversary trim.

Production

Model	Production
Sportsters	33,892
FXD and ST	77,434
Touring	39,492

The XL1200C could also be had in the Midnight Red and Champagne Pearl 95th anniversary trim.

1998 Model Year Lineup

Model	Engine Type	Displacement	Transmission	Feature(s)
Model 98XLH883	Overhead-Valve Twin	883cc	Five-Speed	Standard
Model 98XLH883	Overhead-Valve Twin	883cc	Five-Speed	Hugger
Model 98XL1200	Overhead-Valve Twin	1200cc	Five-Speed	Standard
Model 98XL1200C	Overhead-Valve Twin	1200cc	Five-Speed	Custom
Model 98XL1200S	Overhead-Valve Twin	1200cc	Five-Speed	Sport
Model 98FXDL	Overhead-Valve Twin	88 cid	Five-Speed	Dyna Low Rider
Model 98FXD	Overhead-Valve Twin	88 cid	Five-Speed	Dyna Super Glide
Model 98FXD-Conv.	Overhead-Valve Twin	88 cid	Five-Speed	Dyna Convertible
Model 98FXDWG	Overhead-Valve Twin	88 cid	Five-Speed	Dyna Wide Glide
Model 98FLSTC	Overhead-Valve Twin	88 cid	Five-Speed	Heritage Softail Classic
Model 98FXSTC	Overhead-Valve Twin	88cid	Five-Speed	Softail Custom
Model 98FLSTS	Overhead-Valve Twin	88 cid	Five-Speed	Heritage Springer
Model 98FXSTS	Overhead-Valve Twin	88 cid	Five-Speed	Springer Softail
Model 98FLSTF	Overhead-Valve Twin	88 cid	Five-Speed	Fat Boy
Model 98FLTR	Overhead-Valve Twin	88 cid	Five-Speed	Road Glide
Model 98FLTRI	Overhead-Valve Twin	88 cid	Five-Speed	Road Glide w/ Fuel Injection
Model 98FLHT	Overhead-Valve Twin	88 cid	Five-Speed	Electra Glide Standard
Model 98FLHTC	Overhead-Valve Twin	88 cid	Five-Speed	Electra Glide Classic
Model 98FLHTCI	Overhead-Valve Twin	88 cid	Five-Speed	Electra Glide Classic w/Fuel Injection
Model 98FLHTCUI	Overhead-Valve Twin	88 cid	Five-Speed	Electra Glide Classic Ultra w/ Fuel Injection
Model 98FLHR	Overhead-Valve Twin	88 cid	Five-Speed	Road King
Model 98FLHRCI	Overhead-Valve Twin	88 cid	Five-Speed	Road King Classic w/Fuel Injection

The 1998 FLSTS was offered in Vivid Black with either red or blue trim, as well as the two-tone anniversary paint.

A New Era of Harley-Davidson Power Moves In

1936 was the last year that Harley-Davidson offered a completely new power plant for its machines. The Knucklehead featured overhead valves, and set the stage for the next six decades of engine design. Subsequent motors were loosely based on the lower end of the Knucklehead, with new valvetrains attached. 1999 would witness the introduction of the next big thing for the fabled Milwaukee builder.

The newest motor shares only 18 parts with its predacessor, and is enhanced in almost every dimension. Displacement has risen from 1340 cc's, which is just over 80 cubic inches to 1450 cc's for a new total of 88 cubic inches. Hence the "Twin-Cam 88" moniker. The new slang would become the "Fathead."

In order to meet with both styling and noise guidelines, a different method needed to be employed for driving the camshaft. After several explorations, a twin-cam layout was agreed upon. This simplified the mechanics and provided a quieter, less troublesome method of pushrod activation. The valves are still mounted on top of the cylinders, but now reside beneath a split housing. The housing allows access to the valves, while the motor is still in the frame. Valve position is unchanged from the Evo motor, but reshaped combustion chambers provide better burning of the air/fuel mix. The resulting 9.0:1 compression ratio does require premium fuel, but it's a small price to pay for the added performance. The Dyna models fitted with the new motor will breath through the same Keihin carburetor as the Evo, while some of the other models will get fuel injection.

The crankshaft of the 88 weighs 2 lbs. more than the Evo's, and utilizes a crankpin 40 percent larger. Almost every internal bearing was enhanced to meet with the needs of the bigger, stronger motor.

Design of the all-new cases was the result of thousands of hours on a computer. Every component was tested on a computer screen for maximum strength before it became real.

Cooling fins on the cylinders are larger than ever before to combat heat under extreme conditions, and oil is sprayed on the bottom of the pistons to assist in keeping temperatures within boundaries. Cylinder bore was increased by 1/4 inch to 3.75, and the thickness of the casting would allow performance motors to reach a displacement of 1550 cc's.

Lubrication was provided and improved with an internal, crank-driven geroter oil pump.

The shape of the new air cleaner might be described as a football with flattened ends, but it is easy to tell the new design from the old. Depending on the model it's mounted to, it can be finished in chrome or black crinkle paint.

An overall increase of nearly 10 hp was gained over the Evo, but more importantly the Twin-Cam 88 provides Harley-Davidson with a motor that can live on for many years to come.

Harley-Davidson reached new heights with the Twin-Cam 88.

The 1999 FLHRI embodied the spirit of the giant touring models, but was a more compact package.

1999

The new Twin-Cam 88 stole most of the headlines for the model year, but other changes were afoot. Not all models received the newest motor, and there were again changes to the lineup.

The Sportster clan introduced another member in the XL883 Custom. All of the Sportsters would remain Evo powered, but the Custom featured several bits to set it apart. Up front was a 21-inch spoked wheel. A single speedometer rested between the grips of the flat drag bars, and the forward controls added another bit of attitude.

The 1200 Sport was the recipient of a performance-enhanced motor for 1999. The better-performing engine added to the existing sporting nature of the suspension. To help slow the Sport model, four-piston calipers grabbed a trio of 11 1/2-inch brake rotors mounted to the cast-spoke wheels.

The Dyna models would all be fitted with the new Fathead motor, and a previous model would return for the new year. The FXDX, or Dyna Super Glide Sport, was previously the FXDS. Powered by the new motor, the FXDX delivered a new level of performance to the sporting variant. As with all the Dynas for the year, a 40mm Keihin carburetor was on duty at the fuel delivery point. Cast wheels were the factory default, but wire rims could be added as an option. The Dyna line also received a new taillight assembly that was sealed to eliminate internal condensation from forming, and ran off of a circuit board, instead of the old wiring.

Two new Softail models were also shown for 1999. The FXST Softail Standard listed for only $11,999, and was available only in black. The second model, clothed in an all-black motif, was the FXSTB Night Train. Three different black finishes were applied to the Night Train. Wrinkle, texture, and gloss made their way onto the new model. Anything that wasn't black was finished in chrome.

The Night Train, like all the other ST models was still motivated by the Evo motor, but the darkened engine and sheet metal added a touch of drama. The 16-inch solid disc rear wheel was teamed up with a 21-inch front wire wheel, and a pair of disc brakes did the slowing.

The full line of Softails were fitted with upgraded electronic speedometers that allowed for on-board diagnostics.

Touring machines would all receive the latest 88 power plant, but only selected models would be available with the latest in electronic fuel injection. The biggest FL models were assisted by the addition of an integrated rear brake reservoir, and a master cylinder located near the pedal. Road Kings got the electronic speedometer complete with diagnostic functions.

1999 Model Year Lineup

Model	Engine Type	Displacement	Transmission	Feature(s)
Model 99XLH883	Overhead-Valve Twin	883cc	Five-Speed	Standard
Model 99XLH883	Overhead-Valve Twin	883cc	Five-Speed	Hugger
Model 99XL883C	Overhead-Valve Twin	883cc	Five-Speed	Custom
Model 99XLH1200	Overhead-Valve Twin	1200cc	Five-Speed	Standard
Model 99XL1200S	Overhead-Valve Twin	1200cc	Five-Speed	Sport
Model 99XL1200C	Overhead-Valve Twin	1200cc	Five-Speed	Custom
Model 99FXD	Overhead-Valve Twin	88 cid	Five-Speed	Dyna Super Glide
Model 99FXDX	Overhead-Valve Twin	88 cid	Five-Speed	Dyna Super Glide Sport
Model 99FXDL	Overhead-Valve Twin	88 cid	Five-Speed	Dyna Low Rider
Model 99FXDS-Conv.	Overhead-Valve Twin	88 cid	Five-Speed	Dyna Low Rider Convertible
Model 99FXDWG	Overhead-Valve Twin	88 cid	Five-Speed	Dyna Wide Glide
Model 99FXST	Overhead-Valve Twin	88 cid	Five-Speed	Softail Standard
Model 99FXSTB	Overhead-Valve Twin	88 cid	Five-Speed	Night Train
Model 99FXSTS	Overhead-Valve Twin	88 cid	Five-Speed	Springer Softail
Model 99FLSTF	Overhead-Valve Twin	88 cid	Five-Speed	Fat Boy
Model 99FLSTC	Overhead-Valve Twin	88 cid	Five-Speed	Heritage Softail Classic
Model 99FLSTS	Overhead-Valve Twin	88 cid	Five-Speed	Heritage Springer
Model 99FLHT	Overhead-Valve Twin	88 cid	Five-Speed	Electra Glide Standard
Model 99FLHTC	Overhead-Valve Twin	88 cid	Five-Speed	Electra Glide Classic
Model 99FLHTCI	Overhead-Valve Twin	88 cid	Five-Speed	Electra Glide Classic w/Fuel Injection
Model 99FLHTCUI	Overhead-Valve Twin	88 cid	Five-Speed	Electra Glide Classic Ultra w/ Fuel Injection
Model 99FLHR	Overhead-Valve Twin	88 cid	Five-Speed	Road King
Model 99FLHRI	Overhead-Valve Twin	88 cid	Five-Speed	Road King w/Fuel Injection
Model 99FLHRCI	Overhead-Valve Twin	88 cid	Five-Speed	Road King Classic w/Fuel Injection
Model 99FLTR	Overhead-Valve Twin	88 cid	Five-Speed	Road Glide
Model 99FLTRI	Overhead-Valve Twin	88 cid	Five-Speed	Road Glide w/ Fuel Injection

The Deuce was a new bike introduced for the 2000 model year, and combined the new twin-cam motor with a variety of factory custom touches.

2000

The new decade would see few changes in the Harley-Davidson catalog but, as always, improvements were made, and yet another new model was rolled out. There was a universal alteration that involved the braking systems. Four-piston calipers were installed, and H-D's patented "uniform expansion," fixed rotor design did away with the required use of separate disc carriers. Improved batteries and sealed, low-maintenance wheel bearings completed the list.

The changes to the XL brigade were minor, and included the installation of blacked-out exhaust pipes on the 1200 Sport model. The 1200 Custom had a larger 4.4-gallon fuel tank and fresh graphics and trim. Five versions of the XL were still available.

The Dyna models had a variety of small changes. The Sport received additional attention to its suspension. The front fork was fully adjustable to fit the rider's preferences, and the rear shocks could also have their rebound and preload adjusted to satisfy almost any riding condition. Blacked-out exhaust tubes, a narrower drive belt, wider rear tire, and cast wheels completed the performance

2000 Model Year Lineup

Model	Engine Type	Displacement	Transmission	Feature(s)
Model 00XLH883	Overhead-Valve Twin	883cc	Five-Speed	Standard
Model 00XLH883	Overhead-Valve Twin	883cc	Five-Speed	Hugger
Model 00XL883C	Overhead-Valve Twin	883cc	Five-Speed	Custom
Model 00XLH1200	Overhead-Valve Twin	1200cc	Five-Speed	Standard
Model 00XL1200S	Overhead-Valve Twin	1200cc	Five-Speed	Sport
Model 00XL1200C	Overhead-Valve Twin	1200cc	Five-Speed	Custom
Model 00FXD	Overhead-Valve Twin	88 cid	Five-Speed	Dyna Super Glide
Model 00FXDX	Overhead-Valve Twin	88 cid	Five-Speed	Dyna Super Glide Sport
Model 00FXDL	Overhead-Valve Twin	88 cid	Five-Speed	Dyna Low Rider
Model 00FXDS Conv.	Overhead-Valve Twin	88 cid	Five-Speed	Dyna Low Rider Convertible
Model 00FXDWG	Overhead-Valve Twin	88 cid	Five-Speed	Dyna Wide Glide
Model 00FXST	Overhead-Valve Twin	88 cid	Five-Speed	Softail Standard
Model 00FXSTB	Overhead-Valve Twin	88 cid	Five-Speed	Night Train
Model 00FXSTD	Overhead-Valve Twin	88 cid	Five-Speed	Softail Deuce
Model 00FXSTS	Overhead-Valve Twin	88 cid	Five-Speed	Springer Softail
Model 00FLSTF	Overhead-Valve Twin	88 cid	Five-Speed	Fat Boy
Model 00FLSTC	Overhead-Valve Twin	88 cid	Five-Speed	Heritage Softail Classic
Model 00FLSTS	Overhead-Valve Twin	88 cid	Five-Speed	Heritage Springer
Model 00FLHT	Overhead-Valve Twin	88 cid	Five-Speed	Electra Glide Standard
Model 00FLHTC	Overhead-Valve Twin	88 cid	Five-Speed	Electra Glide Classic
Model 00FLHTCI	Overhead-Valve Twin	88 cid	Five-Speed	Electra Glide Classic w/Fuel Inject.
Model 00FLHTCUI	Overhead-Valve Twin	88 cid	Five-Speed	Electra Glide Classic Ultra w/Fuel Inj.
Model 00FLHR	Overhead-Valve Twin	88 cid	Five-Speed	Road King
Model 00FLHRI	Overhead-Valve Twin	88 cid	Five-Speed	Road King w/Fuel Inject.
Model 00FLHRCI	Overhead-Valve Twin	88 cid	Five-Speed	Road King Classic w/Fuel Injection
Model 00FLTR	Overhead-Valve Twin	88 cid	Five-Speed	Road Glide
Model 00FLTRI	Overhead-Valve Twin	88 cid	Five-Speed	Road Glide w/ Fuel Inject.

bumps for the Sport this year. The Convertible received a third disc brake. The front forks of the Wide Glide featured a slider valve that delivered a better ride.

In the Softail camp, the new Twin-Cam 88 was installed into a stiffer frame for 2000. The new frame held a counterbalanced motor that ran with less vibration than ever before. The Twin Cam 88B motor helped to absorb some of the rattle that the rubber-framed Dynas already eliminated. The Classic model held fuel in a new 5-gallon container.

The newest member of the club was the Deuce. Built around the new, 34-percent-stiffer Softail frame, and powered by the all-new Fathead B motor, the Deuce delivered a new level of factory custom styling. The fuel tank stretched back to reach the front edge of the saddle, and the rear fender was bobbed on a horizontal plane.

A wide, 17-inch rear tire and solid disc wheel put the power to the ground, and the staggered dual exhaust let the engine breath. A laced wheel at the front accented the available two-tone paint schemes offered.

For the touring fans, not much changed. Minor improvements were made to the saddles to enhance comfort, and the handlebars of the Road King were higher for a more comfortable reach. Road Glides and Electra Glides were also benefactors of the latest in electronic speedometers.

PRODUCTION

Model	Production
Sportsters	46,213
FXD and ST	100,875
Touring	57,504

The 2001 FLTR Road Glide offered plenty of touring capabilities along with a sporty appearance.

2001

With only two years to go before the big Centennial celebration, changes on the '01 models were minor, yet widespread over the whole line.

Sportster changes were found on the inside of the motors, and included the same cylinder liners as the Twin-Cam 88. A more efficient oil pump helped to retrieve oil from the lower regions of the motor at high rpms. Efforts to reduce noise from the engine were made by installing high-contact-ratio cam gears. Like nearly every model in the lineup, the Sportsters were fitted with Dunlop tires designed specifically for their intended machine.

All models outside the Sportster family were now available with electronic security systems to help thwart thieves. Setting off the alarm sounded a loud warning, shut down the starter motor, and killed the fuel delivery system. By adding the additional siren and pager, your bike would scream at the first sign of thievery, as well as send a message to your belt-mounted paging device. Every Big Twin model featured the new Digital Technician system that provided dealers instant information on your bike's troubles, should they occur. Once downloaded from a machine's black box, the data could be sent electronically to Harley-Davidson's central computers for future reference.

A change in the Dyna lineup saw the FXDS- Convertible being replaced by the FXDST, T-Sport model. The T-Sport featured a quickly removable fairing that also had an adjustable windshield. A pair of ballistic nylon saddlebags could expand from 3 to 6 inches wide, and could also be easily removed. Fully adjustable suspension rounded out the distinctive features of the T-Sport.

The Dyna Low Rider had a record-setting seat height of only 25.2 inches, which was achieved by shortening the suspension components and removing a portion of the padding from the saddle. The handlebars reached back to the rider on newly shaped risers, and foot controls fell neatly beneath the rider's boots.

Every model in the Dyna tribe received more easily accessed fuses, a fog-resistant fuel gauge, and smoother shifting gears.

Softails were all available with carburetors or the new electronic fuel injection, as well as a 38-amp charging system. The Heritage Springers lost the fringe on their saddlebags and seats, but gained newly designed paint and graphics.

The family of touring machines all received rubber stops for the side stands, and lost a metal air dam that had previously proven to push engine heat directly onto the rider during hot-weather riding. Enhanced components within the transmission were also employed to provide smoother gear changes.

The Road Glides got a new blacked-out headlight bezel, an enhanced stereo system, and cruise control was a standard feature.

Electra Glide Classic and Ultra models pumped out sound through an improved set of speakers, and the rear-mounted Tour Pak featured sturdier hardware.

2001 Model Year Lineup

Model	Engine Type	Displacement	Transmission	Feature(s)
Model 01XLH883	Overhead-Valve Twin	883cc	Five-Speed	Standard
Model 01XLH883	Overhead-Valve Twin	883cc	Five-Speed	Hugger
Model 01XL883C	Overhead-Valve Twin	883cc	Five-Speed	Custom
Model 01XLH1200	Overhead-Valve Twin	1200cc	Five-Speed	Standard
Model 01XL1200S	Overhead-ValveTwin	1200cc	Five-Speed	Sport
Model 01XL1200C	Overhead-Valve Twin	1200cc	Five-Speed	Custom
Model 01FXD	Overhead-Valve Twin	88 cid	Five-Speed	Dyna Super Glide
Model 01FXDX	Overhead-Valve Twin	88 cid	Five-Speed	Dyna Super Glide Sport
Model 01FXDXT	Overhead-Valve Twin	88 cid	Five-Speed	Dyna Super Glide T-Sport
Model 01FXDL	Overhead-Valve Twin	88 cid	Five-Speed	Dyna Low Rider
Model 01FXDWG	Overhead-Valve Twin	88 cid	Five-Speed	Dyna Wide Glide
Model 01FXST	Overhead-Valve Twin	88 cid	Five-Speed	Softail Standard
Model 01FXSTI	Overhead-Valve Twin	88 cid	Five-Speed	Softail Standard w/Fuel Injection
Model 01FXSTB	Overhead-Valve Twin	88 cid	Five-Speed	Night Train
Model 01FXSTBI	Overhead-Valve Twin	88 cid	Five-Speed	Night Train w/ Fuel Injection
Model 01FXSTD	Overhead-Valve Twin	88 cid	Five-Speed	Softail Deuce
Model 01FXSTDI	Overhead-Valve Twin	88 cid	Five-Speed	Softail Deuce w/ Fuel Injection
Model 01FXSTS	Overhead-Valve Twin	88 cid	Five-Speed	Springer Softail
Model 01FXSTSI	Overhead-Valve Twin	88 cid	Five-Speed	Springer Softail w/Fuel Injection
Model 01FLSTF	Overhead-Valve Twin	88 cid	Five-Speed	Fat Boy
Model 01FLSTFI	Overhead-Valve Twin	88 cid	Five-Speed	Fat Boy w/Fuel Injection
Model 01FLSTC	Overhead-Valve Twin	88 cid	Five-Speed	Heritage Softail Classic
Model 01FLSTCI	Overhead-Valve Twin	88 cid	Five-Speed	Heritage Softail Classic w/Fuel Injection
Model 01FLSTS	Overhead-Valve Twin	88 cid	Five-Speed	Heritage Springer
Model 01FLSTSI	Overhead-Valve Twin	88 cid	Five-Speed	Heritage Springer w/Fuel Injection
Model 01FLHT	Overhead-Valve Twin	88 cid	Five-Speed	Electra Glide Standard
Model 01FLHTC	Overhead-Valve Twin	88 cid	Five-Speed	Electra Glide Classic
Model 01FLHTCI	Overhead-Valve Twin	88 cid	Five-Speed	Electra Glide Classic w/Fuel Injection
Model 01FLHTCUI	Overhead-Valve Twin	88 cid	Five-Speed	Electra Glide Classic Ultra w/ Fuel Injection
Model 01FLHR	Overhead-Valve Twin	88 cid	Five-Speed	Road King
Model 01FLHRI	Overhead-Valve Twin	88 cid	Five-Speed	Road King w/Fuel Injection
Model 01FLHRCI	Overhead-Valve Twin	88 cid	Five-Speed	Road King Classic w/Fuel Injection
Model 01FLTR	Overhead-Valve Twin	88 cid	Five-Speed	Road Glide
Model 01FLTRI	Overhead-Valve Twin	88 cid	Five-Speed	Road Glide w/ Fuel Injection

On a more traditional note, the FXDWG3 was styled upon the existing Dyna Wide Glide.

2002

For the first 98 years of the company's existence, the majority of Harley-Davidson's machines were based on the same time-tested formulas. Changes were evolutionary, not so much revolutionary. One of the new models introduced for 2002 would be different. There were additional alterations made to the balance of the lineup as well, but most would be overshadowed by the VRSCA.

The 1994 model year saw Harley-Davidson once again take to the track with its all-new VR-1000. It was powered by a 60-degree twin-cylinder motor that was liquid cooled. It bristled with the latest technology, but failed to achieve a lot of success on the track. Nevertheless, it planted the seeds that would one day change H-D history.

The VRSCA, or "V-Rod," would embody many of the features found on the VR-1000, only refined and tuned for the street. The heart of the new beast was a 69-cubic inch, 60-degree V-Twin with liquid cooling. Twin overhead cams operated the four valves in each head. All of these features were a first on a Harley-

The bikini fairing added a touch of style to the FXDWG3 and helped move the air around the rider's head.

The 2002 V-Rod was a radical departure from the norm for Harley-Davidson, but well received by the motorcycle public.

Davidson. The crankshaft was a forged, one-piece item, in contrast to the typical three-piece crank used on other Harley motors. Sequential-port, electronic fuel injection kept the new motor fed, while its breath was drawn out through a two-into-one-into-two exhaust system that was more graceful than anything ever seen on a Harley. Running on 11.3:1 compression, the V-Rod produced 115 hp at just over 8200 rpm—another first for a factory Harley.

Encasing this new power plant was a chassis like no other built by Harley. The 67.5-inch wheelbase was the longest ever seen from Milwaukee, as was the 38-degree fork angle. Instead of using the usual backbone style frame, the VRSCA utilized a perimeter chassis that enveloped the motor. The upper frame rails were formed using the latest in hydro form processing to achieve the excessive curvature while retaining strength. The power train

The saddle of the "3" was covered in a textured material that looked like natural ostrich hide, and was dyed to match the theme of the bike.

was held in place using a separate bolt-in segment of frame. The apparent fuel tank was nothing more than a cover for the motor's intake.

The actual fuel receptacle was beneath the saddle, keeping things neat, and providing a lower center of gravity. The radiator shroud, instrument pod, and rear fender section flowed like nothing anyone had seen before, especially on a Harley. The instrument cluster itself was a work of art, and seemed to complete the design theme of the V-Rod. A pair of seamless, solid disc wheels found on no other model also helped to set the VRSCA apart.

Back at the H-D ranch, other changes were being also made.

The XL883R model was a new entrant in the Sportster arena, and provided the sport rider with a new option. Wearing orange and black garb that reflected the XR-750. Wrinkle-black paint was applied to the cases, battery cover, oil tank, and headlight brim, contrasting the bright orange finish on the tank and fenders. All the XL models were fitted with a stiffer exhaust flange that provided a better connection between the pipes and the cylinder heads. The bullet-shaped turn signals found on the Deuce were also applied to the Sportsters for 2002.

A new Dyna model was introduced for 2002. The FXDWG3 was yet another "factory custom" from Harley-Davidson. Mechanicals were the same as on other FXD variants, but the "3" wore a set of distinctive trim. A pair of bikini fairings graced the headlight and lower section of the frame. Perhaps more form than function, they did help to guide airflow. A pair of five-spoke wheels, unique to the 3, were found at both ends. In the middle, a saddle covered with simulated ostrich hide was dyed to compliment the selected color scheme. The grips, mirrors, and forward controls were all machined from billet. Engraved identification plaques helped to tell the world what you were riding. Factory-applied flames added to the package.

Softail variants equipped with electronic fuel injection featured a new three-part temperature control to maintain consistent performance at all temperatures.

The FLH models received extensive modifications to their chassis and suspensions. A larger, stronger, swingarm and a larger rear axle added stiffness to the tail section. Improved air shocks also help to smooth the rear end ride of the big touring models. Up front, cartridge-style forks bolstered handling and braking abilities.

The 60-degree, liquid-cooled V-twin VRSCA featured overhead cams and four valves per cylinder.

The V-Rod's ovoid-shaped headlight and sleek instrument stalk make for interesting conversation.

2002 Model Year Lineup

Model	Engine Type	Displacement	Transmission	Feature(s)
Model 02XLH883	Overhead-Valve Twin	883cc	Five-Speed	Standard
Model 02XLH883	Overhead-Valve Twin	883cc	Five-Speed	Hugger
Model 02XL883C	Overhead-Valve Twin	883cc	Five-Speed	Custom
Model 02XL883R	Overhead-Valve Twin	883cc	Five-Speed	Replaced Sport Model
Model 02XLH1200	Overhead-Valve Twin	1200cc	Five-Speed	Standard
Model 02XL1200C	Overhead-Valve Twin	1200cc	Five-Speed	Custom
Model 02XL1200S	Overhead-Valve Twin	1200cc	Five-Speed	Sport
Model 02FXD	Overhead-Valve Twin	88 cid	Five-Speed	Dyna Super Glide
Model 02FXDX	Overhead-Valve Twin	88 cid	Five-Speed	Dyna Super Glide Sport
Model 02FXDXT	Overhead-Valve Twin	88 cid	Five-Speed	Dyna Super Glide T-Sport
Model 02FXDL	Overhead-Valve Twin	88 cid	Five-Speed	Dyna Low Rider
Model 02FXDWG	Overhead-Valve Twin	88 cid	Five-Speed	Dyna Wide Glide
Model 02FXDWG3	Overhead-Valve Twin	88 cid	Five-Speed	Dyna Wide Glide 3
Model 02FXST	Overhead-Valve Twin	88 cid	Five-Speed	Softail Standard
Model 02FXSTI	Overhead-Valve Twin	88 cid	Five-Speed	Softail Standard w/Fuel Injection
Model 02FXSTB	Overhead-Valve Twin	88 cid	Five-Speed	Night Train
Model 02FXSTBI	Overhead-Valve Twin	88 cid	Five-Speed	Night Train w/ Fuel Injection
Model 02FLSTF	Overhead-Valve Twin	88 cid	Five-Speed	Fat Boy
Model 02FLSTFI	Overhead-Valve Twin	88 cid	Five-Speed	Fat Boy w/Fuel Injection
Model 02FXSTS	Overhead-Valve Twin	88 cid	Five-Speed	Springer Softail
Model 02FXSTSI	Overhead-Valve Twin	88 cid	Five-Speed	Springer Softail w/Fuel Injection
Model 02FXSTD	Overhead-Valve Twin	88 cid	Five-Speed	Softail Deuce
Model 02FXSTDI	Overhead-Valve Twin	88 cid	Five-Speed	Softail Deuce w/ Fuel Injection
Model 02FLSTC	Overhead-Valve Twin	88 cid	Five-Speed	Heritage Softail Classic
Model 02FLSTCI	Overhead-Valve Twin	88 cid	Five-Speed	Heritage Softail Classic w/Fuel Injection
Model 02FLSTS	Overhead-Valve Twin	88 cid	Five-Speed	Heritage Springer
Model 02FLSTSI	Overhead-Valve Twin	88 cid	Five-Speed	Heritage Springer w/Fuel Injection
Model 02FLHT	Overhead-Valve Twin	88 cid	Five-Speed	Electra Glide Standard
Model 02FLHR	Overhead-Valve Twin	88 cid	Five-Speed	Road King
Model 02FLHRI	Overhead-Valve Twin	88 cid	Five-Speed	Road King w/Fuel Injection
Model 02FLHRCI	Overhead-Valve Twin	88 cid	Five-Speed	Road King Classic w/Fuel Injection
Model 02FLTRI	Overhead-Valve Twin	88 cid	Five-Speed	Road Glide w/ Fuel Injection
Model 02FLHTC	Overhead-Valve Twin	88 cid	Five-Speed	Electra Glide Classic
Model 02FLHTCI	Overhead-Valve Twin	88 cid	Five-Speed	Electra Glide Classic w/Fuel Injection
Model 02FLHTCUI	Overhead-Valve Twin	88 cid	Five-Speed	Electra Glide Classic Ultra w/ Fuel Injection
Model 02VRSCA	Overhead-Cam Twin	69 cid	Five-Speed	V-Rod w/Fuel Injection

This '03 FXDWG is finished in Sterling Silver and Vivid Black—one of the Anniversary color schemes offered to mark the 100th year.

2003

This year would mark the 100th year of uninterrupted production for The Motor Company—an achievement that no other motorcycle manufacturer could claim. Harley-Davidson had survived two World Wars, The Great Depression, and a corporate merger, and still came out with flying colors. Sure, there were a few black eyes and skinned knees along the way, but these things will happen when you're in business for a century.

Several versions of air-cleaner markings were used to announce the centennial.

A pair of badges were seen atop the fuel tank.

Saddles of several models were also adorned with birthday trim, as seen here on the Softail Deuce pillion.

Numerous applications of commemorative markings are found on the motor cases of the '03 models.

The 2003 models would be largely unchanged, but were available in a myriad of Anniversary trim. Every unit built would wear some form of birthday garb in an effort to drive home the importance of the date. It would be another 100 years before H-D could mark its bicentennial.

The Sportsters benefited from new mirrors for '03, but little else was changed. The 1200 Sport got chrome exhaust to accent the black-and-silver Anniversary look, but was otherwise untouched.

Changes to the FXD clan were basically limited to birthday trim, but the FXDWG had a wider, 150 series rear tire, and repositioned foot pegs. The Dyna Low Rider also rolled on the new, wider rear tire. The FXDX Dyna Super Glide Sport glittered with new chrome pipes to compliment the blacked-out power plant.

Over in the Softail neighborhood, modifications were also minor, aside from the array of birthday badging, engraving, and paint. The Fat Boy's and Softtail Standard's rear tires grew to the latest 150 series rubber for a wider footprint. The Softail Deuce had a 160 series tire wedged under its rear fender.

The Road Glide received a CD player as part of its standard features, and gold cast wheels were included in the Anniversary trim for 2003.

The fuel-injected Electra Glide Standard was treated to the improved EFI system that was added to the balance of the touring rigs the previous year. The Electra Glide Classic and Ultra models also received the CD player as part of their basic gear.

The V-Rod was trimmed in a silver-and-black ensemble, but was otherwise unaltered from the '02 version.

2003 Model Year Lineup

Model	Engine Type	Displacement	Transmission	Feature(s)
Model 03XLH883	Overhead-Valve Twin	883cc	Five-Speed	Standard
Model 03XLH883	Overhead-Valve Twin	883cc	Five-Speed	Hugger
Model 03XL883C	Overhead-Valve Twin	883cc	Five-Speed	Custom
Model 03XL883R	Overhead-Valve Twin	883cc	Five-Speed	—
Model 03XLH1200	Overhead-Valve Twin	1200cc	Five-Speed	Standard
Model 03XL1200C	Overhead-Valve Twin	1200cc	Five-Speed	Custom
Model 03XL1200S	Overhead-Valve Twin	1200cc	Five-Speed	Sport
Model 03FXD	Overhead-Valve Twin	88 cid	Five-Speed	Dyna Super Glide
Model 03FXDX	Overhead-Valve Twin	88 cid	Five-Speed	Dyna Super Glide Sport
Model 03FXDXT	Overhead-Valve Twin	88 cid	Five-Speed	Dyna Super Glide T-Sport
Model 03FXDL	Overhead-Valve Twin	88 cid	Five-Speed	Dyna Low Rider
Model 03FXDWG	Overhead-Valve Twin	88 cid	Five-Speed	Dyna Wide Glide
Model 03FXST	Overhead-Valve Twin	88 cid	Five-Speed	Softail Standard
Model 03FXSTI	Overhead-Valve Twin	88 cid	Five-Speed	Softail Standard w/Fuel Injection
Model 03FXSTB	Overhead-Valve Twin	88 cid	Five-Speed	Night Train
Model 03FXSTBI	Overhead-Valve Twin	88 cid	Five-Speed	Night Train w/ Fuel Injection
Model 03FLSTF	Overhead-Valve Twin	88 cid	Five-Speed	Fat Boy
Model 03FLSTFI	Overhead-Valve Twin	88 cid	Five-Speed	Fat Boy w/Fuel Injection
Model 03FXSTS	Overhead-Valve Twin	88 cid	Five-Speed	Springer Softail
Model 03FXSTSI	Overhead-Valve Twin	88 cid	Five-Speed	Springer Softail w/Fuel Injection
Model 03FXSTD	Overhead-Valve Twin	88 cid	Five-Speed	Softail Deuce
Model 03FXSTDI	Overhead-Valve Twin	88 cid	Five-Speed	Softail Deuce w/ Fuel Injection
Model 03FLSTC	Overhead-Valve Twin	88 cid	Five-Speed	Heritage Softail Classic
Model 03FLSTCI	Overhead-Valve Twin	88 cid	Five-Speed	Heritage Softail Classic w/Fuel Injection
Model 03FLSTS	Overhead-Valve Twin	88 cid	Five-Speed	Heritage Springer
Model 03FLSTSI	Overhead-Valve Twin	88 cid	Five-Speed	Heritage Springer w/Fuel Injection
Model 03FLHT	Overhead-Valve Twin	88 cid	Five-Speed	Electra Glide Standard
Model 03FLHTI	Overhead-Valve Twin	88 cid	Five-Speed	Electra Glide Standard w/Fuel Injection
Model 03FLHR	Overhead-Valve Twin	88 cid	Five-Speed	Road King
Model 03FLHRI	Overhead-Valve Twin	88 cid	Five-Speed	Road King w/Fuel Injection
Model 03FLHRCI	Overhead-Valve Twin	88 cid	Five-Speed	Road King Classic w/Fuel Injection
Model 03FLRTI	Overhead-Valve Twin	88 cid	Five-Speed	Road Glide w/ Fuel Injection
Model 03FLHTC	Overhead-Valve Twin	88 cid	Five-Speed	Electra Glide Classic
Model 03FLHTCI	Overhead-Valve Twin	88 cid	Five-Speed	Electra Glide Classic w/Fuel Injection
Model 03FLHTCUI	Overhead-Valve Twin	88 cid	Five-Speed	Electra Glide Classic Ultra w/ Fuel Injection
Model 03VRSCA	Overhead-Cam Twin	69 cid	Five-Speed	V-Rod

An abundance of badging was used on the 2003 models, and the tank-mounted emblem was the most prominent.

Harley-Davidson Racing

This 1924 FHAC model was one of the dominant machines Harley-Davidson created in the days of board track racing.

This segment of the book will present a very general overview of Harley-Davidson's racing history. Volumes can, and have, been written by better men than myself on the subject, but I wanted to at least provide an outline of the fabled efforts made during the course of H-D history.

As early as 1911, private owners were campaigning their Harley-Davidsons on tracks across the country. They didn't have factory race bikes, and weren't sanctioned by the manufacturer. These men simply wanted to experience the thrill of riding their two-wheeled machines around performance circuits to appease their own thirst for speed. Harley's involvement ended once the sale was completed at the dealership, but the company was evidently proud of the fact that its equipment was winning races. In 1913, Harley-Davidsons finished in the top three positions in a 225-mile race from Harrisburg, Pennsylvania, to Philadelphia and back. The new machines of the time were proving to be both fast and dependable.

Three years later, in 1914, The Motor Company chartered its own factory race team for the first time. In 1915, the team had scored 26 victories, and 1916 added an additional 15 marks in the "win" column. These races were being run on board tracks and flat tracks, as well as in FAM events.

World War I put a temporary end to racing in the U.S., but Harley-Davidson would return to the tracks as soon as peace had been restored. On the famous sands of Daytona Beach, Harley machines posted speeds of over 100 mph, and an average speed of over 100 was accomplished in 1921 on a California board track. It seemed that racing did well for the company, as race victories translated into sales in the showroom.

Exotic four- and eight-valve motors were slipped into minimalist frames, and riders ran at top speed with no brakes at board track events. The Harley-Davidson "Wrecking Crew" was a dominant force during the heyday of board track racing, as it claimed victory after victory with its Milwaukee-built race machine.

The tracks were comprised of 2-inch-wide timbers turned vertically and sandwiched together. The races were inherently dangerous, and the track itself posed a many risks as the racing itself. Several riders and spectators lost their lives before this form of racing was banned.

Along with board track racing, hill climb, flat track and enduro events gave racing fans plenty of variety. Harley-Davidson produced machinery to compete in every form of racing, and found success more often than not.

World War II again curtailed racing events as the country's focus remained on the conflict overseas. As with the first World War, once peace had been restored, the country went racing. A new form of sanctioned racing was designed by the AMA, and the events were held nationwide. Harley-Davidson rider Joe Leonard won the very first National Championship in 1954, and was followed by Brad Andres in 1955. The next four years saw another Harley-mounted rider dominating the National events. Carroll Resweber racked up an impressive list of first-place finishes that amounted to a 98-percent success rate.

Land speed racing was yet another form of competition that attracted a unique kind of pilot. Turning and handling were of minimum concern—all-out speed was the key. A new record of 177.225 mph was set in 1965 by George Roeder, aboard a bullet-shaped rocket powered by a 250cc Harley Sprint motor.

The drag racing world was also growing, and a twin-engined, Harley-powered drag bike ridden by Joe Smith set a new record at only 8.20 seconds in the quarter mile in 1974.

Flat track racing was also dominated by Harley-Davidson in the late '70s as three consecutive world championships were added to the H-D record books.

A new form of racing was created by Harley-Davidson so its 883cc Sportsters could prove their mettle on a track along with other similar machines. The AMA/CCS 883 Twin Sports class was born, and allowed riders of many skill levels to take their race-prepped Sportsters on a series of road racetracks across the country.

A new type of Harley race machine was also unveiled for the 1994 season. Powered by an all-new, 60-degree V-Twin that displaced 1,000 liquid-cooled cubic centimeters, the VR-1000 was an amazing tool for the road race circuits. Miguel Duhamel piloted a VR-1000 to a fourth-place showing at Brainerd in its first year of competition.

The VR shared no components with street-bound Harleys, but was allowed to race due to the 50 copies built as "street-legal" models. Although not legal in the USA, they were within the boundaries, and raced on venues around the country. While never achieving great success themselves, the VR-1000s did lead to the wildly successful V-Rod, introduced for the 2002 model year.

The 1927 FHAO made things tough on the competition by improving the breed of already successful board track machines.

The Peashooter had proved its worth on venues all across the USA, and the 1935 model was the last of the breed.

The 1948 WR was often modified for use on flat tracks, and also made a name for itself by winning races on a consistent basis.

Powered by an Italian 250cc motor, the 1968 CR250 was a star in the single-cylinder class of racing.

The XR-750, seen here in 1977 form, was introduced in 1969 and instantly became the bike to ride. The heads were later used on the XR-1000 street machine sold at dealerships.

The VR-1000 was rolled onto tracks in 1994, and is seen here in "street-legal" trim. Although not legal in the U.S., it still fell within AMA rules and was campaigned with limited success.

This is the race-level VR-1000. Although it never achieved the success that it had been ticketed for, it did lead to the introduction of the popular V-Rod.

Bibliography

Facts, figures and historical data for this title were gathered from a variety of sources. In addition to period advertising, dealer brochures, service manuals and promotional materials, the following were used to create the book you are now reading.

Books

Birkitt, Malcolm. (1994). *Harley-Davidson Electra Glide.* Osprey Automotive. London, England.

Bolfert, Thomas C. (1991). *The Big Book of Harley-Davidson.* Harley-Davidson, Inc. Milwaukee, WI.

Brown, Roland. (1996). *Encyclopedia of Motorcycles.* Smithmark Publishers. New York, NY.

Carroll, John & Stuart, Garry. (1994). *Harley-Davidson 45s Workhorse and Warhorse.* Osprey Automotive. London, England.

Conner, Rick. (1996). *Harley-Davidson Data Book.* Motorbooks Int'l. Osceola, WI.

Girdler, Allan & Hackett, Jeff. (2001). *Harley-Davidson In The 1960s.* Motorbooks, Int'l. Osceola, WI.

Girdler, Allan. (1992). *Harley-Davidson The American Motorcycle.* Motorbooks, Int'l. Osceola, WI.

Girdler, Allan. (1987). *Harley Racers.* Motorbooks, Int'l. Osceola, WI.

Girdler, Allan. (1986). *Illustrated Harley-Davidson Buyer's Guide.* Motorbooks, Int'l. Osceola, WI.

Harley-Davidson. (1994). 1903-1993 *Harley-Davidson, Inc. Historical Overview.* Harley-Davidson. Milwaukee, WI.

Hatfield, Jerry. (1996). *Illustrated Antique American Motorcycle Buyer's Guide.* Motorbooks, Int'l. Osceola, WI.

Hatfield, Jerry. (1997). *Illustrated Buyer's Guide; Harley-Davidson Classics 1903-1965.* Motorbooks, Int'l. Osceola, WI.

Hatfield, Jerry. (1990). *Inside Harley-Davidson.* Motorbooks, Int'l. Osceola, WI.

Marselli, Mark. (1994). *Classic Harley-Davidson Big Twins.* Motorbooks, Int'l. Osceola, WI.

Wagner, Herbert. (1999). *Classic Harley-Davidson, 1903-1941.* Motorbooks, Int'l. Osceola, WI.

Wilson, Hugo. (1995). *The Encyclopedia Of The Motorcycle.* Dorling Kinersley. New York, NY.

Wright, David K. (2002). *The Harley-Davidson Motor Company - A 100 Year History.* Car Tech, Inc. North Branch, MN.

Periodicals

Cycle. Ziff-Davis Publishing. New York, NY.

Cycle Guide. Cycle Guide Publications. Torrance, CA.

Cycle World. Hachette Filipacchi Media U.S. Inc. Newport Beach, CA.

The Enthusiast. Harley-Davidson, Inc. Milwaukee, WI.

Ironworks. Hatton Brown Publishers, Inc. Montgomery, AL.

Motorcycle Collector. Don Emde. Laguna Niguel, CA.

Motorcyclist. Primedia, Inc. Los Angeles, CA.

Rider. Ehlert Publishing Group, Inc. Maple Grove, MN.